How Can You Represent Those People?

How Can You Represent Those People?

Edited by

Abbe Smith
and
Monroe H. Freedman

palgrave macmillan

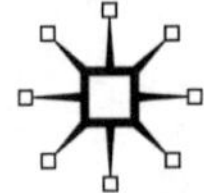

HOW CAN YOU REPRESENT THOSE PEOPLE?

First published in 2013 by
PALGRAVE MACMILLAN®
in the United States—a division of St. Martin's Press LLC,
175 Fifth Avenue, New York, NY 10010.

Where this book is distributed in the UK, Europe and the rest of the world, this is by Palgrave Macmillan, a division of Macmillan Publishers Limited, registered in England, company number 785998, of Houndmills, Basingstoke, Hampshire RG21 6XS.

Palgrave Macmillan is the global academic imprint of the above companies and has companies and representatives throughout the world.

Palgrave® and Macmillan® are registered trademarks in the United States, the United Kingdom, Europe and other countries.

ISBN: 978–1–137–31193–1 (hc)
ISBN: 978–1–137–31194–8 (pbk)

Library of Congress Cataloging-in-Publication Data

How can you represent those people? / edited by Abbe Smith and Monroe H. Freedman.
pages cm
Includes index.
ISBN 978–1–137–31193–1 (hardcover :alk. paper)—
ISBN 978–1–137–31194–8 (pbk. : alk. paper)
1. Defense (Criminal procedure)—United States—Personal narratives. 2. Criminal defense lawyers—United States. 3. Criminal justice, Administration of—United States. 4. Trial practice—United States. 5. Criminal justice, Administration of. 6. Defense (Criminal procedure) I. Smith, Abbe. II. Freedman, Monroe H.

KF9656.H69 2013
345.73′05044—dc23 2013006150

A catalogue record of the book is available from the British Library.

Design by Newgen Knowledge Works (P) Ltd., Chennai, India.

First edition: August 2013

D 10 9 8 7 6 5 4 3 2

For our families:
The Greenbergs, McKowns, Smiths, and Sterns
and
The Freedmans, Izquierdos, Lodhis, and Tobias,
and
For our clients

CONTENTS

Preface

"How can you represent those people?" All criminal defense lawyers are asked this question—by family, friends, and folk of all sorts. The query is such a part of the criminal defense experience that it is known as "the question." Posed by the genuinely perplexed as well as the hardened heckler—often at a cocktail party when the defender has a drink in hand and his or her guard down—the lawyer tries not to seem bored or peeved while offering a range of replies: personal, professional, political. What is really being asked is, "How can you represent people you know to be guilty?" Not guilty shoplifters, marijuana possessors, drunk drivers, or political protesters—these could be us, our children, our parents. Not the wrongly accused or convicted either—even the harshest critics understand defending the innocent. The Question refers instead to the representation of guilty criminals who have committed acts of violence or depravity.

There are no right answers to The Question or related questions. Each lawyer has his or her own reasons for doing the work. This book is the first collection of answers to The Question ever assembled. The contributors are some of the most experienced and thoughtful criminal defense lawyers and teachers in the country—old and young, male and female, white and black. They explain simply and powerfully why they represent "those people."

As we mark the fiftieth anniversary of *Gideon v. Wainwright*, the US Supreme Court case that guaranteed the right to counsel in criminal cases in this country, we should likewise mark the important work of criminal lawyers. Although we remain far from fulfilling the promise of *Gideon*—that people accused of crime will be well represented no matter how much money they have—the voices in this collection inspire us to do better.

Some contributors speak poignantly of their own experiences with injustice as underlying their commitment to indigent defense. Angela Davis shares a story of racism from her childhood in Georgia, Vida Johnson a story about her grandparents' struggles with the Ku Klux

Klan in Mississippi. Others, like Tucker Carrington and Ann Roan, acknowledge their own relative privilege and good fortune but find themselves drawn to the poor accused nonetheless. William Montross and Meghan Shapiro write about their experience representing people on death row, and the toll capital defense takes on clients, their families, their lawyers. Two contributors, David Singleton and Robin Steinberg, run organizations. Singleton shares his experience representing sex offenders while trying to keep the Ohio Justice Policy Center afloat, while career defender Steinberg talks about what led her to indigent defense and ultimately to create the Bronx Defenders, one of the most innovative public defender offices in the country. Joseph Margulies and Alice Woolley provide a historical and political context for representing "those people." Former federal prosecutor Paul Butler turns the focus on prosecutors with his version of the "how can you" question. Criminal defense icons Alan Dershowitz, Michael Tigar, and Barbara Babcock point to law, philosophy, politics, and personality to explain how they represent "those people." We, the coeditors, contribute chapters as well, offering our own reasons for defending people, even those who do very bad things.

Prominent criminal lawyer Edward Bennett Williams once noted that, like other criminal lawyers, he took on difficult cases for unpopular clients, "not because of my own wishes, but because of the unwritten law that I might not refuse." The lawyers in this collection could not refuse either. Moreover, they could not be prouder to champion the very worst of "those people."

Acknowledgments

We thought it might be a good idea to put together a collection of chapters on the all-too-familiar question "How can you represent those people?" We were lucky that the criminal lawyers we most wanted to include in this project—experienced and thoughtful practitioners willing to think hard about the question—were eager to join us.

We are especially pleased to have gathered together such a varied group of contributors. The authors range in age from their late twenties to mid-eighties, practice in all parts of the country, and come from public defender offices, private law practice, public interest organizations, and academia. Half are women; a quarter are African-American.

We thank Barbara Babcock, Paul Butler, Tucker Carrington, Angela Davis, Alan Dershowitz, Vida Johnson, Meghan Shapiro, David Singleton, Joseph Margulies, William Montross, Ann Roan, Robin Steinberg, Michael Tigar, and Alice Woolley for their wonderful, often very personal, chapters.

We also thank Jenelle DeVits, Anna Selden, Max Sirianni, and Lisa Spar for excellent research, editorial, and formatting assistance; Burke Gerstenschlager, Farideh Koohi-Kamali, Lani Oshima, and Luba Ostashevsky at Palgrave Macmillan for their belief in this project and wise counsel throughout the publication process; and Dean Eric Lane, Maurice A. Dean School of Law, Hofstra University, and Dean William Treanor, Georgetown University Law Center for their generous support.

We couldn't be prouder of the final product.

1

"Defending the Guilty" after 30 Years

Barbara Babcock

In 1983, I published "Defending the Guilty,"[1] a piece that lives on in citations and classrooms. Perhaps it's the provocative title, or the story of Geraldine, the essential client, that has made the article popular. For this volume, I've spruced up the diction and added some reflections from the life of Clara Foltz, the founder of the public defender movement. The chapter also draws on my memoir-in-progress, *Recollections of a Woman Lawyer.*

I always wanted to be a criminal defense lawyer, which was even more unusual for a woman in the early 1960s than wanting to be a lawyer at all. Reflecting back now, I have no insights on the source of my ambition. Maybe it sprang from my Christian upbringing, my innate sympathy for the underdog, my love for the Robin Hood stories. Nothing really adds up. Criminal defense was a rare goal for men too at the time, especially at elite schools like Yale. Along with this set ambition, I also had a fixed belief that lawyers had a high moral duty to defend—the more heinous the crime, the greater the duty.

In his book, *One Man's Freedom*, published while I was in law school, the famous defense lawyer Edward Bennett Williams confirmed my instincts when he wrote of taking on "difficult cases for unpopular clients... because of the unwritten law that I might not refuse."[2]

John Ely, a classmate who went on to become a distinguished law professor, disputed the "unwritten law." He thought that only if the lawyer was the last one on earth was he obligated to represent the client he disliked or whose cause he disapproved. In the manner of law students everywhere, we argued heatedly. Fifty years later, I can still remember walking along the winter streets of New Haven, furious at

John for claiming that he might refuse to defend some dreadful criminal. Who did he think he was? Defense of the defenseless, the guilty, and even the indefensible was already my religion.[3]

Given my passion about defending, it seems fortuitous that *Gideon v. Wainwright*[4] should come down the year I graduated from law school. In one of its most far-reaching and important decisions, the Warren Court held that lawyers were necessities in criminal cases and that due process required an attorney even for the accused who could not pay. The most salient years of my career would be spent at the Public Defender Service, established in Washington, DC, to fulfill the mandate of *Gideon*.

My years at "the agency," as we always called it—from 1966 to 1972—were exciting and happy, including the four years I served as director. Paradoxically, they were also the most frazzled and anxious time of my life. Often I felt alone, standing between the client and powerful pneumatic forces that threatened to sweep us both away. The work was endless because there was always something more that might be done. Filing a motion, finding a witness, or stopping by the jail for a chat on a Sunday afternoon could mean the difference between victory or defeat, between freedom and prison.

A few years ago, I was remembering (in an oral history) what it felt like to be a public defender:

> I was always tired, and driven, and in a rage (that I was repressing) because it seemed that no one in power could see the injustice that was happening and the necessity of providing real defense lawyers and doing it right away...But the thing was it was fun, there wasn't that rigid work/play distinction. I loved what I was doing, even though I was just tremendously wrought up all the time when I look back on it.[5]

One of the daily stressors was the constant question: How Can You Defend Someone You Know Is Guilty? Everyone asks it—benign old aunts, eager young students, the gardener, the grocery store clerk, and lately even the oncologist. Today, 40 years after I last appeared in court, interviewers still bring up the subject. Every defense lawyer develops an answer to keep at the ready for the inevitable, existential query. I wrote *Defending the Guilty*, with its sardonic title, on the twentieth anniversary of *Gideon*, to offer a list of responses I had used or heard.

The Garbage Collector's Answer. Yes, it is dirty work, but someone must do it. We cannot have a functioning adversary system without partisans for both sides. A defense lawyer keeps the system clean by holding the police and the prosecutors to high standards. True, his methods are often unrefined and he may use rough tactics and searing cross-examination, but essentially his work is the same as that of any skilled trial lawyer, civil or criminal, who arranges, argues, and even orients the facts with only the client's interests in mind.

The Constitutionalist's Answer. It is noble work. The Right to Counsel is here invoked—to the best effect still by Anthony Lewis, speaking on the "dream of Gideon" of "a vast, diverse country in which every [person] charged with crime will be capably defended, no matter what his economic circumstances, and in which the lawyer representing him will do so proudly, without resentment."[6] Or as Clara Foltz, the founder of the public defender, put it, speaking of the duty of the government to provide counsel for the indigent, 70 years before Gideon: "Let the criminal courts be [reorganized] upon a basis of exact, equal and free justice."[7]

The Civil Libertarian's Answer. The criminally accused are the representatives of us all. When their rights are eroded, the camel's nose is under and the tent may collapse on anyone. In protecting the constitutional rights of criminal defendants, we are only protecting ourselves.

The Legal Positivist's Answer. Truth cannot be known. Facts are indeterminate, contingent, and, in criminal cases, often evanescent. A finding of guilt is not necessarily the truth, but instead is a legal conclusion arrived at after the role of the defense lawyer has been fully played.

The sophist would add that it is not the duty of the defense lawyer to act as fact finder. Were she to handle a case according to her own assessment of guilt or innocence, she would be in the role of judge rather than advocate.

The Philosopher's Answer. There is a difference between legal and moral guilt; the defense lawyer should not let her apprehension of moral guilt interfere with the analysis of legal guilt. The usual example is that of the person accused of murder who can respond successfully with a claim of self-defense. The accused may feel morally guilty but not be legally culpable. Foltz would add that all the accused are presumed innocent by sacred principles of law and should be treated accordingly until a final verdict or plea.

The Oddsmaker's Answer. It is better that ten guilty people go free than that one innocent is convicted. The risk of acquitting the guilty is the price of our societal concern for sparing the innocent.

The Political Activist's Answer. Most people who commit crimes are themselves the victims of injustice. This statement is true generally when those accused are oppressed minorities. It is also often true in the immediate case because the defendant has been battered and mistreated in the process of arrest and investigation. Moreover, the conditions of imprisonment may impose violence worse than that inflicted on the victim. A lawyer performs good work when he helps to prevent the imprisonment of the poor, the outcast, and minorities in shameful conditions.

The Social Worker's Answer. This reason is closely akin to the political activist's reason, but the emphasis is different. Those accused of crime, as the most visible representatives of the disadvantaged underclass in America, will actually be helped by having a defender, regardless of the actual outcome of their cases. Being treated as a real person in our society (almost by definition, one who has a lawyer is a real person) and accorded the full panoply of rights and the measure of concern afforded by a lawyer can promote rehabilitation. Because the accused comes from a community, the beneficial effect of giving him his due will spread to his friends and relatives, decreasing their anger and alienation.

The Humanitarian's Answer: The criminally accused are men and women in great need, and lawyers should come to their aid. That great icon of the criminal defense bar, Clarence Darrow, wrote in his autobiography:

> Strange as it may seem, I grew to like to defend men and women charged with crime. It soon came to be something more than the winning or losing of a case. I sought to learn why one goes one way and another takes an entirely different road...I was dealing with life, with its hopes and fears, its aspirations and despairs. With me it was going to the foundation of motive and conduct and adjustments for human beings, instead of blindly talking of hatred and vengeance, and that subtle, indefinable quality that men call "justice," and of which nothing really is known.[8]

The Egotist's Answer. Defending criminal cases is more interesting than the routine and repetitive work done by most lawyers, even those engaged in what passes for litigation in civil practice. The heated facts of crime provide voyeuristic excitement. Actual court appearances, even jury trials, come earlier and more often in one's career than can be expected in any other area of law. And winning, ah winning, has great significance because the cards are stacked for the prosecutor. To win as an underdog, and to win when the victory is clear—there is no appeal from a "Not Guilty" verdict—is sweet.

My Answer. Though many of the answers overlap, many do not. For instance, one can be a successful defender without a drop of social worker in her veins, or love the work without any particular attachment to the development of the law. My point is only that, whatever the rationale, the defender, unlike most professionals, must have one. My own reason for finding criminal defense work rewarding and important is an amalgam in roughly equal parts of the social worker's, the humanitarian's, and the egotist's reason and is encapsulated in a story.

I once represented a woman, I will call her Geraldine, who was accused under a draconian federal drug law of her third offense for possessing heroin. The first conviction carried a mandatory sentence of five years with no possibility of probation or parole. The second conviction carried a penalty of ten years with no probation and no parole. The third conviction carried a sentence of twenty years on the same terms. Geraldine was 42 years old, black, poor, and uneducated. During the few years of her adult life when not incarcerated by the state, she had been imprisoned by heroin addiction of the most awful sort.

But even for one as bereft as Geraldine, the general practice was to allow a guilty plea to a local drug charge, which did not carry the harsh mandatory penalties. In this case, however, the prosecutor refused the usual plea. Casting about for a defense, I sent her for a mental examination. The doctors at the public hospital reported that Geraldine had a mental disease: inadequate personality. When I inquired about the symptoms of this illness, one said: "Well, she is just the most inadequate person I've ever seen." But there it was—at least a defense—a disease or defect listed in the Diagnostic and Statistical Manual of that day.

At the trial I was fairly choking with rage and righteousness. I tried to paint a picture of the poverty and hopelessness of her life through lay witnesses and the doctors (who were a little on the inadequate side themselves). The prosecutor and I almost came to physical blows—the angriest I have ever been in court. Geraldine observed the seven days of trial with only mild interest, but when after many hours of deliberation the jury returned a verdict of "Not Guilty by Reason of Insanity," she burst into tears. Throwing her arms around me, she said: "I'm so happy for you."

Embodied in the Geraldine story, which has many other aspects but which is close to true as I have written it, are my answers to the question: "How can you defend someone you know is guilty?" By direct application of my skills, I saved a woman from spending the rest of her adult life in prison. In constructing her defense, I became intimate with a life as different from my own as could be imagined, and I learned from that experience. In ways that are not measurable, I think that Geraldine's friends and relatives who testified and talked with me were impressed by the fact that she had a "real" lawyer provided by the system. But in the last analysis, Geraldine was right. The case became my case more than hers. What I liked most was the unalloyed pleasure of the sound of "Not Guilty." There are few such pure joys in life.

The story of Geraldine is one of my urtexts—I've told it at least once or twice a year for decades, regularly in criminal procedure and sometimes in civil procedure as well. Recalling the thrill of that verdict also brings to fond memory Judge William B. Bryant. He was the first African-American judge on the US District Court in DC, as he had been the first federal prosecutor there, a job he left to become a criminal defense lawyer.

In the cold marble precincts of that court where most judges felt it beneath their dignity to preside over trials for street crimes, Judge Bryant alone fully appreciated the difficult work of a defender. His courtroom was also wonderfully civilized—he listened to both sides with sympathy and intelligence, and best of all, a certain enjoyment of the human predicament in which we were all enmeshed. His good humor leavened the irate adversary exchange in Geraldine's case. When the prosecutor asked for a recess because I had "threatened" him, Judge Bryant responded with unfeigned interest: "What on earth did she say?" (In one of many angry moments, I had said I would get him disbarred if he asked another question inviting inadmissible evidence.)

Though outside the courthouse, I had some friends who were prosecutors, in trial they were usually the enemy—even more so in this case because the prosecutor AUSA had denied the customary plea bargain. After hearing a rumor that he simply wanted the experience of a trial against me, I offered to turn the case over to another defender. But he claimed that Geraldine was a dealer who deserved a long prison sentence and refused the merciful plea.

Drawing Judge Bryant from the random assignment system was one of the few lucky things that had ever happened to Geraldine, and to her lawyer it felt like a form of insurance. I was sure the judge would avoid imposing the mandatory 20 years of hard time by taking the case from the jury and granting a judgment of acquittal. And I knew also that there would be plausible grounds for it because the government bore the ultimate burden of proving sanity beyond a reasonable doubt, a hard one to meet.

My confidence in the judge's compassion led me into an experiment in jury selection—that I once heard Edward Bennett Williams recommend. He scorned the services of jury consultants (though he hired them) and advocated putting the first 12 in the box. "If you do your job they will do theirs," he said. I had always wanted to try it and see if it would impress a jury in my client's favor to be accepted without probing inquires into their beliefs and prejudices. But I was afraid to experiment in an actual case until this golden opportunity. After the acquittal I expected from the judge, I would be able to question the jurors about their reaction to the absence of voir dire. So, as soon as 12 people were seated, I announced: "The defense accepts this jury."

The dramatic move threw the prosecutor off his game. Expecting that jury selection in an insanity case would take some hours, he had no witnesses ready and only a rough opening statement. My early tactical advantage paled during the trial, however, because this unselected jury just looked so bad. They were diverse enough, but, regardless of race or gender, they shrugged and sneered and slept as I presented the evidence of my client's horrendous childhood and of the toll on the development of her personality from many years of heroin addiction. Juror number six in particular distressed me. I can see her today—a large Germanic woman with thin lips whose hair looked like it was cut around a bowl. Every time I looked at her, she rolled her eyes and shook her head.

The only thing that sustained me during the seven dreary days of trial was the expectation that the judge would direct the verdict. But instead he sent the jury out to deliberate and told me privately to "keep the faith." When at last they announced "Not Guilty by Reason of Insanity" and Geraldine acted as if my life had been the one saved, Judge Bryant started laughing. He laughed so hard that he almost fell off his high bench.

He continued laughing when Juror number 6 joined Geraldine and me: "Well, we went out 11–1 for conviction, but I was finally able to bring them around," she declared. Single-handedly she had led the jury to see that Geraldine should be treated and not punished. Her eye-rolls and head-shakings were indications of empathy. Since that verdict I have joined my hero, Judge Bryant, in believing in the ultimate wisdom of the jury and in its often mysterious deliberative process.[9] The Geraldine story has a number of such lessons, but the subtext is always the fun and satisfaction, the glory and goodness of defending. Perhaps its triumphal tone roused the critics who complain that it is dishonest and does not reflect the real life of defenders. Women charged with nonviolent crimes are not the usual clients, happy endings are rare, and one could spend a lifetime in the work and never have a case like Geraldine's. Some people also use the story to illustrate the insensitivity of white elites like me, charging that Geraldine was objectified, her secrets and sorrows revealed without her approval or participation. But this reported criticism does not bother me because I knew Geraldine approved of what I was doing.[10]

A more jarring censure arose some years ago when I told the story in a speech at Indiana Law School. As usual, I joked a little about the ridiculous diagnosis (inadequate personality) and its treatability (zero). But I was not implying that insanity was an illegitimate defense in Geraldine's case. Mental illness caused by profound, untreated addiction was a valid claim that I could have presented solely through lay witnesses if I had not found experts to agree. My main point in telling the story that night was the absurdity of the system and the need for a zealous creative defense lawyer to save the client from its extremities. As always I was proselytizing, trying to attract young people to the work, especially to the defense, by showing how much intellectual and forensic enjoyment there can be in such a case and what a difference an individual lawyer can make.

To my surprise, and dismay, in the comment period, Indiana professor William Hodes compared the Geraldine defense to that in the O. J. Simpson murder trial.[11] He suggested that both Simpson's and Geraldine's defenses were fabricated by highly skilled defense lawyers going to the outer barricade of zealous representation. I had constructed an insanity defense for a guilty drug dealer, and "the dream team" (O. J's lawyers) had implied that the racist LA police had framed him for murder and demanded that the jury "send a message" to the people of the city with a not guilty verdict. Professor Hodes praised the defense performances in both cases and implied that the not guilty verdicts showed the workings of our justice system at its best.

I could not accept the compliment or comparison. To me, the trial of O. J. Simpson was a travesty and the verdict a miscarriage of justice. There is not enough space here to compile the errors and missteps on every side in the trial, but I believe that if the judge, jury, and prosecution had done their jobs, there would have been a guilty verdict.[12] To my students at the time, I explained that juries are imperfect human institutions that make mistakes. But years later, I still find it painful that the jury failed in the O. J. case so publicly.

Did the defense lawyers do anything wrong, dishonest, or unethical in putting the police on trial instead of O. J. Simpson? Attacking the police is a familiar tactic used especially by defense lawyers who view their work partly as guardians of the criminal justice system. Certainly the defense team did not commit established wrongs like suborning perjury or manufacturing evidence. On the other hand, some capable and ethical defense lawyers would not think there was sufficient connection between the racism of the police and framing Simpson for murder, enough of a foundation for the far-ranging questions allowed by the judge.

The issue of what a defense lawyer may honestly and ethically do in "defending the guilty" is subtle and inherent in the omnipresent question. Indeed, it was present at the creation of public defense. When researching the life of Clara Foltz, the nineteenth-century founder of the movement, I studied the authorities available to her on the subject of representing the so-called guilty client. Thomas Cooley's *Constitutional Limitations* was the best known of these.[13] He advised that a lawyer who, after he has begun his representation, becomes convinced of his client's guilt must nevertheless continue his advocacy to assure that "a conviction is not secured contrary to law."[14]

But Cooley went on to say that in this situation "how persistent counsel may be in pressing for the acquittal of his client, and to what extent he may be justified in throwing his own personal character as a weight in the scale of justice, *are questions of ethics rather than of law*."[15] In other words, the law demands that the attorney continue his representation, but how eager and ardent he should be in the defense is entirely up to the individual lawyer. After identifying the "ethical" question, however, the great jurisprude did not even attempt an answer. He said that counsel must not use fraud or falsehood "even in a just cause" and at the same time that it was wrong to accept "the confidence of the accused, and then [betray] it by a feeble and heartless defense." Cooley implied a middle ground between these two, but locating that ground has proved difficult for academics and practitioners alike.

Clara Foltz found it in the presumption of innocence; she believed that a defense lawyer should live out the law's presumption and consider her client guiltless until the contrary was proved.[16] Monroe Freedmen and Abbe Smith, the editors of this volume, have been the major modern proponents of robust representation along the client-centered lines that Foltz suggested.[17] Others propose that lawyers should take into account their roles as officers of the court and citizens concerned with public justice when choosing their tactics.[18] "Defending the Guilty," published so long ago, was meant as a contribution to this discourse, although admittedly it elides the ethical issues inherent in the question of how to defend the guilty.

I elided the issues in practice as well; I managed to represent hundreds of people charged with serious crimes without confronting the harrowing moral dilemmas posited in the debates over defense ethics. For instance, not once in my practice did a client admit his guilt and then demand to testify falsely. Using techniques gleaned from what I saw when working as a paid lawyer, I did not advise the client at the outset that he must tell me the truth. Instead, I would say: "I don't want to know now from you whether you are, or feel, guilty. I intend to investigate the government's case, and talk to witnesses who might help you. Who are these? And how did you get arrested?" For my indigent clients, I would turn to collecting information to get them released pending trial.

I would investigate possible defenses, file motions to suppress, and gather favorable information generally so that we had something to bargain with beyond the client's trial right. But unless there was a decent defense, it was too risky to roll the dice at trial, hoping for an anomalous, merciful, or mistaken verdict. A judge who has heard the witnesses and the full account of the crime will tend toward a heavier sentence than one who has only the limited information presented at a guilty plea. And though it is wrong (indeed unconstitutional), some judges will penalize the accused for insisting on his trial and for presumably committing perjury if she testifies and is convicted.[19]

Most of my clients understood these things as well as I did. When we disagreed about going to trial, it was mostly in cases where I thought we had a fighting chance and that I would enjoy myself. Naturally, these were also the cases in which the prosecutors offered the best pleas—and usually the clients jumped at them. Preparing the defendant to enter a plea was soon enough for me to learn from him about his actual guilt.

In the cases that went to trial, I always managed to develop at least a reasonable doubt, coupled with the atavistic desire simply to win. Once or twice I represented clients I thought were factually innocent—but usually the prosecutor would drop such cases before trial. I enjoyed considerable success with juries, based I think on projecting my faith in my clients and my belief in the evidence and arguments. As Thomas Cooley would say, I "threw my own personal character as a weight in the scale of justice."

I didn't discuss any of this in the original "Defending the Guilty" article. Thirty years ago, I did not want to engage in the ethical quandaries of defending. I still don't want to discuss them—as if those were the important issues confronting the criminal justice system. In the 1983 article, I used a classic rhetorical gambit by arguing that the question itself was wrong. It should not be "how can you defend" but "how can you fail to defend." That is still the real question today.

Almost 50 years after *Gideon* and more than a 100 after Clara Foltz first urged the pressing need for a public defender in 1893, the representation of the indigent accused remains woefully inadequate. Most defender offices (not all, but most) are overwhelmed with caseloads and clients they cannot serve adequately, no matter the amount of their skill or devotion.[20] Sometimes the failure of the criminal justice system to provide adequate defense services appears willfully defective.

Take Judge Richard Posner's "hardheaded" (his description) approach: after acknowledging the poor quality of much indigent criminal defense, he wrote that the lawyers nevertheless "seem to be good enough to reduce the probability of convicting an innocent person to a very low level. If they were much better, either many guilty people would be acquitted or society would have to devote much greater resources to the prosecution of criminal cases. A bare-bones system for defense of indigent criminal defendants may be optimal."[21] His premise that few innocent people are convicted seems wrong in light of the many much-publicized exonerations in recent years, and even the guilty often serve unjust sentences because of ineffective assistance of counsel.

Faced with a criminal justice system in disarray, surprisingly like that of today, Foltz believed that a public defender who was equal in skills and resources to the public prosecutor could make great changes. Her vision was one of equal adversaries, bearing each other mutual respect and regard, a fair judge, an honest jury—all engaged in the same task, to assure "exact, equal and free justice." And she promised in return "the blessings which flow from constitutional obligations conscientiously kept and government duties sacredly performed." I believe that if we can only summon the political will, the promise holds true today.

NOTES

1. Barbara Allen Babcock, "Defending the Guilty," *Cleveland State Law Review* 32 (1983–1984). 175.
2. Edward Bennett Williams, *One Man's Freedom* (Atheneum: New York, 1962), 12–13.
3. For more on the debate between John and me, see Barbara Allen Babcock, "The Duty to Defend," *Yale Law Journal* 114 (2005): 1489.
4. 372 U.S. 335 (1963).
5. "Oral History of Barbara Babcock," by LaDoris Cordell, *ABA Commission on Women in the Profession*, February 8, 2006, http://www

.americanbar.org/content/dam/aba/directories/women_trailblazers/babcock_interview_4.authcheckdam.pdf.
6. Anthony Lewis, *Gideon's Trumpet* (New York: Random House, 1964), 205.
7. Clara Foltz, "Public Defenders," (lecture, Congress on Jurisprudence and Law Reform, Chicago World's Fair, 1893) in *Albany Law Journal* 48 (1893).
8. Clarence Darrow, *The Story of My Life* (New York: Da Capo Press, 1996), 75–76.
9. Barbara Babcock and Ticien Sassoubre, "Deliberation in 12 Angry Men," *Chicago-Kent Law Review* 82 (2007) (commentary on the workings of the jury).
10. Most of all, Geraldine wanted to avoid another long prison sentence. An acquittal on the grounds of insanity would mean a sentence to a mental hospital until no longer dangerous to herself or others. Since her diagnosis of inadequate personality disorder described a condition neither treatable nor dire, she was likely to be (and was) out of the hospital in months rather than years.
11. W. William Hodes, "Rethinking the Way Law Is Taught: Can We Improve Lawyer Professionalism by Teaching Hired Guns to Aim Better?" *Kentucky Law Journal* 87 (1999): 1050 (describing the talk at Indiana on September 29, 1997).
12. See, for example, Barbara Allen Babcock, "In Defense of the Criminal Jury," in *Postmortem: The O. J. Simpson Case*, ed. Jeffrey Abramson (New York: Basic Books, 1996) (drawing on articles I wrote during the trial for the LA Times); Barbara Allen Babcock, "Protect the Jury System, Judge was the Problem," *Los Angeles Times*, October 8, 1995, http://articles.latimes.com/1995-10-08/opinion/op-54586_1_jury-system.
13. Barbara Allen Babcock, "Inventing the Public Defender," *American Criminal Law Review* 43 (2006); Thomas M. Cooley, *A Treatise on the Constitutional Limitations Which Rest upon the Legislative Power of the States of the American Union*, 2nd ed. (Boston: Little, Brown, and Company, 1871).
14. Cooley, *A Treatise on Constitutional Limitations*, 361–362.
15. Ibid., emphasis supplied.
16. Babcock, "Inventing the Public Defender," 1305–1307 (describing Foltz's position).
17. Monroe H. Freedman and Abbe Smith, *Understanding Lawyers' Ethics*, 4th ed. (New Providence, NJ: LexisNexis, 2010). Both have written many articles on aspects of zealous representation. Monroe Freedman's 1966 article was the first modern treatment of the issues and laid the foundation for the debate that followed. Monroe H. Freedman, "Professional Responsibility of the Criminal Defense Lawyer: The Three Hardest Questions," *Michigan Law Review* 64 (1966).
18. William H. Simon, "The Ethics of Criminal Defense," *Michigan Law Review* 91 (1993).

19. Barbara Allen Babcock, "Taking the Stand," *William and Mary Law Review* 35 (1993): 1–19.
20. Norman Lefstein, *Securing Reasonable Caseloads, Ethics and Law in Public Defense* (Chicago: American Bar Association, 2011), http://www.americanbar.org/content/dam/aba/publications/books/ls_sclaid_def_securing_reasonable_caseloads.authcheckdam.pdf (documenting the dire condition of public defense, and calling the profession to action).
21. Richard A. Posner, *The Problematics of Moral and Legal Theory* (Cambridge, MA: Harvard University Press, 1999), 163–164.

2

How Can You Prosecute Those People?

Paul Butler

Introduction

Defense attorneys are frequently asked the "cocktail party" question: "how can you represent those people?" Prosecutors are rarely asked "how can you prosecute those people?" It's a good question—and maybe harder to answer, in many respects, than the defense attorney question. It is interesting that we do not demand the same moral accountability from prosecutors that we do from defense attorneys about the work they have chosen.

But people do ask prosecutors sometimes. When I was a prosecutor, the people who asked it were usually African-Americans. I would not call it a cocktail party question because the people who asked generally weren't the cocktail party type. They were poor and working-class folks whose sons or grandbabies had gotten caught up in the criminal justice system. I'll call it the "courthouse hallway" question because that was the usual forum.

The courthouse hallway question often was an accusatory look rather than a form of words. It came from relatives of the person on trial, defense attorneys, and sometimes, if I hadn't done my voir dire right, jurors. It made me feel like I was the one on trial, like I had done something wrong.

The question also seemed like a kind of racial profiling; I thought I got the question more because I am African-American, although perhaps that was just my guilty conscience. This is what the question seemed to signify: now was the first time that a professional black man had ever paid much attention to their kid and it was only because that professional black man—me—was trying to get the kid locked up.

Here I will provide a brief account of how I could have—and did—prosecute those people, and then compare the debate about the ethics of defense work to the new debate about the ethics of prosecution work. I will also examine some morally problematic aspects of the work of prosecutors and conclude with a brief comparison of the ethics of defense versus prosecution in an age of mass incarceration and extraordinary racial disparities in punishment.

How and Why I Prosecuted Those People

I became a prosecutor because of my experiences as a young African-American man. The times I wasn't being harassed by police and security guards, I was being harassed by other young black men. Stopped and questioned by the former, robbed of my lunch money by the latter.

I wanted to use my law school education to address the two most vexing criminal justice issues for blacks—overenforcement of the law and underenforcement of the law—at the same time. So I joined the US Department of Justice as a trial attorney.

My plan was to go in as an undercover brother. It's the classic liberal response—to infiltrate the oppressor to try to create change from the inside. I thought nobody would be in a better position to make a difference than me.

Young black men are the most frequent victims of crime and the most likely to be charged with crimes. I could have responded the way that lots of my brothers do—by not trusting anybody. You walk through your hood and you glare at the dope boys on the corner, who make your community feel unsafe. Then, when the squad car slowly rolls by, and the cops take a good look at you, you glare at them too.

But I was an idealist. And being a prosecutor seemed to be the perfect solution to the long-standing concerns that African-Americans had about both civil rights and public safety. In the segregated neighborhood in Chicago where I grew up, blacks made the same claims about law enforcement that they do now. The times that my neighbors were not complaining about how the police treated them, they were complaining that the police were never there when they needed them.

These claims seemed contradictory, but they were both accurate. And unfortunately things have not changed much now, when the United States has almost 1 million black people in prison.

The African-American prosecutor lives at the intersection of crime control and racial disparities in criminal justice. Most fail, as I did, to make the difference they hope to make because their tool—locking people up—is too blunt an instrument. In the adversarial system of American criminal justice, prosecutors are forced to choose a side. So they end up enforcing selectively applied criminal laws, defending the police, and locking up a lot of black people.

Who gets prosecuted in the United States is politicized and racialized. The cities that have the highest number of incarcerated blacks are often the same as the ones with the most African-American prosecutors.

But when African-American prosecutors talk among themselves and say, "I wouldn't trust this guy in a dark alley," they could be talking about the police as easily as their most recent defendant. Black prosecutors are still black, which means they have their own stories about being racially profiled.

People ask if, when I was a prosecutor and I got stopped by the cops, I told them what I did for a living. Yes, but it didn't always make a difference. It didn't make a difference the time I told the cop that I was a prosecutor, and he smirked and said, "So you probably know this already"—and then he read me my *Miranda* rights.[1]

I became a prosecutor because I wanted to help victims, and not be one—of the police or of another black man. The police have a name for black on black crime: routine homicide. The closure rate on those cases is often less than 50 percent.

So there is a crying need for law enforcement interventions that actually work to keep communities of color both safe and free. I have explained elsewhere why my work as a prosecutor did not facilitate that effort.[2]

Here I want to examine why, given the vast inequities and draconian punishment that mark the American criminal justice regime, defenders—the people who resist this regime—are challenged more than prosecutors—the people who uphold it.

The Morality of Prosecution Work: A New Debate

The discussion about the ethics and morality of prosecution can be traced to Abbe Smith's seminal article "Can You Be a Prosecutor and a Good Person?"[3] Professor Smith wrote: "We live in an extraordinarily harsh and punitive time, a time we will look back on in shame. The rate of incarceration in this country, the growing length of prison terms, the conditions of confinement, and the frequency with which we put people to death have created a moral crisis. Although, arguably, all those who work in the criminal justice system have something to do with its perpetuation and legitimacy, prosecutors are the chief legal enforcers of the current regime."[4]

In her book *Arbitrary Justice*, Angela Davis took prosecutors to task for practices that perpetuate racial disparities and recommended legal and policy interventions that might reduce those disparities.[5] In a chapter in my book *Let's Get Free: A Hip-Hop Theory of Justice*, I argued that "the adversarial nature of the justice system, the culture of the prosecutor's office, and the politics of crime pose insurmountable obstacles for prosecutors who are concerned with economic and racial justice."[6] That conclusion has been vigorously contested by many current and former prosecutors, some of whom have engaged me in public debates on the topic.

Legal scholars, and former defense attorneys, James Forman and Jonathan Rapping, have also written critically about the morality of prosecution under the present conditions of American criminal justice.[7] In "Who's Guarding the Henhouse?," Professor Rapping castigates the prosecutor's office because it has become "more focused on conviction rates than the quality of the case resolution; has lost sight of the humanity of the people it prosecutes; and has minimized the import of the fundamental protections that are the foundation of our democracy." He states that "the ethical prosecutor should refuse to charge cases that the system is not funded to handle responsibly."[8]

So there is a growing critique of the morality of being a prosecutor in the United States in the twenty-first century. But that debate and the other debates about how defense attorneys can morally represent people accused of crimes are never recognized as related. In the next part, I want to flip the script by suggesting that some of the moral concerns expressed about defense attorneys are equally applicable to prosecutors.

INNOCENCE AND GUILT

The most serious moral concern that many people have about defense attorneys is that they defend people who are guilty of the crime. Of course, the opposite is true of prosecutors: they sometimes prosecute, and even obtain convictions of, people who are innocent. While no well-meaning person desires this result, no one could deny that it occurs.[9]

The US system of justice is based on the idea that we prefer the guilty to go free rather than the innocent to be convicted. This ideal is most famously expressed in the "Blackstone ratio" that it is "better that ten guilty persons escape, than that one innocent suffer." Thus when the defense attorney helps a "guilty" person go free, she is actually upholding an important principle of our democracy. The prosecutor who convicts an innocent person, on the other hand, subverts this ideal. It is strange, then, that "wrongful" acquittals seem to inspire more questioning about the role of the lawyer than wrongful convictions.

Perhaps the reason for the distinction goes to the intent or knowledge of each lawyer. Defense attorneys, the argument might be, sometimes know their client is guilty, whereas a prosecutor would not know that the defendant she is prosecuting is innocent.

I never prosecuted anyone who was innocent. I don't think. But of course I would say that, I was a prosecutor. Like most people drawn to this work, I possess a moral certainty about some things I cannot actually know.[10] In the cases I prosecuted I think the defendants were guilty based on the evidence (and because 90% of the time, they pled guilty). The evidence is usually collected by the police, so my belief in the defendant's guilt also requires a certain amount of trust of the police. Yet the Supreme Court has described police officers as "engaged in the competitive enterprise of ferreting out crime," and for that reason they require judicial oversight when they seek search or arrest warrants.[11]

Prosecutors don't usually have time to second-guess the police or even to corroborate their work. An empirical study of prosecutor workloads found that in Houston, the average prosecutor handles 1,500 cases a year, in Las Vegas, 800, and in Chicago between 800 and 1,000.[12] Professor Jonathan Rapping estimates that "with caseloads this high, the prosecutor who works fifty hours a week for fifty weeks per year will be able to devote between 1.66 and 3.125 hours to each case each year."[13] Thus the prosecutor's "knowledge" of guilt is mainly secondary and not well-informed. It hardly seems the basis for the quality of information that any of us would desire in making a life-altering decision.

The risk of wrongful conviction is compounded by the bias that a defendant in a criminal case experiences from the moment he enters the courtroom. Moreover, prosecutors have more trials than almost any other litigator and they are often exceptionally able advocates. I believe, for example, that I have the skills that would allow me to get a conviction of an innocent person of a crime. Indeed, there is a saying that is a favorite of some prosecutors—one hopes it is said facetiously: "Convicting the guilty is easy. Convicting the innocent is the real challenge." In addition, defendants have little recourse once they are found guilty. Appeals are almost always focused on legal errors, not innocence. Indeed Supreme Court justice Antonin Scalia has stated, "This Court has *never* held that the Constitution forbids the execution of a convicted defendant who has had a full and fair trial but is later able to convince a habeas court that he is 'actually' innocent."[14]

In sum, prosecution incurs the risk of wrongful convictions, and this risk upsets democratic norms in a way that does not occur when a defense attorney wins an acquittal for someone who actually committed a crime. It is troubling, then, that the rhetoric about the morality of helping obtain inaccurate verdicts focuses on defense attorneys and not on prosecutors.

Helping Victims

The discourse about the ethics of criminal practice is sometimes framed by a good/evil dichotomy that is not particularly elucidating. Nowhere is this more evident than in the "prosecutor as protector of victim" trope. If prosecutors help victims, then what do defense attorneys do?

As a matter of trial practice, we know what defense attorneys do to victims. Defense attorneys interrogate victims, they cast doubt on their credibility, and they paint them as unobservant or malicious or complicit. In this narrative, the victim is presented as powerless, exploited, injured. Anybody who had a conscience would treat her with respect, and that is the opposite of how defense attorneys behave.

This narrative is incomplete, and to the extent it casts prosecutors as the victim's protector, it is misleading. As a prosecutor, I had several occasions to tell victims, "I don't represent you." The prosecutor's client is the government, not the victim. Victims are simply witnesses, with all the baggage that implies. Usually she is the star witness, so your most profound hope is that she doesn't mess up your case. In order to prevent that from happening, prosecutors "prepare" witnesses. This may involve coercion, for example subpoenaing people to make them come to court even if they don't want to. It may involve harsh questioning or threats. The victim is supposed to tolerate it, based on the understanding that it's all in the service of punishing her victimizer.

Of course, people should be punished when they hurt others. The point is that in their zeal to prove that a crime occurred, prosecutors don't necessarily treat victims with dignity and kindness. For both sides, the victim is more or less a prop. This is disturbing to hear because we know that she is also a human being. But the trial lawyer's responsibility is to truss, manipulate, and fashion her into the teller of the story that the lawyer has created. People understand that this is what the defense attorney is doing, and that is a reason some people complain about defense attorneys. But prosecutors are also guilty of this sin.

In a more fundamental sense, defense attorneys are also helping victims—their clients. Virtually every person who commits a violent crime has been a victim at some point as well.[15] This is not to excuse the crime, but rather to place the act in a larger context, a context more like the real world, and less like the artificial constructs of "evidence" that the courtroom allows.

In the real world, the determination of "defendant," "victim," and "witness" is more random than it seems in the courtroom. "On any given Sunday," Lenese Herbert used to say when she was a prosecutor, "someone who is a victim today could have been a defendant yesterday and might be a witness tomorrow."[16] If it's the Sunday that she's the victim, she gets solicitude. If, on the other hand, it's the Sunday that she's the defendant, she is widely despised.

"Those People"

In the cocktail party question, "how can you represent those people?," "those people" are generally understood to be the guilty, as the preceding section discussed. But prosecutors also have clients. They represent "people" as well. Sometimes literally, as in New York and Illinois, which style their criminal cases "The People versus [the name of the defendant]." Otherwise, the prosecutor represents the people in the form of the state, like "California v. O. J. Simpson," or the "United States versus Bernie Madoff." What are the moral issues involved in representing "those people" in criminal prosecutions?

The Supreme Court, in some death penalty cases, has suggested that *the people* the prosecutor represents are emotional and vindictive. They need to be represented by a lawyer, the court says, because otherwise they might take matters in their own hands.[17] In their name, the prosecutor exacts a vengeance, thus circumventing the need for a lynching.

In drug cases, on the other hand, The People are situated differently than in violent crime cases. In drug cases The People are white, and middle class, and hypocrites, some of them. They tolerate a war on drugs selectively waged against low-income African-Americans. Others use drugs just as much, or more, but they don't get prosecuted. The prosecutor is a key component of the machinery of this discrimination. How can she, knowing this, represent those people?

In *The Collapse of American Criminal Justice*, the late Harvard law professor William Stuntz described the American body politic as believing that "a healthy criminal justice system should punish all the criminals it can."[18] This perspective is the result of antiblack political appeals and sensational news broadcasts rather than a reasoned analysis of public safety. Of course, in a democracy, people have the right to make bad public policy. I simply want to point out that in the US punishment regime, just as the defense attorney's client may not have clean hands, the prosecutor's client may at times have motives that are ill-informed and even discriminatory.

Two Troubling Aspects of How Prosecutors Do Their Work

Thus far I have explained how three moral critiques of defense attorneys—that their work leads to inaccurate verdicts, that they treat victims unfairly, and that they represent people with antisocial interests—can also be applied to prosecutors. Now I will briefly identify some other qualities of prosecution that should give us pause about whether the work can be done ethically. This inquiry also will be in the service of elevating the *courtroom hallway question* to the central place that the *cocktail party question* presently enjoys in the discourse about the morality of criminal law practice.

Coercing Guilty Pleas

US Supreme Court justice Anthony Kennedy has stated that "criminal justice today for the most part is a system of pleas, not a system of trials."[19] More than 90 percent of people who are charged with crimes end up pleading guilty. This is not because many of these defendants do not want to go to trial. Rather it is because prosecutors overcharge, in order to force the defendant to plead guilty to receive a lesser sentence.

In *Bordenkircher v. Hayes,* the Supreme Court blessed this practice.[20] Paul Hayes was charged with writing a bad check for $88.30. The prosecutor told him that he would recommend a sentence of five years if he pled guilty. If, on the other hand, he made the government go through the bother of a trial, the prosecution would seek life imprisonment.[21] Hayes went to trial, was convicted, sentenced to life, and the Supreme Court affirmed. The court recognized, however, that "the breadth of discretion that our country's legal system vests in prosecuting attorneys carries with it the potential for both individual and institutional abuse."[22]

Prosecutors have not taken the court's admonition about the potential for abuse to heart. Rather they have embraced the court's disinclination to regulate their discretion. Offering choices like those that Mr. Hayes was offered are routine practice for prosecutors, with horrific consequences. A reasonable innocent person, facing such a choice, might reasonably decide to plead guilty. Indeed, unless one's case would almost certainly lead to an acquittal, it might border on recklessness not to plead guilty. What prosecutors do, every day, is force people to give up one of their most precious constitutional rights, and one that is almost uniquely American, the right to trial by jury. This is not a necessary component of prosecutor's work; it simply makes their jobs easier. Comparing the moral critique of defense work, it is hard to find an analogue.

Dehumanization of Defendants

Some defense attorneys answer the cocktail party question by saying that it is not difficult to represent accused persons because defense attorneys get to know their clients as human beings. Remembering Sister Helen Prejean's admonition that "people are more than the worst thing that they have ever done in their lives," Rapping reminds us that criminal defendants are "sons and daughters, mothers and fathers, brothers and sisters. They may be cooks, sanitation workers, artists, or hairdressers. They are whole human beings with a lifetime of experiences that shape and define them."[23]

For prosecutors, on the other hand, defendants are the worst thing that they have ever done in their lives, or at least the most recent bad thing that landed them in criminal court. Few of us would want to be judged on this basis, but that is what prosecutors do. There is a certain level of hypocrisy; for example, prosecutors force defendants to suffer criminal consequences for some offenses, like drug crimes, and it is hard to believe that they would want the same for their family members or friends. The dehumanization of defendants by prosecutors is attributable in part to the adversarial system, which makes championing the defendant's cause the defense attorney's job. We can also blame the high caseload that most prosecutors carry; even if there was the inclination there, there is not the time to get to know the defendants as human beings. No matter that the prosecutor is the key player in a process that will fundamentally alter the life of the defendant.

What kind of expertise should be required when one human being wields so much power over another human being? How much knowledge should these persons be required to demonstrate about the role of poverty and race discrimination in causing people to make bad decisions? How much empirical data do they need on the most effective intervention of the state when someone has made a mistake? Exactly what bad acts by the defendant justify the unspeakable cruelties of the prisons to which prosecutors send people? And, in the absence of satisfactory answers to the questions, why are prosecutors called the "good guys?"

Racial Justice

Eric Holder, the first African-American Attorney General, was also the first black chief prosecutor in the District of Columbia. He had a famous question that he asked prospective prosecutors in interviews: "How are you going to feel about sending so many young black men to jail?" Holder's question recognized that, for better or worse, this is the everyday work of many prosecutors.

I will conclude my chapter with a short meditation on the comparative racial equality components of prosecution and defense. If defense is racial justice work, then what is prosecution?[24]

Prosecutors assert a claim on this front as well as defense attorneys'. As I have already mentioned, one reason I became a prosecutor was to help to remedy the problem of underenforcement of the law in the African-American community. The prosecutor's racial justice intervention is to bring the equal protection of the law. This is a laudable goal, but it must be balanced against the reality that the criminal justice system is the primary legal manifestation of racial subordination in the United States.[25] The problem is that the prosecutor's instrument—prison—is too blunt. She needs a scalpel but she uses a sledge hammer.

Prosecutors labor in a system that produces extraordinary race disparities. The result of her work is a selective enforcement of certain criminal laws that has resulted in more African-Americans under criminal justice supervision than there were slaves in 1850.[26] Even if prosecutors have been successful in helping minority communities receive the protection of the law—and I believe that they have—this does not ameliorate the substantial problems caused by overenforcement (especially of drug laws in the African-American community, and the "crimigration" laws against Latinos).

For example, officers of the New York Police Department, in certain neighborhoods, stop black and Latino men for virtually any reason, and they rarely find anything incriminating. In one neighborhood, the cops made over 40,000 stops, and found just 25 guns—a hit rate of less than 0.1 percent.

Meanwhile, violent crime in that community is going up. The tragedy of racial profiling is not only that it's ineffective, but it's also that it makes many of its victims hate the profilers—whether they are police, security guards, or neighborhood watchpeople. And that causes a breakdown in trust that makes public safety even more problematic.

The main work of prosecutors in this regime is to defend the police and their tactics. If the police were actually making the community safer through their rough tactics, perhaps we could reluctantly tolerate it. But they are not. Can being complicit with a justice system this racially skewed, and this ineffective, ever be morally justified?

Conclusion

Perhaps the pat conclusion of this comparison of questions—the cocktail party defense question and the courthouse hallway prosecution question—should be that both sides have a role to play. Defense attorneys are moral actors and so are prosecutors. Both are important and necessary components in the American regime of crime and punishment.

But that conclusion is trite. It is not as nuanced as justice. It's not as complicated as equality. It's not as deep as truth.

A refrain frequently heard in prosecutor's closing statements is that people should be responsible for their choices. They should be held accountable. I want to say that this applies to the lawyers in the courtroom as well as defendants on trial. Defense attorneys and prosecutors have made choices motivated and constrained by ambition, personality, luck, and morality, among other things. They work in a system that some people have compared to slavery, to Jim Crow segregation, to an American gulag. They help implement, or fight against (or maybe defense attorneys do both[27]), the largest and most draconian punishment regime in the history of the world.

For people who are concerned about social justice or racial justice or economic justice, the answer to the question "how can you defend those people?" should be clear. This doesn't automatically lead to the conclusion that defense work is the best way to challenge the system, but there should be no doubt that individual human beings—"clients"—desperately need help. But for people concerned about civil liberties and equality under the law, "how can you prosecute those people?" is a more troublesome question. If the people you care most about are victims, and you have a relatively narrow view of what it means to be a victim, there is perhaps a coherent answer. But people with more expansive visions of social justice might require a more persuasive justification.

The "smart on crime" movement led by some progressive prosecutors, like Craig Watkins, District Attorney of Dallas, Texas; Kamala Harris, the Attorney General of California; and Cyrus Vance, Jr., District attorney of New York County, is limited reason for optimism. This movement focuses on reserving incarceration for violent crime, and repairing relationships between the police and disaffected communities. The US Department of Justice, under Attorney General Eric Holder, has also promoted reconciliation between law enforcement and African-Americans.

One day the answer to the question "how can you prosecute those people?" might be as persuasive as the answer to the question "how can you defend those people?" The reality that the first question isn't even asked much—outside the affected communities—demonstrates how far we are from that day.

NOTES

1. Paul Butler, *Let's Get Free: A Hip-Hop Theory of Justice* (New York: The New Press, 2009), chap. 1.
2. Ibid., chap. 6.
3. Abbe Smith, "Can You Be a Good Person and a Good Prosecutor?," *Georgetown Journal of Legal Ethics* 14 (2001).
4. Ibid., 355.
5. Angela Davis, *Arbitrary Justice, The Power of the American Prosecutor* (New York: Oxford University Press, 2007).
6. Butler, *Let's Get Free*, 101–102.
7. Jonathan A. Rapping, "Who's Guarding the Henhouse? How the American Prosecutor Came to Devour Those He is Sworn to Protect," *Washburn Law Review* 51 (2012).
8. Ibid., 518.
9. For example, almost three hundred people have been exonerated through postconviction DNA evidence since 1989. See "Facts on Post-Conviction DNA Exonerations," The Innocence Project, accessed September 28, 2012, http://www.innocenceproject.org/Content/Facts_on_PostConviction_DNA_Exonerations.php.
10. See Abbe Smith, "Are Prosecutors Born or Made?" *Georgetown Journal of Legal Ethics* 25 (2012).
11. Johnson v. US, 333 U.S. 10, 14 (1948).
12. Adam M. Gershowitz and Laura R. Killinger, "The State (Never) Rests: How Excessive Prosecutorial Caseloads Harm Criminal Defendants," *Northwestern University Law Review* 105 (2011).

13. Rapping, "Who's Guarding the Henhouse?" 539.
14. In Re Davis, 130 S. Ct. 1, 3 (2009) (emphasis in original).
15. This is sometimes referred to as the "cycle of violence." See Abigail A. Fagan, "Relationship between Adolescent Physical Abuse and Criminal Offending: Support for an Enduring and Generalized Cycle of Violence," *Journal of Family Violence* 20 (2005).
16. Butler, *Let's Get Free*, 111.
17. See Greg v. Georgia, 428 U.S. 153 ("In part, capital punishment is an expression of society's moral outrage at particularly offensive conduct. This function may be unappealing to many, but it is essential in an ordered society that asks its citizens to rely on legal processes rather than self-help to vindicate their wrongs.").
18. William J. Stuntz, *The Collapse of American Criminal Justice* (Cambridge, MA: Harvard University Press, 2011), 55.
19. Lafler v. Cooper, 132 S. Ct. 1376, 1388 (2012).
20. 434 U.S. 357 (1978).
21. Hayes was subject to a mandatory life sentence based on a "three strikes" law. Ibid., 359 n. 3.
22. Ibid., 365.
23. Rapping, "Who's Guarding the Henhouse?" 559–560.
24. For example, see Angela J. Davis, "There but for the Grace of God Go I," and Vida Johnson, "Defending Civil Rights," in this volume.
25. Michelle Alexander, *The New Jim Crow* (New York: The New Press, 2010).
26. Ibid., 175.
27. Monroe H. Freedman, An *Ethical Manifestor for Public Defenders*, 39 Valparaiso L. Rev. 911 (2006).

3

How Can You Defend Those People?

Tucker Carrington

For a period of time when I worked as a public defender, this was the rhythm of my daily life: At the end of each day of a four-month, multiple-defendant homicide and conspiracy trial, I walked the half block from the H. Carl Moultrie I Superior Courthouse in Washington, DC, to the north exit of the Judiciary Square Metro Station.[1] There, at the top of the escalator, I would meet my wife and our 18-month-old son. My wife was finishing her last semester at Georgetown Law School. She had purposely chosen classes that met in the evening so our schedules would be in sync. Or, out of sync, depending on how you choose to look at it. She'd give me a quick kiss, a bottle of breast milk, and the stroller. And our son. As she went off to class, he and I would take the escalator down to the Metro for the trip home.

Attorneys—especially those who deal on a daily basis with live clients—have to struggle with some version of cognitive dissonance from time to time. Public defenders likely more than most. My struggle was making the transition from representing gang members whose ineptitude was matched only by their lethality to reading *Tikki Tikki Tembo* for the umpteenth time out loud to my son on the Red Line at rush hour. When the two of us arrived home, I'd feed him supper and then sing him to sleep while lying beside him in his Ikea crib-bed. Most nights I'd fall asleep, too, still in my suit, my feet resting on the floor. When my wife got home, I'd get up, pretend for a few minutes that I was interested in what had happened during her day, and then spend several hours preparing for the next day of trial.

As hectic as that period of my life was, I was wise enough to know that it was special too. I somehow knew that the intensity of the experience would likely never be matched, especially given what it was in service of: my indigent accused clients, and, in whatever corners of time I had left in my day, small but sincere efforts to sustain the love and welfare of my family.

It was therefore with particular regret that I left my job at the Public Defender Service for the District of Columbia (PDS). My decision was only supposed to be temporary—I was taking a "leave of absence," I told everyone—to teach prospective public defenders in a fellowship program and criminal clinic students at Georgetown Law School. But the truth was that I was looking for a way out of trial work, or at least the steady diet of it, to make a transition to something else. Precisely what that was going to be I couldn't say. Starting and directing an Innocence Project—in Mississippi, no less—is hardly the destination I envisioned. But what I could say was that with two young children—we had a daughter in the meantime—and a wife, who by then was a practicing attorney herself and who was doing more than her fair share of holding hearth and home together, we were getting to the end of our collective rope.

A few weeks before I left PDS, I tried my last case. Like every other case I handled, I wanted the best possible outcome for my client. But I also wanted something else out of it, too: something for me. What I wanted was some sign, a capstone even, that my time as a public defender had been well-spent—that I had become a skilled advocate, exhibited unwavering fidelity to my clients, and met the standard set by PDS: "the best representation that money can't buy."

As it turned out, I had picked a pretty poor case to hitch my hopes to. It was a fairly pedestrian codefendant murder case—pedestrian in the sense that it was more or less indistinguishable from the dozens and dozens of other similar murders that take place each year in our nation's capital. My client was female, the codefendant, male—which made the case somewhat unusual, I suppose—but in almost every other regard it was pretty straightforward: a drug deal gone bad that led to a stabbing. I had inherited the case from another lawyer in the office who had had it for some time before becoming pregnant and taking time off to have her baby. After almost a year of pretrial calendaring dates and status conferences, the prosecutor got pregnant too—and the case was continued for another year and a half.

Over that period there were a lot of court dates where not much happened. But at each one the judge would always ask whether there was any additional business that needed to be addressed. Without fail my client would lean over to me—she was about a foot and a half shorter than I—and tell me to inform the judge that she needed to be transferred immediately to St. Elizabeths Hospital.

Congress established St. Elizabeths in the mid-1800s for the treatment of patients with mental illness, including those charged with criminal offenses deemed in need of evaluation or treatment. Among some of its notorious patients were poet Ezra Pound and would-be presidential assassin John Hinckley. Located on the bluffs overlooking the Potomac and Anacostia rivers, the older part of the hospital has one of the most beautiful views of downtown DC that can be found anywhere. Several of the original buildings are architectural treasures, and so are the Frederick Olmstead and Calvert Vaux designed grounds. By the time I was practicing, however, the old St. Elizabeths had gone to seed and what remained was a bizarre mix of the decrepit and the new—contemporary clients with forensic mental health issues locked in underfunded, antiquated, columned wards with screened sleeping porches. I once went to visit a client there and walked into a time-capsule—a ward where the entire patient population was engaged in "dance therapy." It was a coed affair, the lights down low, permanent-resident patients decked out in 1970s-era *Soul Train* garb, Isaac Hayes on the stereo. Think *Shaft* crossed with *One Flew Over the Cuckoo's Nest.*

Given the limited choices available to my client, it was paradise. Especially compared to the DC Jail.

I would glance down at my client after every one of her St. Elizabeths requests. She'd look up at me. We got along well.

"You're crazy, alright," I'd lean down and whisper in her ear. "Like a fox." She'd laugh, one hand self-consciously covering her near toothless mouth.

At one point I asked her what she expected me to tell the judge in support of the request—what it was, precisely, that qualified her for an extended stay at St. Elizabeths. She paused and thought for a moment and then told me that the judge would definitely think she was crazy if I told him she had named her three children "Yesterday," "Today," and "Tomorrow."

As far as I knew she had no children. There was no record of children at any rate—not in my file, nor the notes and materials from the previous lawyers. I didn't challenge her on that; I let it pass. But I did tell her that naming children "Yesterday," "Today," and "Tomorrow" was probably not the kind of act that would get her transported from the DC Jail to St Elizabeths. What I also thought—but did not say—was that naming one's children "Yesterday," "Today," and "Tomorrow" was any number of things: odd, self-indulgent, even cruel, but not crazy.

Whatever it was she was selling, I wasn't buying. I was certain that no one else would either. As her lawyer, I declined to communicate her request to the judge.

What flowed from that decision—a very minor one in the grand scheme of a serious felony trial that, in most respects, was going to determine how my client would spend the rest of her life—is my answer to this book's title: *How Can You Represent Those People?*

* * *

In its most immediate and obvious context, my refusal was simply the result of my considered legal opinion that her request bordered on being frivolous; it had no hope of being granted. But at a much more sophisticated level—one, I imagine, where a person's lifetime of good and bad acts are toted up and calculated—it was much more than just that. It was something perilously close to a failure of moral imagination. At the very least it was a reminder of my—our—too frequent stubbornness to cop to our own rampant solipsism. Our inability to exercise, in other words, what the poet Kelly Cherry has described as "the faculty that lifts you out of your body and sets you down in someone else's skin"[2]—that offers a way out of that very human condition.

I have to admit right away to feeling somewhat uncomfortable answering this question about how it is I defend those people. In taking a moment to explain my unease I want to do two things: first, come clean about a few things, and, second, sharpen and individualize my ultimate answer to why it is that I do this work.

First, to come clean. In all candor, much of my day-to-day motivation as a public defender—about defending those people—was about as conventional as it gets. I was simply taking advantage of an embarrassment of riches. To work at one of the best public defender offices in the country, with a stable of investigators, law clerks, and helpful engaged colleagues and a low caseload, was a no-brainer. And let's not kid ourselves—it was a pretty good living. I arrived at PDS in the flush years of the mid to late 1990s. President Clinton had folded much of the District's perennial fiscal shortfall into the federal government's bulging coffers, and along with that came a significant rise in salary and benefits. A public defender with health insurance? And a 401(k)? Who knew?

I also did it because I found it personally interesting. Professor Barbara Babcock, who has contributed her own chapter to this collection, identified many years ago several motivational categories that she believed characterized public defenders: "The Garbage Collector," "The Positivist," "The Political Activist," "The Social Worker," and "The Egotist."[3] They all sounded pretty great to me, and, depending on the day and my level of outrage, I could easily fit into one or more. Every case seemed to offer either a new problem to solve or, at the very least, to demand a different solution to the same one. It was a chance to be creative; be responsible for important issues; ensure civil rights; stand up to injustice; speak truth to power. Nice work if you can get it.

The second point I want to make is that the mere asking of this question seems to demand some grand answer that I'm unable—and unworthy—to provide. I can't and won't pretend to compete with the moving and powerful experiences of some of my fellow contributors: Professor Vida Johnson, for example, whose grandparents were firebombed by the Ku Klux Klan in Laurel, Mississippi, because her grandfather was active in the National Association for the Advancement of Colored People (NAACP) and Voters League; or Professor David Singleton, who has single-handedly built one of the premier civil rights organizations in the Midwest based on his deep empathy for clients forced into a life of marginalized, second-class citizenship.

Once a public defender colleague, who, like me, is white and privileged, went with several defender friends to speak to a group of high school students about why they had decided on public defense as a career path. As my friend recounted the incident, she said that her fellow lawyers each took a few minutes to explain briefly their individual journey to becoming a public defender. One of our friends described being pulled over by a state trooper on a family vacation in Florida for no reason other than "driving while black." Another described a childhood surrounded by civil rights icons. My friend was panicking. How could she compete with these narratives?

She's not alone.

Another friend and lawyer—roughly the same age as I am—describes growing up in Richmond, Virginia, where I also grew up, and taking the bus each day to an after-school program for gifted inner-city kids. She was from a single parent home; her mother cleaned houses for a living. Needless to say, our paths never crossed in Richmond. Day after day, year after year, trip after trip to the program, where she started on the path to becoming a first-rate lawyer, she watched as kid after kid on the bus got devoured in the maw of the criminal justice system, or, worse, died an early and violent death. She speaks for them, she says, every time she opens her mouth in court on behalf of a client.

Who is it, I often wondered, that I speak for?

In some respects, even asking the question risked certain sense of entitlement. My good friend and former PDS colleague James Forman tells this story about an experience he had with his father, the late, great Student Nonviolent Coordinating Committee leader and civil rights icon, James Forman, Sr.:

> It was 1984, the summer before I entered Brown University. My parents had divorced when I was young, and my dad's idea of a good father-son bonding experience was to attend the Democratic National Convention in San Francisco and then drive together to Atlanta, where I lived with my mom. From California to Texas, we mostly rehashed our ongoing political argument: he supported Walter Mondale and thought it was nuts that I was drawn to Jesse Jackson. As we approached Louisiana on I-20, his mood began to change. He grew tense and withdrawn. After looking at the speedometer—I was driving 65 MPH in a 55 MPH zone, as I had done the whole trip—he told me to slow down because "we don't want to get stopped around here." I knew of course that he had grown up in Mississippi and Chicago and had been part of the southern civil rights movement. I was raised with the stories—Emmett Till, Chaney, Goodman and Schwerner—and always the reminder that "those are just the ones people remember." But the good guys had won in the end, right?
>
> I wanted to stop and call my mom to let her know how long it would be until we reached Atlanta. My dad told me we could only stop at a Howard Johnson's, a Motel 6, or an Amoco. Moreover, we could only stop once we were in a city. "It can wait until we get to Jackson," he said. "That's stupid," I replied. "It will be late then. Why wake her?" Seventeen years old and headstrong, I turned off at an exit in Mississippi and pulled over at a rundown gas station. A man was behind the counter and another was filling his tank near us. I went to the phone booth while my dad kept watch, peering out into the Mississippi night. I was placing the collect call with the operator when every light in the gas station went out. It was pitch black. My dad hit the headlights and turned the ignition. He screamed, "Get in the car! Now!" I dropped the phone and ran to the car while he leaned on the horn.
>
> We never discussed what happened that day. In my mind, though, I was sure I was right—sure that, in 1984, black people didn't get attacked for no reason at a gas station just off the interstate. Not even in Mississippi. But I was equally sure that this wasn't really the point, or at least not the main point. After more than twenty-five years (plus a substantial motive to repress memories of the incident), the details are a little blurry, but I still remember clearly the look on my dad's face when I returned to the car and got on the highway. He was terrified in a way that I had never seen. I cried myself to sleep that night, in a Howard Johnson's near downtown Jackson. I was overwhelmed with a boy's shame at watching his father laid low, and the double burden of knowing that I had helped bring it about.[4]

James's point is a critical one: we should be careful about drawing analogies or claiming mantles that aren't rightly ours.

But if he's correct, where does that leave me? My motives, as I've described, are—most days anyway—mixed. I've never had one of these personal, epiphanic moments of social injustice that set so many of my wonderful and able colleagues on their path. Who am I to think that I can even speak for my clients?

* * *

The murder trial quickly turned into a bit of a disaster. DC is one of the few remaining jurisdictions that more or less allows trial by ambush. Witness' names are redacted from police reports and the rules of discovery do not require witnesses to be identified prior to trial. Prosecutors, among others, claim the practice is good public policy: it cuts down on witness reluctance and intimidation. Others argue that, on balance, open-file discovery is both more efficient and frequently results in fairer dispositions.[5] Regardless of what opinion one holds, it is demonstrably true that the practice makes defending difficult cases even more challenging.

I was surprised that the government presented as its first witness an uninvolved eyewitness who had watched most of the fight from his unobstructed second floor window. It was the kind of witness that is so frustrating to have to deal with at a trial: first of all because there is little that can be done to blunt the force of his testimony—but also because had I been made aware of this witness during pretrial discovery my advice to my client would have been different, and much sharper. In all likelihood I would have explained to her that an uninvolved eyewitness who incriminated her would likely play an important part in any jury's verdict. In this particular case, it would have led to my trying to get my client to accept the plea offer and shave as many years as possible from what was sure to be a lengthy sentence.

As it was, she was facing a felony murder charge—which carried a 30-year sentence. My client was in her late forties and not in terribly good physical health. It would have quite likely amounted to an unsurvivable sentence were she to be convicted. And, after this eyewitness finished testifying, I thought the odds of that happening were pretty good.

I got along well with the prosecutor. I explained why she should have alerted me to the witness, what it meant to the case, to my ability to have adequately explained the quality of the plea offer, and so forth—and miraculously got the original plea offer back. I went to the jail a couple of times over the weekend and in no uncertain terms told my client that she needed to take the plea offer. I offered several reasons—but foremost among them was my firm belief that she was going to be convicted. The plea offer was not great; she was going to have to serve somewhere between 12 and 20 years, as best I could figure. But that *was* a survivable sentence. A conviction and sentence in the range of 30 years was not. She agreed. I called the judge's chambers and arranged a plea for the following Monday morning.

Before court convened on Monday, I went back to the cellblock to make sure we were still on the same page.

We weren't.

She no longer wanted to plead. She didn't really offer much of a reason—a combination of what sounded like a mix of innocence or vitiated culpability, minor differences with the factual bases of the plea, her original commitment to going to trial, and not wanting to stop now. I told her that I thought her decision was a huge mistake—that her concerns were irrational and in conflict with all of the unimpeached evidence in the case. It was a mistake, I said to her, that she would likely pay for with her life. She was unmoved.

It was my habit in moments like those to tell myself that there was a story in it somewhere—some lesson that would help me process the issue: "You can lead a horse to water," came to mind; so did, more charitably to the client, several thoughts about what I could have done to be a better lawyer, to have gotten through to my client in her moment of greatest need. Whatever the thoughts were, though, they were mostly about me, or, to the extent that they were about how my client's rash decision would affect her, they were how I might have done something to avoid a train wreck that all of us were going to be involved in.

But nothing I did or said could convince her to change her mind. So we continued with the trial.

* * *

Explaining how I can represent those people also makes me uncomfortable for other, more substantive, reasons. As posed, the question itself seems both presumptuous and too narrow at the same time. Presumptuous because it assumes that "those people" want and need our representation. I'm willing to concede that, as an amorphous group, the underprivileged, poor, and beleaguered minority can use as much assistance as they can get, ours and others'. But the less abstracted and more individualized they become, the more any assumption about a client's wants or needs runs afoul of much of what

I think ought to be at the center of the attorney-client relationship, namely significant client autonomy. It seems too narrow inasmuch as it gives short shrift to the possibility that "those people" may, in the course of the representation, have something to offer themselves—to us, their lawyers, and to the community at large.

And so precisely what is it that our clients have to offer us?

Not money, surely, and not much in the way of other tangible effects, either. (That said, some of my most prized possessions are a hand-fashioned cross made from copper wire; a sculpture of a voluptuous nude woman carved from the DC Jail commissary soap; and, from a disgruntled client whose trial I lost, a letter addressed to: "Tucker Carrington, Attorney at Flaw.") Instead, what our clients can offer us is a way out of our solipsism. This path forward, so to speak, is an experience that I think all defenders have experienced to one degree or another. The most obvious example are the stories: the ones our clients tell us, the ones they've lived.

The problem, though, is that creating narrative is our job; not our clients'. Or so we believe. Mostly this is a good thing. We expend a lot of effort trying to tell the stories of our clients' lives—to show that they are something other, and more—than the worst thing they may have done. But in that effort we sometimes lose our way. Among the other things that get sacrificed is the truth. Sometimes the truth—and the dignity that comes from hewing to it—is all that's left to our clients.

I should pause here, perhaps, and make the point that the fact that I now represent "innocent"—as opposed to potentially culpable—clients makes no fundamental difference. For one thing, innocent clients do not generally spring fully formed out of our postconviction relief applications. To read the appellate opinions on these cases is to read a record that is replete with a version of guilt. The trial record is generally no better. Until the moment that a court reverses a conviction, being the director of an innocence project is in many ways the functional equivalent of my job as a public defender. For another, though, the reservoir from which clients—innocent and guilty alike—draw their stories is the same. *They* are the same: the poor, the disenfranchised, the accused.

Once I was sitting in a courtroom in DC Superior Court where I watched as case after case was called and handled by a very kind judge. It was a misdemeanor calendar, so for the most part the offenses were fairly petty and nonviolent—simple drug possession, shoplifting—the daily grind of a part of the District that few who live and work there are really aware of. Books have been written about the people who pass through that courtroom on a daily basis; the millions of dollars spent and legislation and federal and state programs put into place to help; the political divisions established over these people and their plights—all of them in their own way an effort at narrative control.

Anyway, I walked into an ongoing saga. A young African-American male who had been convicted was engaged in a conversation with the judge. Or, more accurately, she was trying to engage him in a conversation that he was participating in only minimally, if that. I wasn't paying much attention at first; my thoughts were occupied by my own business there. But the hearing dragged on and I started paying attention. Evidently, the judge had told the defendant some weeks before that if he could read a book between the date of his conviction and the sentencing date and report on the book to the court, she would look very favorably upon his abilities to turn his life around, work hard in school, and be successful.

After much prodding, the judge got the young man to disclose that he had, in fact, been reading a book, but that he wasn't quite finished with it. She assured him that his good-faith effort might be enough to get him an extension on his assignment as long as he was willing to speak with her in some depth about what he was reading and whether he liked it.

"What's the name of the book?" she asked him.

He couldn't remember.

Impatient, she asked if he could describe a bit of what it was about.

Silence.

"Anything," the judge offered.

"It was about sports," he said.

The judge was clearly relieved. At last, you could almost hear her thinking: Now we have something to work with.

"Do you like sports," she asked him.

If silence counts as assent, then he enjoyed them a lot.

"What was the book about specifically?" she asked.

"Sports," he said.

"Yes, but what about sports? How to play them? A certain team? Sports star?"

"Stars," he answered. And, then, to everyone's surprise, he offered up something else: "Black sports stars."

Pouncing on the opportunity—Life lessons! Role models!—the judge perked up. "That's terrific," she said. "Who was profiled?"

"Huh?"

"Named. Who were some of the black sports stars written about in the book?"

"I can't remember."

"You can't. Not even one? Michael Jordan? Tiger Woods?"

Silence.

"Anyone?"

"Babe Ruth," he finally answered.

The most palpable reaction was the prosecutor's. She was absolutely beside herself; as best I could tell she viewed the defendant and his choices, from the moment he had been arrested until this one, as an exercise in thumbing his nose at authority. Her refusal to view the world on anything other than her own terms was to engage, in a phrase from Professor Abbe Smith, in "a kind of moral fascism."[6] Not that anyone else was doing much better. The judge remained more or less implacable, but she was finished bending over backward. The defendant's lawyer was embarrassed. The spectators—mostly lawyers and court personnel—were stifling laughter.

Everyone was missing the point—had been missing it all along. At some level everyone was engaged in his or her own narrative charade. The prosecutor was engaged once again in an effort to lock up yet another of DC's young black males on behalf of the spurious war on drugs. The judge, wiser by degrees, was doing her part to ease her conscience no matter what the result. The defense attorney, and I'd venture to guess most of us, were thinking that we'd been there, done that—hung out to dry in open court by a client's act of poor judgment.

Everyone was missing the point, that is, except for the defendant. I'm convinced that he knew—or knew as well as anyone could in his position—precisely what he was doing. He was being honest, and in that effort dragging the rest of us along with him as best he could. He was telling us about himself, who he truly was, where he'd been, where he was going, and none of us was listening very well. We were, in spite of ourselves and our reactions, in the presence of a certain kind of mastery: an individual's ability to tell us with absolute clarity and economy of word and gesture, a story—his story, and ours in relation to it—of his young life.

* * *

My cocounsel and I completed the trial, delivered the closing argument, and then waited for the guilty verdict that we knew was coming. Sure enough, the jury returned fairly quickly. They walked into the courtroom, just as convicting juries do—stoically, somberly, without glancing at us.

And then they proceeded to acquit our client of all charges.

As an experienced public defender I have had plenty of practice—and consider myself fairly adept—at maintaining my composure even in the face a surprising turn of events. My head was swimming. I acted like it wasn't. When I went back to the cellblock to speak with my client she was smiling.

"If I had taken your advice," she said, "I'd be finishing my first week of a fifteen year sentence." It was true. Had she taken my advice—my considered, experienced, and in every way except the way that it really mattered, *correct*, advice—she would have indeed been in for a very long stint in prison. Against all odds, she had given herself her life back.

"You're right about that," I said. Because, really, what else could I say?

"You're crazy," I said to her, meaning, I think, that she wasn't.

"That's what I've been trying to tell you," she said.

And then she laughed and threw her arms and hands out at me. Go on, get out of here, she was saying. She was done. She was already on to the next thing.

I gathered my trial boxes, placed them on my wheeled cart, and walked into the corridor outside of the courtroom, all the while trying to make sense of things, attempting to put my own gloss on how this could have happened, in this, my final trial as a public defender. Once again falling so quickly and so easily into the trap of developing my own self-serving, self-comforting narrative. I certainly was not looking for and in fact was wholly *undeserving* of it—those stories, those moments that our clients offer up—what Flannery O'Connor, whose genius lies in large part in capturing what I'm talking about, once described as sometimes nothing more than a gesture that transcends any neat allegory or moral lesson, that forces us out of the comfort of our own self-satisfied logic, and, in some special instances, makes "contact with mystery."[7]

And so it was in that way that I emerged from the courtroom to be embraced by people I had never seen before and had every reason in my version of my world to believe did not exist: my client's three children, who thanked me for giving them their mother back, and then introduced themselves as Yesterday, Today, and Tomorrow.

NOTES

1. An earlier, and somewhat different, version of this chapter was written and delivered as an address at the fiftieth anniversary celebration of

Georgetown Law Center's E. Barrett Prettyman Program, July, 2011 in Washington, DC.

2. Kelly Cherry, *The Exiled Heart, A Meditative Autobiography* (Baton Rouge: Louisiana State University Press, 1991), 30.
3. Barbara Babcock, "Defending the Guilty," *Cleveland State Law Review* 32 (1983).
4. James Forman, "Racial Critiques of Mass Incarceration: Beyond the New Jim Crow," *New York University Law Review* 87 (2012): 139–140.
5. For background, see Robert P. Mosteller, "Exculpatory Evidence, Ethics, and the Road to the Disbarment of Mike Nifong: The Critical Importance of Full Open-File Discovery," *George Marshall Law Review* 15 (2008) (arguing for open-file discovery in criminal cases); Editorial, "Justice and Open Files," *New York Times*, February 27, 2012, http://www.nytimes.com/2012/02/27/opinion/justice-and-open-files.html (urging open file discovery in both federal and state criminal cases as the only way to ensure that favorable evidence will be disclosed to criminal defendants in compliance with *Brady v. Maryland*).
6. Abbe Smith, "Can You Be a Good Person and a Good Prosecutor?," *Georgetown Journal of Legal Ethics* 14 (2001).
7. Flannery O'Connor, "On Her Own Work," in *Her Mystery and Manners: Occasional Prose*, ed. Sally Fitzgerald and Robert Fitzgerald (New York: Farrar, Straus and Giroux, 1969), 107–118. See also, Flannery O'Connor, "Prefatory Comments to a Reading of 'A Good Man Is Hard to Find,'" (lecture, Hollins College, October 14, 1963).

4

There but for the Grace of God Go I

Angela J. Davis

I've listened to many public defenders talk about why they represent poor people charged with crimes. Some of them talk about being inspired by the experience of a brother, cousin, or friend who was arrested and treated unfairly in the criminal justice system. Others speak of a desire to protect the constitutional rights of individuals and fight the power of government. Still others are motivated by a desire to help the poor and disadvantaged.

My own motivations have never been totally clear to me. I didn't personally know anyone who was arrested until after I graduated from college. Fighting the government was unheard of in the household of my father, Master Sergeant Eddie Jordan, a career army man who served his country for 30 years. My parents taught me to help those less fortunate than we were, but they never mentioned people who were in jail or prison. Yet looking back, I cannot imagine doing anything else. My work as a public defender is the most important thing I have ever done or will ever do. When I have tried over the years to explain why I feel so strongly about the work, I have struggled. But now when I look back at my life growing up in the segregated south, it all makes sense.

"I Want to Be a Civil Rights Lawyer"

I was born in Fort Benning, Georgia, and grew up in a little town in Alabama called Phenix City. When I was a child I didn't know what a public defender was, and the first lawyer I ever met was one of my college professors. But I knew what lawyers did, and I decided that I wanted to be one during the summer of 1965. I didn't know it then but what happened that summer was probably the main reason I became a public defender. I was nine years old.

We lived on 10th Avenue—a short street with two churches, a hair salon, and a corner store. All of the families on our street were African-American and working class. The homes were modest but well kept. My dad had joined the army at a young age and received his GED there. My mom was a maid for a white family. Most of our neighbors had similar jobs. The mother of one of my best friends owned the hair salon on our street. Our family attended one of the churches.

I had three older sisters who were nine, ten, and twelve years older. By the time I was ten, they had all left home to attend Howard University in Washington, DC. Except during the summers when my sisters would sometimes come home, I was an only child. Despite their absence, they continued to be big sisters from afar, indoctrinating me with the radical poetry, books, and music they collected during their days at Howard. I think I was the first black girl in Phenix City to wear an Afro.

During the summer of 1965, I had just finished third grade. I was too young to get a job, so I spent my days playing with friends. We rode our bikes and hung out at each other's homes. My parents worked during the day, so my sister Jackie, who had come home that summer, helped look after me.

My friends and I loved to ride our bikes, but it wasn't easy to ride a bike on the street where I lived, 10th Avenue. Our little street was paved, but the sidewalk was not. There wasn't even a walking path on the sidewalk, which was hilly, uneven, and strewn with rocks; riding on the sidewalk was impossible. My parents wouldn't allow me to ride my bike in the street so my friends and I decided to ride our bikes over on Dillingham Street. And that's when the trouble began.

Dillingham Street was perpendicular to 10th Avenue. In fact, the corner store and the church we attended were at the corner of Dillingham and 10th Avenue. Dillingham Street was a long street with nice, paved sidewalks and gentle rolling hills—perfect for bike riding. The houses were similar to the houses on 10th Avenue, but a little larger and nicer. All the families on Dillingham Street were white.

It made sense to ride bikes on Dillingham Street. It was a public sidewalk right around the corner. We didn't think twice about it. But the white kids who lived on Dillingham Street didn't want us in their neighborhood because we were black. They yelled at us as we rode by—"Stay on your own street! Go back to where you belong!" We ignored them, and kept riding our bikes on Dillingham Street—now suddenly determined to do so.

The white kids decided to step up their game. They made barricades on the sidewalk to obstruct our path, piling rocks and tree branches and other booby traps across the sidewalk. But instead of turning back, we would stop, get off of our bikes, remove the debris, and keep riding. It was our very first experience with—and childhood version of—peaceful resistance.

The battle of wills went on for days—my friends and I would start riding our bikes on Dillingham Street, stop at the barricade of rocks and branches, remove them, and keep riding while the white kids looked on and yelled insults at us. One day, when I tossed one of the rocks off the sidewalk, one of the white girls claimed I hit her with it. I was sure I had not, but if I did it was certainly an accident. Words were exchanged—"I did not," "You did so," "No I didn't"—until things escalated into physical fighting, each of us flailing our arms at each other while our respective friends cheered us on. The flailing reflected my level of expertise. Fighting was not my style. I never got into fights, at least not physical ones. It didn't last very long because a man came out of the house next door and yelled, "You little niggers get on back to where you belong!" We got on our bikes and tore out of there at breakneck speed, back to 10th Avenue where we gathered in the back yard of one of my friends.

While we were contemplating our next move, a boy from the neighborhood ran up and cried, "Angela, the police are out front looking for you!" At first I laughed at what could only be a joke, but the frightened look on his face told me otherwise. I followed him around to the front yard to find a police car and two police officers walking toward me. I immediately burst into tears. All the neighbors were standing on their front porches staring at me. I was shocked and ashamed and afraid. My sister Jackie came running from our house and confronted the police officers. She demanded to know where they were taking me. One of the officers said, "We're just taking her home to her parents." Jackie pointed at our house, which was just down the street, and said, "We live right there. I can take her home." But the police wouldn't have it. They ordered me to get in the back of the police car. I was hysterical. Thankfully, Jackie got in the cruiser with me.

In less than a minute, we arrived at our house, which was literally half a block away. My parents were standing in the front yard. I still remember the look on my father's face. He was furious—and it was clear that his anger was directed at me, not the police. He said, "Don't worry, officer. I'll take care of her. This won't happen again." The police left and I ran inside.

I honestly don't remember my punishment, though I'm sure it was severe. I do remember lying on my bed, sobbing hysterically and deciding then and there that I was going to be a civil rights lawyer. I wasn't quite sure what civil rights lawyers did, but I knew that they were working with Martin Luther King to fight the injustices of the segregated south. And what I had just experienced was injustice. I hadn't done anything wrong. In fact, I thought I had done exactly the right thing. I was forbidden from riding in the street, so I had biked on a public sidewalk paid for, in part, by my parents' taxes. The city chose to pave the sidewalks in the white neighborhoods, not the black ones, but they were public sidewalks and I had the right to use them. I had not thrown a rock at anyone, and I certainly didn't initiate the fight that ensued. If anything, I was attacked for no reason and defended myself. Yet I somehow ended up in the back seat of a police car, terrified and embarrassed. And instead of protecting and defending me, my father piled on more punishment. I couldn't wait to get out of Phenix City and go to law school.

The road from small town Alabama to the Public Defender Service for the District of Columbia (PDS) was not a straight one. After graduating from Howard University, I went to Harvard Law School. My first year of law school was not the experience I expected. For the first time in my life, I was alone in a city with no family or close friends. I wasn't able to secure housing on campus so I felt isolated from the other students. Most of the required first year courses—property, torts, and civil procedure—seemed foreign and irrelevant to me. But I did love constitutional law and criminal law. These were the issues that inspired me to go to law school—liberty, equal protection, and due process.

During my second year of law school, I was introduced to fall recruitment. This was the season during which second year students were interviewed for summer associate positions, primarily with law firms. Harvard didn't have a public interest career advisory office then, so I was a bit lost. I wasn't interested in big-firm practice, but my classmates all thought I'd be crazy to forego the opportunity to work at a firm for a summer. Among other things, I would make lots of money. And I did need the money. So I signed up for an interview. It was a disaster. I couldn't even feign interest in this firm that did work I found boring and unappealing. I ended the interview early.

Instead, I accepted a summer position in the US Attorney's Office for the District of Columbia. It was an eye-opening experience. I worked for a team of three prosecutors. At least two of them seemed fair and I learned a lot. Maybe I would become a prosecutor, I thought to myself. All of the crime victims were African-American and they were just as oppressed and abused by the criminal justice system as the defendants. Maybe I could make a difference as a prosecutor. I would dismiss the cases where police violated the Fourth and Fifth Amendments, give decent plea offers to worthy defendants, and argue for modest sentences in all but the most serious cases.

I was so naïve.

In my third year of law school, I enrolled in a law clinic and started representing clients. I took a trial advocacy course and learned how to cross-examine witnesses. Finally, I was acquiring the skills to do the work I wanted to do. Although I hoped to get into the Criminal Justice Clinic, I was assigned to the Civil Clinic instead. Nonetheless, I acquired valuable skills and learned what it meant to zealously represent clients. I joined the Civil Rights-Civil Liberties Law Review, a progressive, social-justice-oriented law journal, and the Prison Legal Assistance Project, a student-run organization that provided representation for Massachusetts prisoners in disciplinary and parole hearings. Law school was starting to make sense to me.

After law school, I was a law clerk for the chief judge of the District of Columbia Court of Appeals. I read transcripts of criminal trials, learned a lot about criminal law in the District of Columbia, and most importantly, discovered PDS. PDS lawyers were always the best—both the trial lawyers in the transcripts and the appellate lawyers who argued before the Court of Appeals. They were smarter and noticeably more zealous than other lawyers. I wanted to be one of them. As my one-year clerkship drew to an end, I knew I had to make some decisions.

I decided to apply to both the US Attorney's Office and PDS.[1] At the time, I still believed I could do as much good as a prosecutor as I could as a defender. I was sure about a few things: I wanted to serve poor people; I wanted to help black people; and I wanted to do it in the criminal justice system—not just by making sure the system was fair, but by doing everything I could to extricate my people from a destructive system. Even before all the studies had come out,[2] I knew that too many black men were in prisons and jails, many of whom didn't deserve or need to be there, even if they were guilty of committing a crime. I wanted to do whatever I could to change what was becoming an epidemic of incarcerating black people. I thought I could do that as either a defender or a prosecutor.

As a public defender, the fight would be clear and obvious. I would zealously represent my clients at every step of the process to free them from the criminal justice system or at least get them the best result possible. I yearned to fight that battle. I had no qualms about representing the guilty because I didn't care whether my clients were guilty or innocent—either way, they didn't deserve what the criminal justice system had to offer. It was an ineffectual, discriminatory, overly harsh system, and I was prepared to fight it.

So how could I even consider being a prosecutor? Even then, I understood the vast, almost limitless power and discretion of prosecutors.[3] As a prosecutor, I could dismiss cases and support alternatives to incarceration. My summer at the US Attorney's Office taught me that there were good and bad prosecutors—some who actually cared about their responsibility to "seek justice"[4] and others who only sought convictions. I learned that many of the victims of crime were very much like the defendants—poor, black, and disadvantaged. Some even had criminal cases of their own. Some of the prosecutors genuinely cared about the victims, and others treated them as poorly as they did the defendants. Rarely did any of them show any empathy for the defendants. I saw a need for a different kind of prosecutor—one who would be a champion of justice for everyone—victim and defendant alike. I would be that prosecutor.[5]

My thoughts about being a prosecutor made sense in theory. But after doing a bit of research, I learned that they only made sense *in theory.* No entry-level prosecutors would ever be able to do what I hoped to do—at least not if they wanted to stay employed. Chief prosecutors vary in how much discretion they give to lower-level assistants, but rarely would low-level prosecutors be able to exercise this much discretion, at least not in the way I imagined. I withdrew my application from the US Attorney's Office and prayed for an offer from PDS. I was lucky that my prayers were answered.

A combination of my personal experience and life story brought me to PDS, but the clients kept me there. They motivated and inspired me every day of the 12 years I spent at PDS. However, there were other factors that kept me in the fight for a dozen years. The clients were number one, but the prosecutors were a factor as well. As loyal as I was to my clients, I was equally appalled by the misconduct and abuse of discretion by prosecutors and wanted to do something about it.

My Clients: "There but for the Grace of God Go I"

From the moment I started at PDS, I knew it was where I was supposed to be. I spent the first six weeks of the job in an intensive training program along with six other lawyers, learning everything from trial advocacy skills, to developing a case theory, to the ins and outs of the DC Superior Court. Charles "Tree" Ogletree was the training director for my "class." Tree, and the other lawyers at PDS, made us feel as if we were soldiers in an army for justice. By the time the training program was over, I felt like the knight in shining armor on the PDS T-shirts—ready to charge across the street to court and slay anyone and everyone who came between my client and freedom.

When I started at PDS in 1982, the first assignment for new lawyers was juvenile court. Since the most a juvenile could be incarcerated was two years in a juvenile facility,[6] juvenile court seemed the most appropriate assignment for brand new lawyers. Even though my clients were not facing the same harsh sentences as adult clients, I represented them with the same zeal as my colleagues in criminal court.

Representing juveniles was complicated. My job was to vigorously pursue the interests of my clients. But when the client was 13 or 14 years old, did they really know their "interest?" Certainly keeping them out of Oak Hill (the juvenile facility) was the first goal, but then what? Most of them had less than ideal living arrangements and many had learning disabilities, substance abuse problems, and mental illness. Fortunately, PDS provided the services of social workers who pursued available resources to help juvenile clients. They would often recommend special schools that could provide services my clients needed. But what if the client didn't want to go to the school? Suppose they wanted to go back to the environment likely to bring them back into juvenile court, or even adult court if they were 16 or 17?[7] Most of these special schools were in places far from the District of Columbia. Some of these kids even preferred going to the dreadful juvenile facility where they would at least be near family and friends. I would never advocate for a result that my client didn't want, so if I wasn't able to convince the client that he or she should go to the special school, I would be forced to advocate for a result that was sometimes unrealistic—probation, for example—knowing that the judge would simply commit the kid to Oak Hill. It was difficult.

Then there were the parent issues. The parents of my juvenile clients were often absent—fathers almost always and sometimes mothers, too. When the mothers were available and interested, they would want to know what was going on with their children. But my ability to share information was limited. I understood that attorney-client confidentiality means nothing to the parent of a child in trouble. I imagined myself in the shoes of some of these mothers, and I knew that I would be just as adamant about wanting to know every detail about my child's case.

In my years as a public defender, I never had the least qualm about representing any of my clients—juvenile or adult. It didn't matter what they were charged with, and I never even thought about whether they were innocent or guilty. It didn't matter to me—I was going to represent them with the same zeal and commitment either way. With juvenile clients, I couldn't understand why everyone didn't feel the same way. Can we ever give up on a child? No matter what they may have done, don't we owe it to ourselves to try to rehabilitate a child? I firmly believed that any child could be saved.

The juvenile client that had the greatest effect on me was my first—Albert Hicks.[8] Albert was charged with a misdemeanor—a simple assault in which he and two adults were alleged to have gone into the home of an acquaintance and beaten him up. My client said that he had not participated in the assault and had done nothing to help the adult codefendants. I believed him. I investigated the case thoroughly, and worked day and night preparing for trial. We went to trial before the Honorable Gladys Kessler, a tough but fair-minded judge.[9] She found him "involved"—guilty—seconds after I gave my closing argument.

I was devastated. In hindsight, there was no logical reason for me to believe I could possibly obtain an acquittal for Albert. Acquittals by judges are rare, especially in juvenile cases. And our defense theory wasn't the strongest. But I was young and idealistic—and maybe a little foolish. I had bonded with my client and wanted to free him from the juvenile justice system. With his record, there was a pretty good chance he would end up at Oak Hill. I couldn't help but feel that his conviction—called an adjudication of delinquency—was my failure.

It wasn't over. There was still the disposition hearing.[10] I put all my energy into getting the best possible result for Albert. I had my work cut out for me. Albert had a juvenile record a mile long, and I found out that he had been charged as an adult for an armed robbery in nearby Prince George's County, Maryland, where, amazingly, he had received a probationary sentence. (For some reason none of this got in the way of my believing Albert's story.) In juvenile court, in order to sentence a child, the judge must find that the child committed a delinquent act and that he is in need of care and rehabilitation.[11] If the judge is convinced that the child does not need care and rehabilitation, she may dismiss the case "for social reasons." If she finds that he is in need of such care and rehabilitation, she may either place him on probation or commit him to the Department of Youth Rehabilitation Services (DYRS).

I decided on an unconventional strategy for the disposition hearing. There was no way Judge Kessler was going to put my client on probation in view of his juvenile and adult record. I decided to file a Motion to Dismiss for Social Reasons. This was unusual because these motions were ordinarily filed in cases where the juvenile was a first offender and there was lots of evidence that he was ordinarily a well-behaved, exceptional kid. There would be letters from teachers, pastors, and community members praising the child for his good grades and good works. There was no such evidence in support of dismissal for Albert. Instead, my motion suggested the opposite. I argued that because Albert had such a long juvenile record and now even an adult record, there was really nothing the juvenile system could do for him. His adult probation would be revoked in Prince George's County, so why send him for a period of incarceration at Oak Hill where he couldn't be helped anyway?

Not surprisingly, Judge Kessler didn't buy it. She committed him to DYRS for a period of two years—the maximum sentence he could get. Again, I was devastated—more so than after the trial. There was nothing else I could do for Albert. I had tried so hard to get a good result for him, yet I failed him at every step of the process. I told Albert that I was sorry and that I would come to Oak Hill to see him soon. I held it together long enough to make it out of the courtroom. I ran to the restroom where I burst into tears. What kind of lawyer was I anyway? That poor kid relied on me and this was the best I could do? The door of the restroom opened and Mrs. Hicks, Albert's mother, walked in. She came over, hugged me, and said, "Miss Davis, don't worry about Albert. He'll be alright." She wasn't crying. I thought, "something is wrong with this picture. I should be comforting *her*. I need to get it together."

But I really liked this kid. I didn't care that he had a long record of criminal behavior and had done a lot of bad things. He wasn't a bad *person*. He was smart and talented, and gentle and kind, despite his criminal behavior. There was no excuse for his behavior, but there was definitely an explanation. Albert's family was poor. He had never known his father, and almost every adult around him was involved in the criminal justice system. As smart as he was, the DC public school system had failed him. Albert's mother did the best she could, but she was a single mother with several other children. Albert had no positive mentors and knew no life other than the one he had. Even though I grew up relatively poor, I had had so many more opportunities. I had parents who were not educated, but who had high standards for their children and worked hard to send us to good schools. I grew up in a racist, segregated town, but I had good role models who instilled in me the value of education as the great equalizer. I had strict parents who made me behave. And I had a big sister who rescued me from the police. Albert had none of these things. There but for the grace of God go I.[12]

Despite losing that first trial, I learned a lot. There were the obvious lessons—things I could have done differently at trial or the disposition hearing. But I also learned a lot about myself. My hardships growing up paled in comparison to Albert's. I was downright *lucky* compared to Albert—even the nine-year-old version of me trembling in the back of the police cruiser. Why did I make it out and not Albert? He was no less deserving. Life was not fair, but I was going to do my damnedest to make it fairer for the Alberts of the world. I knew I would be doing this work for a very long time.

There were many other juvenile clients who touched my life and whose lives I hope I made a little better, at least for awhile. There was James, the juvenile who was a pyromaniac. He burned down an entire strip mall in northeast DC—fortunately in the middle of the night when no one was there. It took the police some time to figure out he'd done it because he was on the scene, talking on a police radio in perfect police lingo. He dressed like an adult and looked like one too. They thought he was another cop for several hours! James eventually gave a full confession after the police officers violated his *Miranda* rights. James was brilliant, but he had a serious learning disability. I put on expert testimony about his disability at the motions hearing. The judge had no choice but to suppress the confession and the government was forced to dismiss the case. In the process of preparing for the hearing, I learned not only about James's learning disability but about his mental health issues. The social workers at PDS were able to get services for him. I was happy for James and believed that I left him better off than I found him.

After a year in juvenile court, I moved on to represent adults. Frankly, it wasn't much different. Most of my clients were young—from 18 to 20 years old. They were still kids to me and the issues were the same. But now the stakes were much higher. I started representing clients charged with misdemeanors, but it wasn't long before I was assigned to clients facing felony charges. I couldn't believe I had cried over two years in a juvenile facility! Like my juvenile clients, I had to grow up.

There was young Brandon Jones. Brandon had killed a man in front of witnesses. He was resigned to a lengthy prison sentence. Resigned, that is, until our investigation revealed that there was a viable claim of self-defense. It turned out the man he stabbed had a reputation for violence in the community. He was known to carry a gun. When he stabbed the man, Brandon feared for his own life. Brandon had no idea that he was legally justified in taking the man's life until I explained to him that he had acted in self-defense. He told the jury what happened, and they believed him. It was a happy ending for a young man who was able to go on with his life.

Not all of my clients were as sympathetic as Albert, a child, and Brandon, a man who killed in self-defense. Leonard Brown was a hardened criminal by anyone's definition. He had a long criminal record and had done a lot of time before he was arrested for first degree murder. The case was assigned to a senior lawyer at PDS. I was still relatively inexperienced at the time. The senior lawyer, Michele Roberts, asked me to second chair the case.[13] Michele was one of the best lawyers in the office, so I knew I would learn a lot from working with her. But nothing could have prepared me for this experience.

Michele told me my first day on the case that a "23–110"—ineffective assistance of counsel—motion would be filed in the case.[14] She explained that—no matter how hard we worked on the case—if convicted, this client would accuse us of incompetence. We didn't take it personally.

The government alleged that Leonard had shot and killed a young woman in an apartment building in southeast Washington. What made the case noteworthy was how Leonard was arrested. He was involved in a high-speed chase that went across the DC line into Prince George's County, causing the Prince George's County police to get involved. Leonard was finally caught, but only after he was shot 38 times. He survived. The doctors at the Prince George's hospital couldn't believe it. We knew then that he was a survivor—by any means necessary.

There was never any talk of a plea in Leonard's case. The government didn't offer one and we didn't ask. Leonard was not going to plead guilty to anything, no matter what. This case was going to trial. He was detained at Lorton Prison in Virginia instead of the DC Jail. It was a long trip out to Lorton but we visited frequently. We knew we were dealing with a different kind of client when we called to arrange a visit and were told that "Mr. Brown was not available to see us on the day we requested!" Apparently he was running the prison! We investigated the case inside and out and worked day and night to put on the best defense possible. But there was just too much evidence. As defenders say, the case was a dog.

Despite our best efforts, the trial was painful—like a long, slow guilty plea. Each witness was more damning than the one before. Our cross-examinations were more and more futile. We'd score a small point here and there, only to have the government come back with evidence that canceled out any progress we'd made. Michele and I were so desperate that we wore white suits the day of closing arguments—perhaps a subliminal message of innocence?

The outcome was no surprise. During deliberations, I got the worst jury note in all my years as a public defender. The note read as follows: "Are we required to choose between First Degree Premeditated Murder and Felony Murder or may we convict him of both?" The judge gave them permission to return verdicts of guilty on both charges and they did just that.[15] Mr. Brown was sentenced to a mandatory life sentence.

Just as Michele predicted, Mr. Brown immediately filed a motion alleging ineffective assistance of counsel. We appeared and testified under oath about the work we had done in the case. I felt no anger toward Mr. Brown. He had to do what he had to do. I remember seeing his father at the hearing. The senior Mr. Brown seemed embarrassed. I went over to him during a break and shook his hand. I told him I was sorry about what had happened and wished Mr. Brown all the best. Leonard Brown was someone's son. He was a human being who deserved to be treated humanely and fairly, despite his transgressions. I was proud to represent him.

There were other clients who decided to go to trial and many more who pled guilty. I fought hard for my clients who exercised their constitutional right to a jury trial and equally hard for those who pled guilty. When it was clear that there was no reasonable chance of an acquittal and the government offered a decent plea, I did my best to convince my client to take it. Some of my best advocacy was convincing clients to take pleas in cases where a conviction at trial would mean many more years in prison. But trial or plea, I learned from all of my clients and tried to do something to make their lives better. I'm not sure I always succeeded.

THE PROSECUTORS

My clients motivated me to work hard. But in a very different way, so did the prosecutors. My internship at the US Attorney's Office after my second year of law school in no way prepared me for what I would learn about prosecutorial power and abuse when I began to represent clients. I learned that prosecutors actually control the entire criminal justice system—particularly through their charging and plea-bargaining decisions.

When the prosecutor calls the shots, there is only so much even a good advocate can accomplish. Because over 95 percent of all criminal cases are resolved by guilty pleas,[16] these decisions—what to charge, what plea to accept—mean that prosecutors predetermine the outcome in most criminal cases. Prosecutors have lots of power and discretion with little to no transparency or accountability. Not surprisingly, their decisions sometimes produce unjust, or at least uneven, results.

I knew and understood that prosecutors had to use their discretion in deciding when and what to charge and whether to offer a plea bargain. I knew that they should take into account factors like the seriousness of the offense, the strength of the evidence, the interest of the victim in prosecution, and the defendant's prior criminal record.[17] But it often appeared to me as a defender that these factors were improperly applied, if considered at all. For example, sometimes when victims didn't appear for a witness conference, it had nothing to do with whether he was interested in prosecution. It could mean that he didn't have transportation or couldn't take time from work. As a result, plea offers, or at least better plea offers, might be offered in cases with poorer victims. Did that mean that prosecutors treated our clients more harshly when the victims were middle to upper class? White victims were almost always in this category. Did this mean prosecutors were treating cases differently based on the race or class of the victim? I had no reason to think they were doing this purposefully. But even if it wasn't intentional, the results didn't seem fair.

One case where race and class seemed to play a role involved one of the few white PDS clients. David McKnight was a 25-year-old Georgetown University student who worked as a bartender in a restaurant. His roommate was John Nguyen, a 55-year-old Vietnamese immigrant who worked as a cook in the same restaurant.

One evening McKnight invited a woman friend to the apartment and asked her to spend the night. The woman declined his invitation and left. Mr. Nguyen was in the apartment at the time, and after the woman left, teased McKnight about his failed romance. McKnight, who was already upset, became even angrier. He attacked Mr. Nguyen with a machete. McKnight was a big man and Mr. Nguyen was just over five feet tall. By the time the attack was over, both men were covered with Mr. Nguyen's blood. Ironically, the first ambulance to arrive picked up McKnight, who was barely injured. A second ambulance came for Mr. Nguyen and took him to the hospital where he died later that night.

The case never went to trial. The prosecutor, who was white, called McKnight's lawyer, Bob Gordon, and invited him to identify witnesses who might testify before the grand jury on behalf of McKnight, who claimed that he acted in self-defense. Mr. Gordon was stunned. He had never known a prosecutor to make such an offer. Mr. Gordon identified witnesses who testified before the grand jury about McKnight's good character. A few weeks later, the prosecutor informed Mr. Gordon that the grand jury voted not to indict McKnight.

Prosecutors also control the grand jury process.[18] Although grand jurors have the power to call witnesses independently of the prosecutor, they rarely do. Defense attorneys are not allowed to be present and prosecutors are not required to present evidence that might exculpate the defendant.[19] The prosecutor's behavior in this case was extraordinary.

There was no evidence that the prosecutor took McKnight's race into account in making his decision. But it seemed more than a coincidence that McKnight received such favorable treatment in a murder case. No doubt the prosecutor unconsciously empathized with McKnight as a young college student with a future, but not Mr. Nguyen, a poor Vietnamese immigrant. The fact that Mr. Nguyen had no family or advocate pushing for McKnight's prosecution probably made the decision even easier.

Another case where race, class, and prosecutorial power seemed to play a role involved an African-American client charged with the felony murder of a young white college student from Nebraska. James Robinson was charged with shooting the student during a robbery.

The case received special attention from the very beginning. The victim's family contacted their congressman, and he began to appear at many of the pretrial court hearings, even routine ones. The press followed the case closely, and the congressman gave a television interview about the case. Needless to say, there was no plea offer, and the case was aggressively prosecuted. The prosecutor often chatted with the congressman before and after the court hearings.

Tony Morris, a senior attorney at PDS, was assigned to represent Mr. Robinson. His junior cocounsel was Sara McCarthy. The trial began almost a year later. Soon after the trial began, one of the government witnesses testified to inadmissible, prejudicial evidence, requiring a mistrial. The parties were ordered to appear the next week to pick a new jury and start the trial again.

Over the weekend, the prosecutor's cousin died. Without objection from Tony, the prosecutor was given a new trial date.

The trial began several months later. On the fifth day of trial, I received a distressing phone call. I was now the director of PDS. I learned that the 33-year-old Tony Morris had had a stroke and was in intensive care. Everyone at PDS was shocked and heartbroken. Because of the extraordinary circumstances, I appeared in court to request a mistrial. When I arrived in the courtroom the judge had not yet taken the bench. I went back in the cellblock to inform Mr. Robinson about Tony's condition and request his permission to ask for a mistrial. He agreed. When I went back into the courtroom, I spoke to the prosecutor—an African-American woman I knew pretty well—and let her know that we would be moving for a mistrial. She expressed concern for Tony's well-being but said nothing more.

The judge took the bench and the case was called. I informed the judge of Tony's stroke and moved for a mistrial. The judge asked if the prosecutor opposed the motion. To my surprise, she did. She argued that rescheduling the trial would be too much of an inconvenience for her witnesses and the family members who had traveled to Washington from Nebraska. She suggested that we recess the trial for a few days to see if Tony would be able to continue with the trial. I explained again that he had suffered a serious stroke, was clinging to life in intensive care, and would not return to work for another six to eight weeks, but she persisted in her opposition to the motion. I was stunned. This was the same prosecutor who had asked to reschedule trial because of the death of a cousin, without opposition from Tony.

Although mistrials are granted under less serious circumstances—for lawyers with the flu or a migraine headache—the judge denied my motion. Clearly, the race of the victim, political pressure, and media attention were having an impact.

The judge proposed that junior cocounsel Sara McCarthy finish the trial on her own. But Sara had only two years of experience as a lawyer and had never tried a case before a jury on her own, much less a murder case. The judge was a former PDS lawyer, so he was well aware of the office's practice of pairing junior lawyers with more experienced counsel, primarily as a learning experience, but he paid no heed to my objection, appointed a non-PDS senior trial attorney to the case (giving him the transcript of the previous five days of the trial and a few days to familiarize himself with the case), and kept Sara as second chair. Mr. Robinson was subsequently convicted of all counts.

To this day, I believe that the prosecutor and judge were influenced by the status of the victim's family. That year, there had been a total of 443 homicides in the District of Columbia.[20] Almost all of the victims were young black men with families who loved and cared about them. Many of them had been killed under circumstances more brutal and vicious than in Mr. Robinson's case. Yet this case was prosecuted more aggressively than any other homicide that year.

The exercise of prosecutorial discretion also produced unfair results that sometimes had nothing to do with race or class. Trevor Davis's case provides an example. Mr. Davis was charged with the rape of a young woman who lived in his neighborhood. He and the young woman were both black, as was the prosecutor assigned to the case.

I was assigned to represent Mr. Davis. Despite the fact that he didn't have a record, he was held without bond because of the seriousness of the offense. Mr. Davis proclaimed his innocence from the very beginning. He told me that he knew the complaining witness and she had consented to have sex with him. He also told me that she was totally deaf. According to Mr. Davis, the woman did not speak and she communicated her consent through body language. He claimed that he had never used any force nor had he threatened her and that she willingly had sex with him. I said I would investigate the case and prepare a consent defense.

The first step was to try to get a written statement from the complainant. I received approval to hire a sign language interpreter to accompany my investigator to the complainant's home. The plan was for the interpreter to communicate with the complainant, explain the purpose of the visit and statement, and translate the investigator's questions and the complainant's answers. The investigator would record the statement and the interpreter would "sign" the statement to the complainant and ask her to sign it as true and accurate.

The plan was unsuccessful. When the investigator and interpreter arrived at the complainant's home, her mother came to the front door and informed them that her daughter would not be giving any statements. Witnesses in the District of Columbia may give a statement to the defense team if they wish but they are not required to do so. Prosecutors prefer that government witnesses not give statements to the defense—written or otherwise—because the statements may be used to impeach them if they testify inconsistently at trial. Prosecutors are not permitted to instruct their witnesses to refuse to give a statement to the defense, but they usually do a thorough job of explaining to them that they aren't required to.

We didn't know whether the complainant's mother had made this decision on her own or if the prosecutor had instructed her. I decided to visit the complainant's home to make sure there were no misunderstandings. When I arrived, the complainant's mother came to the door again and gave me a similar message—there would be no statements. Like my investigators, I never got a glimpse of the complainant. However, I did learn a very important fact. The complainant's mother volunteered that her daughter wouldn't be able to give a statement even if she wanted to because she didn't know sign language. When I asked her how her daughter communicated, she informed me that she had taken care of her daughter all of her life and that they had their own way of communicating with each other. She also told me that the prosecutor had not subpoenaed her daughter to the grand jury and he was aware of her inability to understand standard sign language. I thanked her for speaking with me and went back to my office.

Exactly what was this prosecutor doing? If the complainant didn't understand sign language then the prosecutor wouldn't be able to present her testimony to the grand jury. He could present the testimony of the police officer because hearsay (what others said to the officer) was admissible there, but how did the officer know what had happened? Had the mother told him what the complainant had communicated to her? There seemed to be multiple layers of unreliable hearsay. Moreover, hearsay would not be admissible at trial. No judge would allow the complainant's mother to serve as her interpreter because there would be no way to verify the accuracy and reliability of her translation. Only certified interpreters with no interest in the case would be allowed to translate. I was confident that the prosecutor would never prove my client's guilt at trial.

The prosecutor would not return my calls. I left messages explaining the purpose of my call and requesting a meeting. It became obvious that he was purposely ignoring my attempts to communicate with him. When I finally reached him, I told him what my investigation had uncovered, and suggested he dismiss the case. He assured me that he could prove the case and declined to dismiss. He also reminded me that he had nine months to return an indictment.[21] I suspected that he was abusing the grand jury system—pretending to investigate the case to keep my client in jail.

My suspicions were ultimately confirmed. At the end of the nine-month period, I received a notice that the case would not be indicted and my client would be released. I called the prosecutor and was surprised by his admission: "Your client was guilty. At least he did nine months in jail." He laughed, but I didn't find it funny at all. This man had used his power as a prosecutor to act as judge and jury—single-handedly finding my client guilty and "sentencing" him to nine months in jail.[22]

I felt strongly that the prosecutor be held accountable for his behavior. I couldn't prove that he had violated any of the rules of professional responsibility.[23] However, his behavior was plainly at odds with the American Bar Association's Standards for the Prosecution function, which state that a prosecutor should only bring charges that she believes and she can prove beyond a reasonable doubt.[24] Despite strong language in the ABA standards, prosecutors are not penalized for their failure to follow these standards. There is not even a requirement that they consider the standards before making important prosecutorial decisions.

I had no proof that the prosecutor had actually abused the process. I hadn't recorded the phone conversation, and I wasn't sure it would have made a difference. There didn't appear to be a way of holding the prosecutor accountable. The case was dismissed, Mr. Davis had his freedom, and it might not have been in Mr. Davis's interest to pursue an action against the prosecutor if one were possible.

The interesting thing about the prosecutors' behavior in the McKnight, Robinson, and Davis cases is that it is doubtful that any of them engaged in prosecutorial misconduct as courts have defined it. Although their actions appeared to be an abuse of power, none of them engaged in the kind of behavior that has led to professional discipline or a finding that due process was violated.[25] It was quite an eye-opener for me when I discovered the extent of prosecutorial power and the lack of accountability when that power was abused.

Of course there were many instances in which prosecutors did engage in misconduct. The most common form of misconduct was the failure to turn over exculpatory information as required in *Brady v. Maryland*.[26] When I was at PDS, there was constant litigation over what was exculpatory and when such evidence had to be turned over. Many prosecutors waited until just before trial if they turned it over at all. Even when judges found that prosecutors had violated *Brady*, they rarely penalized them. The remedy for a *Brady* violation was usually a brief continuance of trial to give the defense attorney time to investigate. When there were guilty pleas, prosecutors rarely honored their *Brady* obligations.

Not all prosecutors abused their power when I was a defender. There were prosecutors who made fair plea offers. Some even showed humanity toward the accused. However, the culture of the US Attorney's Office for the District of Columbia at the time I worked at PDS was one of winning at any cost—far from the Supreme Court's mandate that the US Attorney's interest "in a criminal prosecution is not that it shall win a case, but that justice shall be done."[27] I often wondered how I could have ever considered pursuing a career as a prosecutor. I wouldn't have lasted long.

My Destiny

My experience growing up in the segregated south inspired my dream to become a civil rights lawyer. In hindsight, I guess I realized that dream. Criminal defenders are civil rights lawyers. I fought for the civil rights of my clients, demanding that they be treated with dignity and respect. Most importantly, I fought for their freedom. I am so grateful that I had the opportunity to work for them.

Today I teach future public defenders and prosecutors. I encourage my students to pursue careers as public defenders, and yes, as prosecutors too. We need zealous and committed public defenders, but we also need ethical prosecutors who believe that pursuing justice doesn't always mean obtaining a conviction. Both roles are important and essential to a fair criminal justice system.

Not everyone can or should be a public defender. You have to be a little crazy (in a good way) to want to do the work. Looking back, I now understand why being a public defender was my destiny. I remain acutely aware that there but for the grace of God go I.

Notes

1. Ironically, when I advise students who apply to defender and prosecutor offices, I usually tell them that applying to both offices at the same time will probably not help them with either.
2. The following reports prepared by The Sentencing Project are just a few of the many articles that discuss the issues black men face in our criminal justice system: Tushar Kansal, *Racial Disparity in Sentencing: A Review of the Literature* (The Sentencing Project, January 2005), http://www.prisonpolicy.org/scans/sp/disparity.pdf; Mark Mauer, *The Crisis of the Young African American Male and the Criminal Justice System*, (The Sentencing Project, April 15–16, 1999), http://www.sentencingproject.org/doc/publications/rd_crisisoftheyoung.pdf; Mark Mauer and Tracy Huling, *Young Black Americans and the Criminal Justice System: Five Years Later* (The Sentencing Project, October 1995), http://www.sentencingproject.org/doc/publications/rd_youngblack_5yrslater.pdf.
3. Angela J. Davis, *Arbitrary Justice: The Power of the American Prosecutor* (New York: Oxford University Press, 2007), 123–141; Angela J. Davis, *Racial Fairness in the Criminal Justice System: The Role of the Prosecutor*, Columbia Human Rights Law Review 39 (2007); Angela J. Davis, "Prosecution and Race: The Power and Privilege of Discretion," *Fordham Law Review* 67 (1998); Bruce A. Green, "Why Should Prosecutors 'Seek Justice'?," Fordham Urban Law Journal 26 (1999); James Vorenburg, "Decent Restraint of Prosecutorial Power," *Harvard Law Review* 94 (1981).

4. Berger v. United States, 295 U.S. 78, 88 (1935) ("The United States Attorney is the representative not of an ordinary party to a controversy, but of a sovereignty whose obligation to govern impartially is as compelling as its obligation to govern at all; and whose interest, therefore, in a criminal prosecution is not that it shall win a case, but that justice shall be done."); see Model Code of Prof'l Responsibility EC 7–13 ("The responsibility of the public prosecutor differs from that of the usual advocate; his duty is to seek justice, not merely to convict."); ABA Standards Relating to the Administration of Criminal Justice, Standard 3–1.2(c) ("The duty of the prosecutor is to seek justice, not merely to convict."); Model Rules of Prof'l Conduct, R. 3.8 cmt. ("A prosecutor has the responsibility of a minister of justice and not simply that of an advocate.").
5. I disagreed then and still disagree with the view of Abbe Smith and Paul Butler that "good people can't be prosecutors." See Paul Butler, *Let's Get Free: A Hip-Hop Theory of Justice* (New York: New Press, 2009), 101–121; Abbe Smith, "Can You Be a Good Person and a Good Prosecutor?," *Georgetown Law Journal* 14 (2001); Kenneth B. Nunn, "The 'Darden Dilemma': Should African-Americans Prosecute Crimes?," *Fordham Law Review* 68 (2000); cf. Lenese C. Herbert, "Et in Arcadia Ego: A Perspective on Black Prosecutors' Loyalty within the American Criminal Justice System," *Howard Law Journal* 49 (2006); Roscoe C. Howard, Jr., "Changing the System from Within: An Essay Calling on More African-Americans to Consider Being Prosecutors," *Widener Law Symposium Journal* 6 (Fall 2000).
6. D.C. Code § 16–2322(a)(1) (2012). A two-year commitment could be extended until the juvenile's twenty-first birthday. D. C. Code § 16–2322(f) (2012). In addition, see D.C. Code § 16–2303 (2012) (establishing that the court retains jurisdiction over the juvenile until he becomes 21 years old) and D.C. Code § 24–901(6) (defining a youth offender as under 22 years old) (2012).
7. Pursuant to D.C. Code § 16–2301(3), a person who is at least 16 years old may be tried as an adult when charged with certain specified crimes.
8. This name and all names in this chapter are pseudonyms.
9. Juveniles in DC do not have a right to a jury trial for any offense, and since it was a simple assault, he would not have a right to a jury trial even if he had been an adult.
10. In juvenile court, the sentencing hearing is called the "disposition hearing."
11. D.C. Code § 16–2317(c) (2012).
12. I learned much later that Albert was convicted of first degree murder as an adult and sent to a maximum security facility. He found out that I had become a law professor and began to write me letters there. Despite how his life turned out, his letters are hopeful and uplifting.
13. PDS had a practice of assigning junior lawyers as cocounsel in first degree murder cases. The practice was good for the clients and the lawyers. The clients received additional representation, the senior lawyer

was provided needed assistance, and the junior lawyer got additional training.

14. D.C. Code § 23–110(a) (2012) ("A prisoner in custody under sentence of the Superior Court claiming the right to be released upon the ground that (1) the sentence was imposed in violation of the Constitution of the United States or the laws of the District of Columbia, (2) the court was without jurisdiction to impose the sentence, (3) the sentence was in excess of the maximum authorized by law, (4) the sentence is otherwise subject to collateral attack, may move the court to vacate, set aside, or correct the sentence.").
15. It is possible for a homicide to be both first degree premeditated murder and felony murder if the jury finds that the defendant intentionally killed the decedent after deliberation and premeditation AND if the murder was committed during the course of and in furtherance of a dangerous felony. The charges merge at sentencing (that is, the sentences for each charge must be served concurrently).
16. Thomas H. Cohen and Tracey Kyckelhahn, *Felony Defendants in Large Urban Counties, 2006* (Bureau of Justice Statistics, 2010), 10, http://bjs.ojp.usdoj.gov/content/pub/pdf/fdluc06.pdf.
17. A.B.A. Standards for Criminal Justice: Prosecution Function § 3–3.9 (1993), http://www.americanbar.org/publications/criminal_justice_section_archive/crimjust_standards_pfunc_toc.html.
18. Davis, *Arbitrary Justice*, 25.
19. Fed. R. Crim. P. 6(d)(1) ("The following persons may be present while the grand jury is in session: attorneys for the government, the witness being questioned, interpreters when needed, and a court reporter or an operator of a recording device."). Although the A.B.A. suggests that "no prosecutor should knowingly fail to disclose to the grand jury evidence which tends to negate guilt or mitigate the offense," courts have held that the government does not have a duty to present exculpatory evidence to the grand jury. A.B.A. Standards: Prosecution Function § 3–3.9(a); United States v. Williams, 504 U.S. 36 (1992) (holding that the prosecutor does not have a legal obligation to present exculpatory evidence to the grand jury); United States v. Stout, 965 F.2d 340 (7th Cir. 1992) (same).
20. Davis, *Arbitrary Justice*, 61–76.
21. D.C. Super. Ct. R. of Crim. P. 48(c) (2009).
22. Davis, *Arbitrary Justice*, 19–41.
23. D.C. Rules of Prof'l Conduct R. 3.8 (2012).
24. A.B.A. Standards: Prosecution Function § 3–3.9(a) ("A prosecutor should not institute, or cause to be instituted, or permit the continued pendency of criminal charges when the prosecutor knows that the charges are not supported by probable cause. A prosecutor should not institute, cause to be instituted, or permit the continued pendency of criminal charges in the absence of sufficient admissible evidence to support a conviction.")
25. D.C. Rules of Prof'l Conduct R. 3.8 ("Special Responsibilities of a Prosecutor") (2012). For examples of the types of prosecutorial misconduct

that result in discipline, see Davis, *Arbitrary Justice*, 123–141; Neil Gordon, "Misconduct and Punishment," *The Center for Public Integrity*, last modified June 26, 2003, http://www.iwatchnews.org/2003/06/26/5532/misconduct-and-punishment; Duff Wilson, "Prosecutor in Duke Case Disbarred by Ethics Panel," *New York Times*, June 17, 2007, http://www.nytimes.com/2007/06/17/us/17duke.html#; Ken Armstrong and Maurice Possley, "Part 1: The Verdict: Dishonor," *Chicago Tribune*, January 11, 1999, http://www.chicagotribune.com/news/watchdog/chi-020103trial1,0,1561461,full.story; People v. Mackell, 47 A.D.2d 209 (N.Y. App. Div. 1975), *aff'd*, 351 N.E.2d 684 (N.Y. 1976) (discussing prosecutorial misconduct that resulted in criminal prosecution); United States v. Pacheco-Ortiz, 889 F.2d 301, 310–11 (1st Cir. 1989) (describing nonjudicial sanctions for prosecutorial misconduct); Price v. State Bar of Cal., 638 P.2d 1311 (Cal. 1982) (suspending a prosecutor from practicing law for five years when he promised to seek a favorable sentence for a defendant if the defendant agreed not to appeal his conviction); In re G. Paul Howes, 39 A.2d 1 (D.C. 2012) (disbarring a prosecutor who wrongfully distributed witness vouchers, failed to disclose the payments to the court or opposing counsel, and intentionally made misrepresentations to the court that the disclosures had been made).

26. Brady v. Maryland, 373 U.S. 83 (1963).
27. Berger v. United States, 295 U.S. 78, 85 (1935).

5

Why I Defend the Guilty and Innocent Alike

Alan M. Dershowitz

Sometimes it takes personal encounters to understand why it is so important for lawyers to defend even very bad people.

Several weeks after the verdict in the O. J. Simpson double murder case, my wife Carolyn and I were walking down Madison Avenue in New York when a well-dressed woman approached us and said, "I used to love you so much, and now I'm so disappointed in you—and my husband would use even stronger words." She explained, "You used to defend Jews like Scharansky and Pollard. Now you defend Jew-killers like O.J." I replied that she was wrong ever to have loved me because she probably didn't understand what I do. A few blocks farther along, a black man hugged me and said, "Great job. I love what you do." I told him not to love what I do or else he would soon be disappointed.

A few years after that, my wife was involved in a minor litigation. The controversy was sent to mediation where both sides were represented by excellent lawyers. The lawyer for the opposing side was anxious to settle the matter, since my wife was clearly in the right, both legally and morally. (We agreed to mediation only because litigation, which we would have won, would have been incredibly time-consuming and expensive.) I was at the mediation to lend support to my wife, who is a psychologist, not a lawyer. The opposing lawyer was, in my view, particularly nice and extremely polite, but he represented his client—a particularly sleazy enterprise—with vigor. At the first recess, my wife, who rarely has a negative word to say about anyone, was furious at the opposing lawyer. With a wry irony, she fumed, "How can he represent those people? Doesn't he know he's on the wrong side? How does he sleep at night?"

My wife smiled at me, acknowledging that she was saying all of the same things that people say about me when I represent clients they believe are guilty, bad, or wrong. Only after she won the case and got a nice settlement did she really calm down. "I guess I'm equating him with his client," my wife said sheepishly. "That's what they always do to you."

Imagine a legal system in which lawyers were equated with the clients they defended and were condemned for representing controversial or despised defendants. Actually, one need not resort to imagination, since history reminds us that only a little more than half a century ago, mainstream lawyers were frightened away from defending alleged Communists who faced congressional witch hunts, blacklisting, criminal trials, and even execution. Senator Joseph McCarthy and the millions of Americans—including many lawyers, law professors, and bar association leaders—who supported this attack on "commie-symp lawyers" made it impossible for decent lawyers who despised communism but who supported civil liberties and constitutional rights for all to defend accused Communists without risking their careers.

I grew up at a time when Julius and Ethel Rosenberg were accused of being Soviet spies who gave the secret of the atomic bomb to our archenemies. They were defended by a Communist ideologue with little experience in criminal cases. He provided an inept defense resulting in a terrible miscarriage of justice that has only recently been confirmed by Soviet intelligence sources. It now seems clear that the government framed Ethel Rosenberg in a futile effort to get her husband, who was a minor spy, to disclose the names of his accomplices (who were major spies). There is no assurance that an able and zealous mainstream lawyer could have saved either or both Rosenbergs from the electric chair, but we should certainly be left with an uncomfortable feeling that McCarthyite attacks on lawyers may well have contributed to a terrible injustice—and some very bad law—in the Rosenberg and other cases during the 1940s and 1950s.

Even one of my favorite books—*To Kill a Mockingbird*—portrays America's most popular fictional character, Atticus Finch, as representing an apparently guilty black defendant who, in the end, turns out to be completely innocent. One must wonder whether the novel would have been as successful or its hero as admired if the accused were guilty. And my other fictional hero, Perry Mason, not only proved all his clients innocent, but also fingered the guilty killer so that perfect justice could be done.

In many parts of the real world, it remains difficult for a despised defendant to be represented by a mainstream lawyer because many nations—even Western-style democracies—lack any tradition of a political or civil libertarian representation. For example, in Israel, which has an excellent legal system, right-wing lawyers tend to represent right-wing defendants (especially "settlers" on the West Bank), while left-wing lawyers tend to represent left-wingers and Palestinians accused of political crimes. (This situation has improved somewhat in recent years, thanks to a developing legal aid system.) This ideological approach to legal representation creates a circular reality in which lawyers are expected to share the political perspectives of their clients. The result is a bar divided along ideological lines that lack a neutral commitment to civil liberties for all. A similar situation prevails in France, Italy, and some other European countries.

Our nation has been blessed with the tradition of a vigorous bar committed to civil liberties for all, regardless of ideology, politics, or the nature of the accusation. John Adams, Abraham Lincoln, and Clarence Darrow have come to personify this approach. Adams represented the British soldiers who participated in the Boston Massacre; Lincoln and Darrow represented the widest assortment of clients, ranging from corporations to common criminals. It would be a terrible tragedy if we were to surrender this noble tradition to those who are so certain about their ability to discover truth that they become impatient with the often imperfect processes of justice. It was the great judge Learned Hand who once observed that "the spirit of liberty is the spirit that is not too sure that it is right."

It is a rare case in which absolute truth resides clearly on one side. Most cases contain shades of gray and are matters of degree. That has surely been true of most of the cases in which I have participated over my career. Even in those that are black and white—either the defendant did it or he did not—there is often room for disagreement, and it is the advocate's role to present the client's perspective zealously within the bounds of law and ethics. Zealous representation requires the lawyer to subordinate all other interests—ideological, career, personal—to the legitimate interest of the client. You are the surgeon in the operating room whose only goal is to save the patient, whether that patient is a good person or a bad person, a saint or a criminal. It is a rare case in which a lawyer knows for sure that his client is guilty and that there are no mitigating considerations. In most of those cases the lawyer will try to persuade the defendant to enter into a plea bargain—not because that is best for society or the legal system, but because it is best for the client.

Having made this general point, it is important to suggest several distinctions among types of legal representation. At the pinnacle of cases that should be defended vigorously without regard to ideology are free speech and criminal matters. Surely those of us who defend the free speech rights of everyone—including extremists on the right and left, purveyors of sexual material, and newspapers that make honest mistakes—should not be deemed to approve of the content of the materials the government seeks to censor. Those of us who opposed efforts by the town of Skokie to censor Nazis did not sympathize with the Nazis; we opposed censorship even of the most despicable and false ideas. It should be equally obvious that those who choose to defend people facing execution or long imprisonment do not sympathize with murder, rape, robbery, or corporate crime. I personally despise criminals and always root for the good guys except when I am representing one of the bad guys. We believe in the process of American justice, which requires zealous advocacy, scrupulous compliance with constitutional safeguards, and the rule of law. We understand that most people brought to trial for serious crimes are factually guilty. Thank goodness for that!

Would anyone want to live in a country in which the majority of criminal defendants were innocent? That may be true of China, Cuba, Iran, and Syria, but it is certainly not true of the United States. And in order to keep it that way, every defendant—regardless of his or her probability of guilt, unpopularity, or poverty—must be vigorously defended within the rules of ethics. If lawyers were to defend only accused criminals whom they believed were innocent, more actually innocent defendants would be convicted. Also, fewer actually guilty defendants would be acquitted. But if we truly believe that it is better for ten guilty defendants to be acquitted than for one innocent to be convicted, then this trade-off is essential.

The scandal is not that the rich are zealously defended; it is that the poor and middle class are not. More resources should be allocated to defending those who cannot afford to challenge the prosecution and to expose the weaknesses of the evidence against them.

There are indeed some innocent people in prison and on death row, and it is no coincidence that most of them are poor and unable to secure effective legal advocacy. That is why I devote half of my time to pro bono cases. Many other lawyers also do a significant amount of free legal representation, but this is not enough to ensure that no defendant faces execution or long imprisonment without zealous advocacy on his behalf. If lawyers are frightened away from taking on unpopular criminal cases, the already serious problem of inadequate representation will reach crisis proportions. There is no surer way of frightening a young lawyer who is contemplating the defense of an accused murderer or rapist than to accuse him or her of being sympathetic to murder or sexual abuse.

Of course, a lawyer has the legal and ethical option of declining to represent an unpopular and despised defendant whom he believes to be guilty. The real question is whether it is desirable for the decent lawyer to exercise that option on the basis of the "politically correct" criterion of the day, which differs over time. Today, it is popular to represent Communists because communism presents no threat, but it is unpopular to represent Islamic fundamentalists accused of terrorism. I believe no lawyer should turn down a constitutional or criminal case simply because the client or cause is deemed politically incorrect, since—among other things—it will lead to the demise of civil liberties and the creation of a bar so divided along ideological lines that the defendants who most need legal representation will be relegated to ideologues who believe that politics and passion are a substitute for preparation and professionalism.

Several years ago, I got into a scrap with the Boston chapter of the National Lawyers Guild, a left-wing group that thought it was wrong to represent accused rapists. They changed their position only after an African-American man was accused of serially raping white women and the defendant claimed he was the victim of racist misidentification and profiling.

Free speech and criminal cases are different from cases that only involve continuing commercial gain from immoral conduct. A lawyer who provides ongoing legal assistance to a cocaine cartel is acting, in effect, as a "consigliere" to a criminal conspiracy. A criminal organization has no legal right to ongoing advice on how to evade arrest and increase illegal profits. Many lawyers regard the cigarette industry as indistinguishable from the "mob" (though recent settlements suggest that even cigarette lawyers can sometimes help their clients do the right thing, if only for self-serving reasons). Corporations that are not facing criminal charges do not have the same Sixth Amendment rights as accused criminals, nor do they have the same First Amendment rights as those confronting government censorship. Still, we are all better off with a legal system under which important rights are not denied anyone without affording them the right to be defended by a zealous advocate. If we move away from the American tradition of lawyers defending those with whom they vehemently disagree—as we temporarily did during the McCarthy period—we weaken our commitment to the rule of law. What is popular today may be despised tomorrow. So beware of an approach that limits advocacy to that which is approved by the feeling of the day.

A recent case in Massachusetts places limits on a lawyer's discretion to decline a case. A feminist attorney who specializes in representing women in divorce cases refused to represent a male nurse's aide who was seeking financial support from his wealthy wife who was a doctor. The lawyer told the man that she did not accept male clients in divorce cases. A panel of the Massachusetts Commission against Discrimination ruled against the lawyer, stating "that an attorney [holding herself] out as open to the public may not reject a potential client solely on the basis of gender or some other protected class." Obviously this situation is different from one in which a lawyer declines a case on political or ideological grounds, but it does suggest that lawyers are not entirely free to decline cases on *any* ground. In selecting clients, a lawyer may be a feminist but not a sexist. The distinction may be subtle, but it is real. Lawyers in Massachusetts, as in other states, are covered by civil rights and public accommodation laws, some of which prohibit discrimination based on religion, creed, and political affiliation. Doctors and dentists are not free to turn away patients who has AIDS or whose politics they despise. It is a fair question to ask why lawyers should have greater freedom to discriminate than do other professionals.

In the end, I hope lawyers will not need laws to tell them that they should represent those most in need of zealous advocacy, without regard to gender, race, ideology, economic situation, or popularity. Such an approach will make for a better legal system and a freer America.

The one thing a lawyer is never free to do is to accept a case and then pursue it without zeal. Although there are no specific criteria for measuring zeal, there certainly are general guidelines. Being someone's lawyer is different from being their friend. For a friend or relative, you may be willing to sacrifice your life, your liberty, or your fortune. You need not—and should not—do that for a client, even a client you like. Zealous advocacy has limits imposed by law, ethics, and common sense. We know what unzealous representation means: just look at some of the capital case lawyers in Texas! Several fell asleep during trial. (In one capital case I appealed, the lawyer fell asleep during the trial, but that was his finest hour, because when he was awake he hurt his client by telling the jury that he didn't believe his testimony!) Others conducted no investigation. (The same lawyer—a former Klansman representing a black defendant accused of killing a white state trooper—refused to conduct any investigation in black neighborhoods.) Many judges prefer underzealous to overzealous lawyers. That's why they appoint the former—who make their job easier, if they define their job as sentencing as many defendants as possible to death. Zealous lawyers—and lawyers deemed "overzealous" by some—are a pain in the ass to some judges. I know. I am one. We make their job harder by contesting every issue, demanding every right, and disputing every prosecutorial allegation, so long as it is in the best interest of the client (both short term and long term). That is the key to defining appropriately zealous advocacy: It must always be in the legitimate interest of the client. Its purpose is not to make you feel good or virtuous, but to help the client win by any ethical and lawful means.

I'm proud to be a criminal defense lawyer who stands up to the government and defends people without regard to their possible guilt or innocence.

6

Why It's Essential to Represent "Those People"

Monroe H. Freedman

Criminal Lawyers Protect All of Us

When he was President of the United States, Richard Nixon created an Enemies List for the purpose of "screwing" those who had displeased him in some way.[1] The list included reporters, political opponents, and pretty much anyone else against whom Nixon held a grudge. Singled out as personal and political enemies, these people were to be subjected to the full force of governmental power, including criminal prosecutions based on slim and suspect evidence.

As Attorney General of the United States, Robert Kennedy circulated a similar list to all federal prosecutors' offices.[2] Kennedy's enemies list included Jimmy Hoffa and Roy Cohn, both of whom had earned Kennedy's personal enmity in years past. Kennedy had hated Hoffa ever since Hoffa had shaken his finger in Kennedy's face and said, "You're nothing but a rich man's kid who never had to make a nickel in his life." Cohn had earned Kennedy's ire when they were both serving on congressional committees pursuing suspected Communists and Communist sympathizers.

Kennedy even created a Get-Hoffa Squad (it was actually called that) in the Department of Justice. Irving Younger, then a young assistant US attorney, was directed to spare no expense to find grounds to prosecute Roy Cohn, including traveling to Europe in search of whatever evidence he could find to justify a prosecution.[3]

Such abuses of the vast powers of government were denounced by Supreme Court justice Robert Jackson, who had also been attorney general of the United States. Jackson observed that the "most dangerous power of the prosecutor" is the power to carry out an investigation of a particular person because it enables the prosecutor to "pick people he thinks he should get rather than pick cases that need to be prosecuted."[4] Supreme Court justice Felix Frankfurter put that kind of selective prosecution among the "most terrible" things a prosecutor can do.[5] In the words of a former chief federal prosecutor, "The power to investigate is the power to destroy."[6]

More commonplace than enemies lists, but no less insidious, are ordinary federal and state prosecutors who abuse the powers of government to advance their own careers. Too often, this is done by amassing a record of convictions based on false evidence, coerced confessions, inaccurate or phony "science," or by blocking legitimate defense efforts to expose the weakness of the government's case or get at the truth.

Criminal defense colleagues and I have represented:

- a defendant who was told that the prosecutor would indict the man's wife and son as criminals if he did not plead guilty;
- people who were convicted by false evidence that was manufactured by the prosecution;
- men, women, and children who were isolated from their lawyers, families, and friends, and interrogated under harsh conditions for hours until, exhausted, frightened, and confused, they falsely confessed;
- people convicted on the basis of falsified or incompetent "scientific" evidence;
- people arrested and prosecuted because of their race, religion, or ethnicity; and
- people who, when they sought evidence of their innocence, had that evidence covered up or blocked by the prosecution.

I don't mean to suggest that the defendants we represent are all innocent. In fact, most are guilty. This is as it should be in a free society. And a strong criminal defense bar, ready to vigorously represent even the worst of "those people," is the only effective way to discourage those who wield government power from abusing it against any one of us—the innocent and guilty alike—who might meet with their disfavor.

Because criminal defense consists mostly in defending guilty people, I have resisted cataloguing numerous victories of Innocence Projects all over the country.[7] Innocence Projects have provided a valuable service in freeing some of the factually innocent people in our prisons and in exposing the ways that flawed prosecutions can succeed.

But defending the innocent is not the defense lawyer's main job. Instead, our job is to provide every accused citizen with the fundamental rights our Constitution has given us. These constitutional rights include protection from invasion of our homes by government agents; protection from unlawful search and arrest; the privilege against being forced to say things that can lead to our own conviction; and the rights to have a lawyer, present witnesses on our behalf, face and challenge our accusers, and have a speedy and public trial before an impartial jury that will judge our guilt or innocence. In representing "those people," therefore, defense lawyers make sure that every one of us has the benefit of all of these rights, not just on paper, but in fact.

Moreover, we are required, ethically and constitutionally, to do that zealously, focusing on the client's rights even against the government. As the Supreme Court has said, "A defense lawyer best serves the public, not by acting on behalf of the State or in concert with it, but rather by advancing the undivided interests of his client."[8]

Nevertheless, a recurring criticism of criminal defense lawyers is not just whom we represent, but the strong advocacy with which we do it. For example, the lawyers for O. J. Simpson were denounced not just because they represented a guilty man, but also for their zealous efforts to get an acquittal.

In particular, Simpson's lawyers were criticized for "playing the race card."[9] The defense lawyers did that by stressing the racism of detective Mark Fuhrman, a principal witness for the prosecution. After Fuhrman had given damning evidence against Simpson, F. Lee Bailey's cross-examination portrayed Fuhrman as a lying racist who used the word "nigger" repeatedly and boasted of arresting black men for no other reason than that they were accompanying white women. As a result, jurors might well have concluded that Fuhrman's testimony against Simpson, who was married to a white woman, was motivated by his hatred of African-Americans.

Although the defense did indeed play the race card, the state of California dealt it, by knowingly employing and promoting an outspoken racist on the police force and by showcasing him as a principal witness for the prosecution. For my part, I would rather live in a society in which a guilty O. J. Simpson goes free than one in which police detectives like Mark Fuhrman wield the enormous powers of the state.

An important by-product of Bailey's exposure of Fuhrman is that it served to cleanse the Los Angeles police force of officers who were abusing their powers. A senior Los Angeles police officer admitted: "Sure, they knew about Fuhrman; they had to know. Lots of people knew... and they turned the other way."[10] Because the race card was successfully played in Simpson's case, however, the LA chief of police finally began to get racist cops off the force, a long-standing problem in the department.[11]

The O. J. Simpson case is only one of numerous cases in which vigorous criminal defense has led to the improvement of law enforcement and prosecution. Zealous defense has also made eyewitness identification more reliable, exposed abusive interrogations that produce false confessions, closed down incompetent and dishonest scientific laboratories, and enhanced police-community relations.[12]

Thus, effective defense helps to assure that the government follows the rules that protect us all. When defense lawyer Michael Tigar was asked why he was representing a man accused of being a Nazi war criminal, he explained: "When the most powerful country on earth gangs up on an individual citizen, accuses him of being the most heinous mass murderer of the Holocaust, and systematically withholds evidence that he is guiltless of that charge, there is something dramatically wrong... I have spent a good many years of my professional life litigating such issues. I am proud to do so again."[13] Tigar also said: "We must remember the Holocaust, and we should pursue and punish its perpetrators. We dishonor that memory and besmirch the pursuit if we fail to accord those accused of Holocaust crimes the same measure of legality and due process that we would give to anyone accused of wrongdoing."[14]

BEING JEWISH

The above reasons are sufficient for me—I believe in them deeply and think they should be sufficient for anyone who believes in a free society. But I have personal reasons as well, relating to the fact that I'm Jewish. Frankly, I have no idea exactly how being Jewish has influenced my commitment to civil liberties and civil rights. I can only say that it's impossible for me to separate being a Jew from the way I feel about these issues.

In explaining this, I don't mean to imply that any of the values I have absorbed as a Jew are not shared by other faiths or even that all Jews would agree with my understanding of these values. I mean to say only that these are my values and that they have influenced my role as a criminal defense lawyer.

Every client, no matter what he has been accused of doing, or has in fact done, is a fellow human being who is suffering. To recognize this is to invoke "rachmanut," or compassion, despite the fact that the suffering may be that person's own fault. According to Jewish tradition, compassion is one of the seven things with which God created the world[15] and it is worthy of emulation.

In addition to the accused, there may well be one or more family members, human beings who are also suffering, often through no fault of their own.[16] A memory that has stayed with me for over half a century is my first visit to meet with a client at the DC Jail. It was cold and snowing. Outside the heavy wooden door of the fortresslike building, huddled against the red stone of the building, was a boy, about eight years old, alone, shivering, and with tears and mucus running down his face. Apparently a member of his family was visiting another relative or friend in the jail. That boy was in effect a collateral victim of whatever his relative had done, or was accused of having done. He was inevitably part of the reason I was at the jail that day.

As the great criminal defense lawyer Clarence Darrow said: In criminal law, "you are dealing with flesh, blood, reputations, shame, disgrace, and honor" as well as with "wives, fathers, mothers and children."[17]

Consistent with the Torah, the five books of Moses, I believe too that a lawyer must respect the client's autonomy, his God-given free will, and that it is the client's life and the client's case, not the lawyer's. As God says in Deuteronomy, "I have set before thee life and death, the blessing and the curse; therefore choose—."[18] And as God tells Moses in Genesis, "Whoever wishes to err may err."[19]

This does not mean that the lawyer should not give the client moral advice based on the lawyer's own moral judgment when it is appropriate to do so. But as the American Bar Association said in 1969, consistent with Jewish values: "In the final analysis—the lawyer should always remember that the decision whether to forgo legally available objectives or methods because of nonlegal factors is ultimately for the client and not for the lawyer."[20]

In addition, each human being has his or her individual dignity which must be respected even if he or she has done things that are deserving of punishment. That is what is meant, I believe, by the idea that each of us is created in the image of God, that there is an aspect of God in each of us which cannot be denied, ignored, or forfeited regardless of our sins and crimes.

My role models are Moses and Abraham.

Moses gave up the enormous privilege and wealth of Pharaoh's household to become the representative of slaves. His compassion led him to advocate for the Israelites, first against Pharaoh and then even against God Himself. After the Israelites' grievous sin of idol worship of the Golden Calf, Moses was so furious that he smashed the sacred tablets of the law. Nevertheless, when God told Moses that He intended to destroy the Hebrew people and make of Moses himself a great nation,[21] Moses put himself between his people and the wrath and power of the Almighty. He urged God to forgive the Israelites or else "blot me, I pray Thee, out of Thy book which Thou hast written."[22] This challenge to the Almighty was far more courageous than the challenges I have made to state power on behalf of an accused or convicted person, but it stands as the ultimate model for me as a criminal defense lawyer.

Abraham, too, is a criminal defense lawyer's model. When God intended to destroy the people of Sodom and Gomorrah, Abraham confronted the ultimate Judge with a question: "Wilt thou indeed sweep away the righteous with the wicked?" More, he audaciously demanded: "Shall not the Judge of all the earth do justly?" Step by step, Abraham then persuaded God to spare the city for the sake of 50, 45, 40, 30, and 20, and, finally, only 10 righteous people.

Of particular note, Abraham's plea was on behalf of non-Jews, and on behalf of people who were strangers to him—all fellow human beings for whom he felt compassion, despite their "exceeding grievous" sinfulness.[23]

CONCLUSION

In a free society, it is vital that there be a counter to the overwhelming power of government, because it is a power that can be easily abused by those who wield that power, individuals who may be more interested in advancing their own ambitions, venting their own hatreds, and satisfying their own prejudices, than they are in respecting our rights and protecting society. In representing "those people," therefore, even those who have committed the worst crimes against other people and against society, the criminal defense lawyer serves each of us by curbing official abuse and preserving the fundamental values of a free society.

Vital though criminal defense is, it can also be grueling. In addition to what is at stake in representing the accused—frequently the client's inhumane imprisonment, and sometimes even the client's death—criminal lawyers also have to deal with public scorn that can go beyond the familiar "cocktail party question." As Clarence Darrow noted, "You must learn to endure criticism and to be callous to spiteful remarks."[24]

Like Moses and Abraham, therefore, a criminal defense lawyer must be able to stand up to enormously powerful forces, as well as endure anxiety and criticism. Nevertheless, as a member of the legal profession, a Jew, and a human being, I am proud to call myself a criminal defense lawyer and have been privileged to represent "those people."

NOTES

1. John Dean, White House counsel, to John D. Ehrlichman, assistant to the president for domestic affairs, memorandum, August 16, 1971, "Dealing with Our Political Enemies."
2. During Robert Kennedy's tenure as attorney general, there were more prosecutions against Hoffa than there were civil rights prosecutions in the state of Mississippi, and more prosecutions against officers of Hoffa's Teamsters Union than there were civil rights prosecutions in the entire country. In view of the fact that Kennedy was said to have had a "commitment" to civil rights, his determination to put Hoffa in jail bordered on obsession. The first product of that extraordinary diversion of government resources was a two-month trial of Hoffa on a mere misdemeanor charge. The prosecutions proliferated from there. See Victor Navasky, *Kennedy Justice* (New York: Atheneum, 1971), chap. 9.
3. Irving Younger, "Memoir of a Prosecutor," *Commentary Magazine*, October 1976, 66. Younger's account has been challenged by Robert M. Morgenthau and others. Robert M. Morgenthau, letter to the editor, "Getting Roy Cohn," *Commentary Magazine*, January 1977, 4. Roy Cohn was in fact prosecuted three times, each time unsuccessfully.
4. Justice Robert Jackson, (lecture, Second Annual Conference of U.S. Attorneys, April, 1940).
5. Martin v. Merola, 532 F.2d 191, 196 (2d Cir., 1976) (Lumbard, J., concurring) (quoting Felix Frankfurter, letter to the editor, *New York Times*, March 4, 1941); McNabb v. U.S., 318 U.S. 332, 343 (1943) (Justice Frankfurter referring to the "awful instruments of the criminal law").
6. Joseph DiGenova, "Investigated to Death," *New York Times*, December 5, 1995.
7. See Abbe Smith, "In Praise of the Guilty Project: A Criminal Defense Lawyer's Growing Anxiety About Innocence Projects," *University of Pennsylvania Journal of Law and Social Change* 13 (2009–10).
8. Polk County v. Dodson, 454 U.S. 312, 318 (1981).
9. The phrase "play the race card" belittles racism (as it is intended to do) when it is used to describe efforts by the defense to counter racism inherent in the prosecution's case. An interesting variation on this theme is recounted in Steven Lubet, "Storytelling and Trials: Playing the 'Race Card' in Nineteenth-Century Italy," *UCLA Law Review* 48 (2001) (describing an effort to counter antisemitism in a prosecution).

10. Kenneth B. Noble, "Many Black Officers Say Bias Is Rampant in Los Angeles Police Force," *New York Times*, September 4, 1995, 6.
11. "The Fuhrman Tapes and the L.A.P.D." *New York Times*, Editorial, August 25, 1995, http://www.nytimes.com/1995/08/25/opinion/the-fuhrman-tapes-and-the-lapd.html.
12. See John B. Mitchell, "The Ethics of the Criminal Defense Attorney," *Stanford Law Review* 32 (1980); Abbe Freedman and Monroe H. Smith, *Understanding Lawyers' Ethics*, 4th ed. (New Providence, NJ: LexisNexis, 2010), 20–21, 306–314.
13. The full discussion by Professor Tigar and me on this subject, including this quotation, is in Freedman and Smith, *Understanding Lawyers' Ethics*, app. A.
14. Ibid.
15. "With SEVEN things the Holy One, blessed be He, created his world, to wit: knowledge, understanding, might, loving-kindness and compassion, judgment and decree." *The Fathers According to Rabbi Nathan*, trans. Judah Goldin (Binghamton, NY: Vail-Ballou Press, 1955), 153.
16. See Serge F. Kovaleski, "Killers' Families Left to Confront Fear and Shame," *New York Times*, February 5, 2012, A1.
17. John A. Farrell, *Clarence Darrow: Attorney for the Damned* (New York: Random House, 2011), 364.
18. Deuteronomy, 30:19. Compare Ezekiel 18:21–24 and 33:12–20; Genesis 4:7.
19. Genesis Rabbah 8:8.
20. *Model Code of Professional Responsibility*, EC 7–8 (1969).
21. Exodus 32:10.
22. Ibid., 32:32.
23. Genesis 18:20–33.
24. Farrell, *Clarence Darrow*, 364.

7

Defending Civil Rights

Vida B. Johnson

Late one fall night in 1967, a group of men placed a bomb under the floor of a parsonage connected to St. Paul's United Methodist Church in Laurel, Mississippi. The men then moved a safe distance away and lit the fuse. The bomb exploded and the kitchen and dining area were blown apart.

That parsonage was the home of my maternal grandparents. My grandfather, Dr. Reverend Allen Johnson, was the pastor of St. Paul's United Methodist. When the bomb exploded, he, my grandmother, and three of their children were asleep.[1] Miraculously, the bedrooms where they were sleeping were not seriously damaged and no one was hurt.

The bombing of my grandparents' home was part of several months of violence by the Ku Klux Klan in Mississippi.[2] Before my family was attacked, a newly built synagogue in Jackson, Mississippi, was bombed, as was the home of a white professor teaching at a Tougaloo College, a historically black college in Tougaloo, Mississippi, who was rumored to have a black mistress. A few days after the bombing of my grandfather's parsonage, the nearby home of a rabbi was bombed and knocked off its foundation—presumably by the same people. Amazingly, no one was hurt in any of the attacks.

My grandfather and his family were targeted because they were African-American, and because my grandfather was a leader in the civil rights movement. He was active in the National Association for the Advancement of Colored People (NAACP) and was a member of the Voter's League. My grandparents, however, did not waiver in the face of the violence. Indeed, the morning after the bombing, my grandmother sent her young children to school so that everyone in town would know the Johnson family was not intimidated.

The animosity toward African-Americans and their struggle to achieve racial equality extended beyond the relatively small group of people directly involved in the bombing. When my Aunt Glenda went to school the morning after the bombing, she was approached by one of her classmates—a white girl with whom she sometimes played on the playground at the recently integrated elementary school. My aunt told the girl that her house had been bombed, but the girl said she already knew all about the bombing because she had overheard her father and other men planning it—down to the details of how they would get the dynamite into place under the building. It never occurred to the girl to warn my aunt or her family before the bomb went off.

This all took place years before I was born, but the story of the bombing was a huge part of our family history. I grew up hearing about it from my grandparents, mother, aunts, and uncles. The story of the bombing and its aftermath was for me emblematic of my grandparents' commitment to equality, a commitment that shaped and inspired me. However, what led my grandfather to advocate for civil rights in the late 1960s led me to defend people accused of crimes. I see my commitment to indigent criminal defense as following in my grandfather's footsteps.

I was just a child when I first heard the story of the bombing. Of course, as a young black child, knowing that there had been so much animosity toward black people, scared me. But, at the time, the blatant and overt racism that my family had experienced also seemed distant. To me, the bombing was the far-off past. The photos and news clippings were in black and white. And I grew up very far away from Mississippi—in San Diego, California. San Diego has only a small black population and there were very few black people in the small prep school I attended on scholarship. The social problems that existed in Mississippi in the 1950s and 1960s seemed a world apart from California in the 1980s. While classmates occasionally said insensitive things to me, nothing was blatantly racist. For the most part, I did not feel that I was treated unfairly—or that my family was being treated unfairly—on the basis of race. The struggles my family faced in Mississippi seemed long ago.

The disconnect between my family's past and my own present began to fade, however, as I finished high school and began college—largely due to the events of the day. The 1992 Los Angeles riots related to the Rodney King case[3] took place shortly before I graduated from high school. Los Angeles and Orange County, where the riots were taking place, are not too far away from San Diego. I heard plenty of fear in San Diego of "those people" making their way down south.

I started college at the University of California at Berkeley just as affirmative action programs all over the country were coming under attack, especially in California. The debate in the University of California system over affirmative action raged throughout my college years.[4] Debates and marches on the issue of affirmative action kept people talking about race all over campus. A long-simmering racial divide on how people view the America legal system also rose to the surface during and after the O. J. Simpson trial in 1995.[5] Television, newspapers, classrooms, and coffee shops all seemed obsessed with race and inequality.

At Berkeley, I had an unexpected reminder of my family's Mississippi experience: my African-American studies class included the story of the bombing in the assigned reading. I learned something new from the textbook: my grandfather had organized a protest at City Hall following the bombing, attended by more than three hundred people, and was involved in a Christmas-time boycott of white-owned stores in downtown Jackson, Mississippi, to demonstrate the importance of African-Americans to Mississippi's economy. How strange and powerful to see my family story in print.

I began to see the connection between my grandfather's fight for civil rights for black people in 1960s Mississippi and what was happening in 1990s California, and wanted to do my part. I wanted to do something meaningful with my life that would make *my* grandchildren proud. I wanted to help other people and fight against unfairness. I decided to go to law school to do civil rights work.

However, my first real-world work on a civil case—during the summer between my first and second years of law school—led me to a prison. I was volunteering with the Louisiana Crisis Assistance Center (now Louisiana Capital Assistance Center) and working on the center's class-action lawsuits on behalf of death row inmates in Mississippi. The inmates were suing the state for access to counsel for their postconviction appeals. My job, along with a few other summer interns, was to meet with and interview our clients—the men on death row at the infamous Parchman Prison.

I learned three lessons that summer that I knew I would not forget. First, that people who are convicted of crimes—even the most serious crimes that result in death sentences—are not monsters. I was initially apprehensive about the clients I would be representing and worried about meeting convicted murderers. I assumed that they would be gruff, aggressive, and frightening. I was wrong. Over the course of the summer I met with nearly two-thirds of the men on death row in Mississippi—housed on Parchman's notorious Unit 32.[6] The men were extremely grateful for the work we were doing on their behalf. They were polite and even kind. There was one man who always brought candy for us that he had purchased in the prison commissary—no doubt at enormous cost to him—every time we came for a visit. And most of them were scared—scared of how little stood between them and the executioner.

Second, even though these men had been convicted and sentenced to death, the evidence against many of them seemed thin or riddled with problems. I had assumed that the ultimate punishment had been reserved for the worst crimes and the strongest, most-airtight prosecution cases. But again my assumption was wrong. The crimes ran the gamut from run-of-the-mill felony murder to a murder of a child. Also, one of the men on Mississippi's death row at the time I was there was subsequently exonerated.[7]

Third, Mississippi's condemned had been treated unfairly. The vast majority of our clients were black, all of them poor. The state was preparing to execute them, and they were depending on *law students* to defend them. While they had been represented by licensed lawyers at trial, in many instances the lawyers had treated the case with less care than a decent lawyer would give a traffic case. We heard stories of lawyers who had barely met with their clients, had done no investigation, had filed no motions, were overly friendly with prosecutors, and were drunk during trial.

My clients that summer—and the inequities they had suffered in the criminal justice system—made me consider criminal defense rather than civil rights work. Indeed, a lot of our clients asked me if I was going to become a criminal defense lawyer once I finished law school. In retrospect, I am sure most of them were just being polite when they asked about my future plans, but at the time I felt they were encouraging me to be a defense attorney.

When I returned to law school, I still believed that I would ultimately be a civil rights lawyer, but I decided to explore criminal defense. The next summer I interned at the San Francisco public defender office. During my final year of law school I enrolled in the juvenile defense clinic. Working in San Francisco and in New York taught me that the problems I had encountered in Mississippi were not limited to the South or to murder cases.

In some ways criminal law practice in San Francisco seemed like a different world. The defense lawyers were great, the prosecutors were not asking for "strikes" as they were in the rest of California,[8] and the city jail was a lot less intimidating than Parchman. But I quickly noticed that, although black people made up less than 5 percent of the population,[9] most of our clients were still black. As it turns out, I was right. An astonishing 50 percent of the men in prison in San Francisco were black.[10] A police operation that occurred the summer I spent in San Francisco also really bothered me. Police officers would dress up like homeless people and hang out in locations where the homeless congregated. The officers would pretend to pass out or be asleep with money visibly sticking out of their pockets in an attempt to catch people willing to take money from an easy target. While it is a worthwhile goal to keep the homeless from being preyed upon, this "sting" resulted in other homeless men being arrested. I just could not get over the resources and money being spent on arrest and prosecution (there were always two undercover officers—one with the money, another close by, and the arresting officers) instead of just helping these men and women get out of homelessness.

I saw the same sorts of things in the juvenile defense clinic. So many kids in New York's juvenile justice system were there for trivial things—throwing snowballs, jumping subway turnstiles, and, in one case, kicking a soccer ball at a police officer. In terms of seriousness, these kids' cases were the polar opposite of the crimes for which the men on death row in Mississippi had been convicted. The kids had something in common, however, with the adult death row inmates: they were poor people of color. There were no rich white children in New York's juvenile justice system. While statistics show that rich kids are just as likely to use drugs[11] (and presumably just as likely to throw snowballs and kick soccer balls) they simply do not get arrested. A rich kid who takes ecstasy or snorts cocaine while the parents are away does not get arrested. A poor kid who smokes marijuana on the street does. When a rich kid gets in a fight at his prep school, the school administration deals with it. When a poor kid gets in a fight at his public high school, the police are called. Whether the privileged kids avoid getting caught up in the legal system because they commit their crimes outside of public eye, or because they receive different treatment from the police, or because—if they do get caught—their parents pay for high-priced alternatives, does not matter. With marijuana use so widespread, and school fights a common occurrence, it is clear that drug use and school spats do not translate into lifelong criminal behavior. However, incarcerating kids might. The end result is a double standard that burdens the poor, nonwhite kids with yet another disadvantage. They are labeled criminals, given a number, and shuffled through the system. They are often taken away from their families, their lives disrupted.

From what I saw in prisons, jails, and juvenile detention centers in Mississippi, San Francisco, and New York—and what I could tell from visiting my clients' families at their homes—the criminal justice system ensnares huge numbers of people and disproportionately affects poor people of color and their communities. My observations were simply a reflection of what was going on throughout the country. More than 2 million Americans—nearly 1 percent of the country's population—are now incarcerated in a prison or a jail.[12] And that number does not include the nearly 100,000 young people detained in juvenile facilities. If you include the people who are on probation or parole, the number grows to over 7 million.[13]

This is not the way it was when my grandparents and others were fighting for civil rights. Back then, the incarceration rate was approximately 100 Americans per 100,000 in the population.[14] That approximate rate had remained steady from the 1920s right up until the mid-1970s.[15] The incarceration rate has multiplied nearly *ten times* since my grandfather and his colleagues won so many battles for civil rights. This phenomenon—one that is unique to the United States—is known as "mass incarceration."[16] And it is the people for whom those battles were fought—people of color—who have suffered the most from the policies of mass incarceration. For example, whites and African-Americans use and sell drugs at roughly the same rates, but African-Americans, who are 12 percent of the population, account for 34 percent of those arrested for drug offenses and 45 percent of those serving time for drug offenses in state prisons.[17] In 2009, more than half a million people were stopped by the police in New York City—87 percent of them were African-American or Latino (and only 1.3 percent of the stops resulted in the recovery of a weapon and only 6 percent resulted in an arrest).[18] A study in Los Angeles revealed that African-Americans were three times as likely to be stopped as whites, and they were 127 percent more likely to be frisked, but African-Americans who were frisked and searched (and Latinos, who were also more likely to be stopped and searched) were *less* likely to have weapons, drugs, or other incriminating evidence on their persons.[19] Similar disparities have been shown throughout the country for stops and searches, as well as arrests, prosecutions, and length of sentences. As a result, a disproportionate number of African-Americans and Latinos are caught up in our criminal justice system. Among white American males, 678 are incarcerated per 100,000 white males in the general population. Among African-American males, 4,374 are incarcerated per 100,000. Among Latino males, 1,775 are incarcerated per 100,000.[20] *One out of every three* African-American males born today will be in prison at some point in his lifetime, as will one of every six Latino males. This is true for only one in seventeen white males.[21]

When I contemplate these figures I am horrified. It is not hard to be. Yet not everyone agrees. Many Americans do not think our criminal justice system locks up too many people. Indeed, when you watch or read the news, it feels like most Americans believe we should lock up more people. If the tables were turned, however, and the projection was that one of every three white baby boys born today would be locked up at some point in his life, there would be a massive outcry to change the system. Instead, mass incarceration continues, the war on drugs—the biggest contributor to mass incarceration—continues, and the racial disparities in the criminal justice system continue.

Mass incarceration has been especially devastating to certain poor, African-American neighborhoods. In Washington, DC—where I now work—many of my clients come from African-American communities where *more than half* of the young black men are in prison, on probation, or on parole. In some neighborhoods there is a visible absence of young black men. I was lucky enough to obtain a scholarship to a private high school where the expectation was that every student would go to college. In the neighborhoods where my clients come from the expectation is that young men will go to prison. The fact that there are now more black men in jails and prisons than in college dormitories should be disturbing to everyone.[22] In the neighborhoods where many of my clients live, the kids who should go to college do not go, the mentally ill and drug addicted who should get treatment do not receive it, and the homeless people desperate for a place to live are not provided one. Instead, most of them will be sent to the one place that does nothing to solve their problems or prevent crime: prison. And when they get out, their criminal record only makes life more difficult for them, their families, and their neighborhoods.[23]

I do this work because the criminalization of the black community has replaced the Jim Crow segregation of my grandfather's time. Human beings lose their freedom. Families are broken apart. Mass incarceration spawns the same kind of economic inequality and marginalization as segregation. Some inmates work for pennies an hour in prison industries. Upon release, convicts are often barred from good jobs—and sometimes even minimum wage jobs. Criminal records often result in eviction from public housing. Federal student loans are denied to those with certain convictions, even juvenile misdemeanor drug offenses. In many jurisdictions prisoners are disenfranchised, and in many states convicted felons are precluded from ever voting or serving on juries.[24] The communities that have been disproportionately affected by incarceration not only suffer the loss of its members, but the census also counts inmates *where they are incarcerated*—often in far-off places with very different demographics. This means that already hard hit communities lose resources and representation in government.

The policies of mass incarceration and over-criminalization of the African-American community threaten so much of what my grandparents and their colleagues fought for: the right to vote, equal representation in government, and equal employment opportunity. While not overtly based on race, the racialized enforcement of our criminal justice policies leads to the same result. Employers may not explicitly refuse employment on the basis of race; instead they use criminal records as a basis for denying or ending employment. Like Jim Crow, our current criminal justice regime virtually ensures that black Americans will have higher rates of unemployment and poverty, fewer and worse educational opportunities, and underrepresentation in democratic institutions. Disturbingly—and yet perhaps not coincidentally[25]—this process of mass incarceration and criminalization began in the mid-1970s, just when the civil rights movement had begun to accomplish so many of its objectives.

When I enter a courtroom to represent an indigent defendant, I am fighting against the same double standards, the same inequities, the same unfairness that my grandparents fought against. The battle remains the same, only the battlefield has changed. In fact, the subject of this book—how can you represent those people?—highlights one very significant way in which the battlefield has changed. Unequal treatment based on criminalization, rather than race, has eliminated the moral authority of those who would fight against unequal treatment. Where blatant discrimination based on race is now morally repugnant to most Americans, this is not so for unequal treatment of people who have been charged or convicted of crimes. Indeed, most Americans seem to believe that people with criminal records should be denied rights and opportunities. Efforts to garner public support for change—through boycotts, marches, or protests—are unlikely to succeed.

There are, however, ways to fight for some measure of equality. One of them is to make sure that when police and prosecutors try to convict a person of a crime and put him or her in prison, that person has a lawyer who will use every legal means to stop them—or at least hold them to the very high burden of proof required in criminal cases. To me, the question is not how can I represent those people, but how can I not?

No doubt people once asked my grandfather and his colleagues why they were causing so much trouble, why they could not just live with how things were? Now, however, people ask how someone could have worked to support the system of segregation—siccing a police dog or spraying a fire hose on protesters because they sought equality, prosecuting a woman just because she sat at a "whites-only" lunch counter, or prosecuting a couple for miscegenation? Perhaps one day, my colleagues and I will not be the only people asking how police and prosecutors can continue to perpetuate a system that has such an astoundingly disparate impact on people of color.[26]

Mass incarceration, particularly of black people and other people of color in this country, is the civil rights issue of our generation. Hopefully we can be as successful in attacking it as my grandfather and his comrades were at attacking the vicious racism they faced. It is because of my family's legacy and my own disgust at our criminal justice system that I am proud to represent "those people."

NOTES

1. My mother, the oldest child, no longer lived at home at that time.
2. Michael Newton, *The Ku Klux Klan in Mississippi: A History* (Jefferson, NC: McFarland, 2010).
3. The LA Riots, as they are known, began April 29, 1992, and lasted six days. Fifty-three people were killed (ten of whom were killed by the police) and millions of dollars were lost in property damage from the looting and arson that took place during this period of unrest. The riots stemmed from a jury acquitting one Hispanic and three white police officers from the Los Angeles Police Department who has been videotaped beating a black motorist, Rodney King, after a traffic stop. Mr. King was tasered, beaten with a baton, and kicked in the head during the beating that was videotaped for ten minutes. For an in-depth discussion of the Los Angeles riots, see The Staff of the Los Angeles Times, *Understanding the Riots: Lost Angeles before and after the Rodney King Case* (Los Angeles Times Syndicate Books, 1996).
4. Race-based affirmative action was abolished in California. This has changed the campus very significantly. At University of California, Berkeley, for example, the minority share of entering freshmen at Berkeley fell from 22 percent in fall 1997 (the last class admitted with race preferences) to 12 percent in 1998. David Card and Alan B. Krueger, "Would the Elimination of Affirmative Action Affect Highly Qualified Minority Applicants? Evidence from California and Texas," *Industrial & Labor Relations Review* 58 (2005): 417.
5. Orenthal James Simpson, or O. J. Simpson, is a former NFL football player who is African-American. In 1995, he was acquitted of the murder of his white ex-wife, Nicole Brown Simpson. Because of his fame as a football star, Mr. Simpson's criminal trial was televised. Because

of his connections and wealth and the high-profile nature of his case, Mr. Simpson had a high-priced legal team and his trial was dubbed, "The Trial of the Century" by many. It is reported that more than half of Americans watched the not guilty verdict. Views on his guilt seemed to come down to race with white Americans largely believing Mr. Simpson had killed his ex-wife and had gotten away with murder, while black Americans believing that a racist Los Angeles Police Department was to blame for his having been accused of the murder. For more information on Mr. Simpson or his trial, see Jeffrey Toobin, *The Run of his Life: The People vs. O. J. Simpson* (New York: Touchstone Books, 1997).

6. Unit 32 has been closed. Erica Goode, "Prisons Rethink Isolation, Saving Money, Lives and Sanity," *New York Times*, March 10, 2012, http://www.nytimes.com/2012/03/11/us/rethinking-solitary-confinement.html?pagewanted=all.
7. Kennedy Brewer was exonerated in 2008 for a 1992 murder and rape that he did not commit. There have been a number of other nondeath row exonerations in Mississippi as well. For more information, see generally *Mississippi Innocence*, directed by Joe York (2011; University, MS: Mississippi Innocence Project), DVD, (documentary film about the exoneration of Kennedy Brewer and Levon Brooks).
8. California's Three Strikes Law comes from the phrase in baseball, "three strikes and you are out." After a person has a felony conviction, their second felony conviction carries twice the maximum penalty as it would otherwise. A person's third strike carries a mandatory sentence of 25 years to prison. These terms do not apply just to violent felony convictions but to any "serious" or violent felony conviction for which the prosecutor requests a "strike." In *Ewing v. California*, the US Supreme Court found that the imposition of a prison term of 25 years to life did not amount to cruel and unusual punishment where Mr. Ewing was convicted of stealing three golf clubs from a country club. 538 U.S. 11 (2003).
9. According to the 2010 census, black people make up just 3.9 percent of the population of San Francisco. Macio Lyons, "Black Population Drops to 3.9 percent in San Francisco," *San Francisco BayView*, February 4, 2011, http://sfbayview.com/2011/black-population-drops-to-3–9-in-san-francisco/.
10. The numbers are even more astonishing now. African-Americans now comprise more than 60 percent of those in prison from San Francisco and black women make up 67 percent of the female prison population. Editorial, "Alarming Percentage of African Americans in San Francisco Jails," *Fog City Journal* (blog), May 5, 2008, http://www.fogcityjournal.com/wordpress/401/alarming-percentage-of-african-americansin-san-francisco-jails/.
11. An estimated 49 percent of whites and 42.9 percent of blacks aged 12 or older have used illegal drugs at some point in their lifetimes; 14.5 percent of whites and 16 percent of blacks have used them in the past year; 8.5 percent of whites and 9.8 percent of blacks have used

them in the past month, according to the 2006 surveys conducted by the US Department of Health. *Results from the 2010 National Survey on Drug Use and Health: Summary of National Findings*, NSDUH Series H-41, HHS Publication No. (SMA) 11–4658 (Rockville, MD: Substance Abuse and Mental Health Services Administration, 2011).

12. Laura E. Glaze, *Correctional Population in the United States, 2010* (Bureau of Justice Statistics, December 2011), 7, app. table 2.
13. Ibid., 3, table 1.
14. Bruce Western and Becky Pettit, "Incarceration & Social Inequality," *Dædalus* (Summer 2010): 9.
15. Ibid.
16. For a powerful discussion of the phenomenon, please see, Michelle Alexander, *The New Jim Crow*, (New York: The New Press, 2010).
17. Marc Mauer and David Cole, "Five Myths about Americans in Prison," *Washington Post*, June 17, 2011, http://www.washingtonpost.com/opinions/five-myths-about-incarceration/2011/06/13/AGfIWvYH_story.html.
18. "NYPD's Stop and Frisk Policy: Unfair and Unjust," *Center for Constitutional Rights*, accessed August 13, 2012, http://www.ccrjustice.org/stopandfrisk.
19. Ian Ayres and Jonathan Borowsky, *A Study of Racially Disparate Outcomes in the Los Angeles Police Department*, (ACLU of Southern California, October 2008).
20. Glaze, *Correctional Population in the United States*, 8, app. table 3.
21. Marc Mauer, "Addressing Racial Disparities in Incarceration," *The Prison Journal Supplement* 91(3) (2011), 88S.
22. Associated Press, "More Blacks, Latinos in Jail Than College Dorms," *The Oakland Tribune*, September 27, 2007, http://www.highbeam.com/doc/1P2-7620897.html.
23. Alfred Blumstein and Kiminori Nakamura, "Paying a Price, Long after the Crime," *New York Times*, January 9, 2012, http://www.nytimes.com/2012/01/10/opinion/paying-a-price-long-after-the-crime.html.
24. There are more than 38,000 punitive provisions that apply to people convicted of crimes, pertaining to everything from public housing to welfare assistance to occupational licenses. More than two-thirds of the states allow hiring and professional-licensing decisions to be made on the basis of an *arrest* alone. Rabiah Alicia Burks, "Laws Keep Ex-Offenders from Finding Work, Experts Say," *American Bar Association News Service,* July 26, 2011, http://www.abanow.org/2011/07/laws-keep-ex-offenders-from-finding-work-experts-say/.
25. Again, for a discussion of why this may not be a coincidence see Alexander, *The New Jim Crow*.
26. For a different perspective on this issue, see Paul Butler, "How Can You Prosecute Those People," in this volume.

8

Ruminations on Us and Them

Joseph Margulies

As a law professor, I have always encouraged my students to look behind the law to the cultural framework into which the law is embedded.[1] This is just a fancy way of saying that by and large, the law is a product of its time, and that to understand the former it pays to wrestle with the latter. I remind myself of this now and again, including when I am asked how I can represent "those people." The cultural assumption behind the ubiquitous question asked of every criminal defense lawyer is that "those people" aren't like "us." Otherwise the question makes no sense. The decision to represent one of us is easy; only the decision to represent one of them is a puzzle. At its root, therefore, the question is really about who is inside the magic circle and who is out, for it is only when one group is perceived as outside the rest that its claims are viewed as a demand on the community, rather than a demand by the community.

It wasn't always this way. In the last half century, the dangerous criminal has been reimagined from one of us—a person for whom society bears some responsibility and who must therefore be reformed and rehabilitated—to one of them, a monster who threatens to inflict untold damage and must therefore be separated from society and whose movements must be carefully monitored. For years, an increasingly bipartisan sentiment has successfully nurtured and manipulated this darker image. The result has been an angry impulse to purge the community of its undesirable elements by sharply increasing the government's power to control those deemed to be a threat—producing what the sociologist David Garland has branded "the criminology of the dangerous other."[2] The question asked by the authors in this collection is part of this larger cultural transformation.

HISTORY

When the United States emerged in 1945 from the nightmare of total war, there was a consensus, at least among cultural elites, that with only rare exceptions, dangerous criminals were not so much born as made. Deviant behavior was widely believed to be substantially caused by social and economic forces, and not merely the result of individual action. Crime was thought to be "merely a form of primitive social protest."[3] End the environmental conditions that gave rise to the protest, it was thought, and the great majority of criminal behavior would disappear.[4] For that reason, crime control was largely synonymous with social welfare and it was foolish to imagine the former without dedication to the latter. "The war on poverty," Lyndon Johnson said in 1964, "is a war against crime and a war against disorder." As for Barry Goldwater, his opponent in the upcoming election, Johnson said there was "something mighty wrong when a candidate for the highest office bemoans violence in the streets but votes against the war on poverty, votes against the Civil Rights Act, votes against major educational bills that come before him as a legislator."[5]

Like any expression of American identity that achieved widespread acceptance, New Deal optimism cast itself in the elastic rhetoric of the American Creed, stressing the communitarian elements of mutual obligation and civic duty in service of the common good. The welfare of the community was thought to be everyone's responsibility, and all shared in the blame when society left broad segments of the population poor, uneducated, and unemployed, and therefore prone to criminality. As the magazine *Commonweal* put it in 1946, "It is vain to write about the particular motivation of an individual who succumbs and commits a crime. The general public maladies that lead or tempt to crime are everybody's fault to the degree that each could, with justly demanded effort, work against the general demoralizing conditions."[6] Because the chaos and decay that inevitably resulted from these "demoralizing conditions" affected everyone, the entire community had an obligation to become part of the solution, and to take what steps they could to achieve greater equality across the country. Only then could the nation realize the greatness of its lofty goals.

The turbulence of the mid-1960s sorely tested this philosophy. In July 1967, after two weeks of deadly rioting in Detroit and Newark, President Johnson established the National Advisory Commission on Civil Disorders, better known as the Kerner Commission. Its conclusions, released in 1968, were a sober indictment of American life cast in the creedal language of communitarianism and equality. "Our nation is moving toward two societies, one black, one white—separate and unequal." And though it was the ghetto that erupted, the commission made clear that blame did not rest solely with the rioters; causes must be found elsewhere. "What white Americans have never fully understood but what the Negro can never forget is that white society is deeply implicated in the ghetto. White institutions created it, white institutions maintain it, and white society condones it." The "deepening racial division" in the country, the commission warned, "threaten[ed] the future of every American." Failure to act will lead to "continuing polarization of the American community and, ultimately, the destruction of basic democratic values."[7]

Yet by the time the Kerner Commission issued its report, the New Deal sentiment it expressed, with its liberal emphasis on an idealized "American community" and its call for a "massive and sustained" commitment of resources to eliminate the inequality, had already begun to collapse. For years, the liberal view had been under attack by conservative intellectuals who derided the entire New Deal philosophy as collectivist drivel and a dangerous assault on both the free market system and the free will of the individual. The iconoclastic Ayn Rand, author of *Fountainhead* and *Atlas Shrugged*, mocked the very notion that there was a "common good," and ridiculed the suggestion that "everybody is responsible for everybody's welfare."[8] But it was not until Barry Goldwater's campaign for the presidency in 1964 that the conservative view of individualism and personal responsibility began to achieve wider circulation in society.

"If it is entirely proper for the government to take away from some to give to others," Goldwater asked in one speech, "then won't some be led to believe that they can rightfully take from anyone who has more than they? No wonder law and order has broken down, mob violence has engulfed great American cities, and our wives feel unsafe in the streets."[9] Though Goldwater lost decisively, his message of "law and order" struck a chord with the electorate. In 1965, the Johnson administration's approach to crime began to move away from its liberal origins. "The problem runs deep and will not yield easy and quick answers," Johnson said. "We must identify and eliminate the causes of criminal activity whether they be in the environment around us or in the nature of individual men... Crime will not wait until we pull it up by the roots. We must arrest and reverse the trend toward lawlessness."[10]

The 1968 presidential campaign continued the trend that Goldwater and other vanguards of modern conservatism had set in motion. The

Republican national platform of that year called upon the country to "think anew about the relationship of man and his government [and] enlarge the opportunity and autonomy of the individual." On crime policy, the GOP insisted, "We must re-establish the principle that men are accountable for what they do, that criminals are responsible for their crimes, that while the youth's environment may help to explain the man's crime, it does not excuse that crime."[11] On the campaign trail, Richard Nixon pressed hard for law and order. The "solution to the crime problem," he said on one occasion, "is not the quadrupling of funds for any governmental war on poverty but more convictions." In the same spirit, he mocked the Democrat Hubert Humphrey as naïve. "Doubling the conviction rate in this country," he said, "would do far more to cure crime in America than quadrupling the funds for Mr. Humphrey's war on poverty."[12]

Yet the liberal explanation for crime was not yet dead, and Nixon continued to acknowledge that civil order required social justice. He resolved the potential tension in his position by tinkering slightly with his message to fit the perceived demands of his audience. As *TIME* magazine observed two months before the election, Nixon "is in favor of 'order with progress' when he speaks in Westchester but for 'law and order' when he is in Houston or Charlotte, N.C."[13] By contrast, running as an Independent, Alabama governor George Wallace was considerably less nuanced. He scoffed at the suggestion that crime had anything to do with a person's upbringing. "If a criminal knocks you over the head on your way home from work, he will be out of jail before you're out of the hospital and the policeman who arrested him will be on trial. But some psychologist will say, well, he's not to blame, society's to blame. His father didn't take him to see the Pittsburgh Pirates when he was a little boy."[14]

During the same period, Democratic politicians steadily joined the movement away from postwar liberalism. The Democratic national platform in 1964 represented the last pure expression of the communitarian spirit of the New Deal. "America is One Nation, One People," it began. "The welfare, progress, security, and survival of each of us reside in the common good—the sharing of responsibilities as well as benefits by all our people." The lengthy document made scant reference to crime except to emphasize its origin in social conditions. "We cannot and will not tolerate lawlessness. We can and will seek to eliminate its economic and social causes." To that end, the platform vowed to use the war on poverty to increase "educational and employment opportunities, turning juvenile delinquents into good citizens and tax-users into tax-payers."[15]

By 1968, the tone had changed unmistakably as the Democrats began to emphasize a different creedal language. Though the Democratic platform in 1968 never used the distinctly Republican phrase, "law and order," it came close when it stressed the need "to strengthen the fabric of our society by making justice and equity the cornerstones of order," and "to uphold the rule of law by securing to all the people the natural rights that belong to them." Elsewhere, the platform candidly acknowledged that "the fact and fear of crime are uppermost in the minds of Americans today. The entire nation is united in its concern over crime." Speaking the ascendant language of individualism, the platform stressed that "anyone who breaks the law must be held accountable." And acknowledging the increased role of the federal government in combating crime, the platform boasted that the Johnson administration had fought "to prevent and combat youth crime," "added more personnel to strengthen the [FBI]," and secured passage of a gun control law that would take "a step toward putting the weapons of wanton violence beyond the reach of the criminal and irresponsible hands." Looking forward, the Democrats promised to "increase the numbers, raise the pay, and improve the training of local police officers," and vowed to ensure the availability in every metropolitan area of "quick, balanced, coordinated control forces, with ample manpower... to suppress rioting."[16]

Responding to the call for crime control, Vice President Hubert Humphrey insisted defiantly that his campaign would not "out-Nixon Nixon, and we're not going to out-Wallace Wallace. We're going to say it like it is." But his message echoed the Democratic platform, calling for more resources for police and courts while maintaining vaguely that order depended on "a policy not of repression but of liberation; a policy not in reaction to fear but in affirmation of hope."[17] In their concrete proposals, Democrats thus found themselves moving steadily closer to the Republicans. And though their rhetoric continued to suggest that crime was linked to social conditions, that link became increasingly ill-defined and abstract. Unsurprisingly, as the conservative and liberal views on crime began to converge, public opinion followed suit and American thought moved steadily toward a single mind. By 1969, "81% of those polled believed that law and order had broken down, and the majority blamed 'Negroes who start riots' and 'communists' for this state of affairs."[18]

The trend continued throughout the 1970s, though the Republican leadership on the issue temporarily derailed in mid-decade as a casualty of the Watergate scandal. But it was Ronald Reagan in the 1980s who gave the conservative view its most emphatic expression and who most successfully aligned the conservative understanding of crime and risk with the rhetoric of the American Creed. Under Reagan, the communitarian sentiment of the New Deal was decisively replaced with the language of individualism and personal responsibility. In his first major address on crime, Reagan attacked "the social thinkers of the fifties and sixties who discussed crime only in the context of disadvantaged childhoods and poverty-stricken neighborhoods."[19] Reagan charted another course. It is "abundantly clear," he said, "that much of our crime problem was provoked by a social philosophy that saw man as primarily a creature of his material environment... Society, not the individual, they said, was at fault for criminal wrongdoing. We were to blame. Well, today, a new political consensus utterly rejects this point of view."[20]

For Reagan, crime had nothing to do with society and everything to do with personal choice and individual responsibility. "Choosing a career in crime is not the result of poverty or of an unhappy childhood or of a misunderstood adolescence; it is the result of a conscious, willful choice made by some who consider themselves above the law."[21] And some people choose crime, Reagan said, simply because they are evil. While men "are basically good," Reagan said when he presented his anticrime package, some are "prone to evil," some in fact "are very prone to evil," and "society has the right to be protected from them."[22] Victory in the war on crime, he insisted, will come only "when an attitude of mind and a change of heart takes place in America—when certain truths take hold again... truths like right and wrong matters; individuals are responsible for their actions; [and] retribution should be swift and sure for those who prey on the innocent."[23]

By the end of the decade, the Republican and Democratic positions on crime were nearly indistinguishable. The Democratic platform of 1988 abandoned the now heretical suggestion that crime could be caused by social conditions and pledged an aggressive role for the federal government in controlling lawlessness. It pledged, for instance, to "wage total war on drugs" by appointing a National Drug "Czar" to coordinate "every arm of every agency of government at every federal, state and local level... to halt both the international supply and domestic demand for illegal drugs now ravaging our country." The federal government, it said, should increase its assistance to law enforcement, reinforce its commitment to crime victims, and "assume a leadership role in securing the safety of our neighborhoods and homes."[24] The Republican platform that year no longer found it necessary to assert the primacy of individual autonomy and personal responsibility; that battle had long since been won. Instead, the GOP contented itself with a laundry list of accomplishments, including the appointment of federal judges who were "sensitive to the rights of victims" and vastly increasing the number of drug arrests and convictions. And the GOP looked forward to continued movement in this direction, including restoration of the federal death penalty, reform of the exclusionary rule "to prevent the release of guilty felons on technicalities," and passage of preventive detention statutes in state courts that would allow "courts to deny bail to those considered dangerous and likely to commit additional crimes."[25]

By 1992, the shift to the conservative perspective on crime was essentially complete. In their respective positions, the two parties vied for no greater distinction than to be toughest on crime, which by now implied little besides a more expansive federal role, stiffer penalties, and greater support for victims. Nothing illustrates the transformation better than the career of Bill Clinton. In 1980, Clinton had lost his bid for reelection to a second term as Arkansas governor. One lesson he took from his defeat was to never again permit a Republican to use crime to outflank him on the right. In 1992, in the heat of the presidential campaign, Clinton made his stand in the case of Ricky Rector. Rector, who was mentally retarded, had shot himself in the head after his crime, which left him partially lobotomized. He had been sentenced to die but by all accounts he was profoundly impaired. Clinton allowed the execution to go forward—indeed, he flew home to Arkansas mid-campaign to make sure the execution would occur as scheduled. Prison guards reported that Rector was so impaired that he said he was saving his pecan pie from his last meal until after his execution. One Democratic activist later told the *Houston Chronicle* that the execution "completely undermines" any Republican attempt to portray Clinton as "out of touch with [the] mainstream public." A New York political observer put the matter thusly: "He had someone put to death who had only part of a brain. You can't find them any tougher than that."[26]

Today, the belief that crime is solely the personal choice of an evil man is all but universal in this country, at least among whites. In January 2011, when Jared Loughner killed 6 and wounded 14 others, including Arizona Democratic representative Gabrielle Gifford, at a public gathering in Tucson called "Congress on Your Corner," some wondered whether a pervasive environment of violent rhetoric by the political Right could have motivated Loughner's actions. Tucson sheriff Clarence Dupnik condemned "the vitriolic rhetoric that we hear day in and day out from people in the radio business and some people in the TV business." Particular attention focused on former Republican vice presidential candidate and right-wing media favorite Sarah Palin, who had released a fundraising appeal in March 2010 using rifle cross hairs to mark the districts where she hoped to defeat a Democrat, including the district of Representative Gifford, and had encouraged her supporters with remarks like, "Don't retreat. Reload!"[27] Palin denounced the attacks. In a statement released on her Facebook page entitled, "America's Enduring Strength," Palin called Loughner "a single evil man," and "a deranged gunman."[28]

Even on the Left, while some observers suggested that an environment that explicitly encouraged violence might have contributed to Loughner's actions, no one dared suggest what in 1961 would have been commonplace: that even without direct incitements, crime can only be understood in light of prevailing social conditions, and that the person who succumbs to the temptations of crime is, at bottom, no different from the rest of us. That view was dead.

So it came to pass that criminal defense lawyers would have to explain how we can represent "those people." The unspoken but unshakeable cultural assumption—that they are not like us—bears down on the client like a machine press of the mind, stamping out all humanity and leaving in its place a cartoon figure of pure malevolence, a phantom that cannot survive in the real world but that lives easily in the fears of an anxious nation. To save the client from this pitiless machine, the criminal defense lawyer must uncover and present the client's humanity, and in that way demonstrate to a skeptical jury that there is no "them," there is only "us." That is the defense lawyer's creed.

The Post-9/11 Era

In the post-9/11 era, the new arch-demon is the Islamic terrorist, whom we have built into a superhuman monster. On the one hand, he is less than human. He is a barbarian who has renounced the conventions of civilized behavior. Whatever kindness we extend to him is because we are benevolent and humane, not because he is deserving. On the other hand, he is also more than human. A zealot and fanatic, he worships a false God that commands him to destroy America and her institutions, and produces in him the unalterable conviction of his ultimate victory, for which he labors tirelessly. In his actions, he is unrestrained by Western morality. He recognizes no ties to society and is eager to sacrifice himself in the slaughter of innocent people. Though he is everywhere, he is invisible; anyone may be a terrorist, and all terrorists are the same. At special camps and schools, the terrorist trains his mind and body to perfection, which endows him with unique talents that make him all but impossible to locate or capture. Even if you manage to capture him, he has rare skills that will allow him to resist all interrogations. And guard him well, for no ordinary jail can hold him. He is not like mortal men.

It is thinking like this that produced the political and social desire for special government powers to track, seize, detain, interrogate, and try suspected terrorists. It accounts, for instance, for the widespread belief that the government had to devise and deploy enhanced interrogation techniques. Otherwise thoughtful public figures argued that because alleged terrorists received resistance training, the United States simply had to torture them.[29] It is likewise behind the notion that the detainees at Guantanamo are so uniquely dangerous that they cannot be safely relocated to any facility in the United States, even a super-maximum security prison.[30] And it provides substantial support for today's immensely popular argument that the criminal law is simply too forgiving, and terrorists too devious, for them to be tried in federal court.

Even people who should know better, who in fact ought to know all about representing "those people," have lost their way in this new thicket. In 2002, Yale University Press published *Why Terrorism Works*, by Harvard law professor Alan Dershowitz, a contributor to this volume. Terrorism works, he wrote, "because its perpetrators believe that by murdering innocent civilians they will succeed in attracting the attention of the world to their perceived grievances." Since that is what terrorists want, society must not give it to them. "We must commit ourselves *never to try to understand or eliminate its alleged root causes*, [emphasis in original] but rather to place it beyond the pale of dialogue and negotiation." These are not people with whom you can negotiate. Instead, "they are like cunning beasts of prey: we cannot reason with them, but we can—if we work at it—outsmart them, set traps for them, cage them, or kill them. The difference is, of course, that they are much smarter than the most cunning of beasts. Indeed, we must operate on the assumption that they are as smart as we are, but more determined, more single-minded, more ruthless, and less constrained by morality, decency, and legality." In a few short sentences, Dershowitz captures the essence of the mythical sub- and superhuman terrorist—less than human, but so much more.[31]

I have represented these "cunning beasts" for more than a decade. I was counsel of record for the petitioners in *Rasul v. Bush*, 542 U.S. 466 (2004), involving detentions of foreign nationals at Guantánamo, and *Munaf v. Geren*, 553 U.S. 674 (2008), involving detentions of US citizens in Iraq. To meet with my clients, I traveled to Iraq twice and have been to Guantánamo more times than I can count. My first trip to Guantánamo was in November 2004, after our victory in *Rasul*. I sat at a steel table in one of the small, wooden boxes that pass for a prison cell. Across from me was Mamdouh Habib, an Australian and my client. By order of the US military, Mamdouh sat with his back to the door, forbidden to face the natural light. His feet were shackled together. The shackles were bolted to the floor. At my request, the guards had unshackled his hands. I had spent all day with Mamdouh, and the day before as well. As I got up to leave, Mamdouh took my arm. "I'm dying here, Joe. I'm going to die here. They'll never let me go home." He had been a prisoner at Guantánamo since May 2002. It was the Saturday before Thanksgiving.

I sat back down. I had represented Mamdouh almost since he arrived at the base, even though for most of that time he did not know he had a lawyer. He was one of four petitioners in *Rasul*, which my colleagues and I filed in February 2002. A few months later, our team was joined by a group from the law firm of Shearman & Sterling, which filed a similar action on behalf of 12 Kuwaiti prisoners. The case reached the Supreme Court in November 2003 as *Rasul and Others v. George W. Bush*, named for Shafiq Rasul, a British prisoner. The Supreme Court ruled in our favor in June 2004. Mamdouh, like the rest of the prisoners at the base, hadn't even known the case was pending. Now, four months after the victory in *Rasul*, he was still at the base. And he had given up hope. He had a wife in Australia, a daughter too young to remember him, and three older children who wondered if they'd ever see their father again. "You don't have the luxury of giving up hope," I told him.

The month before my visit, the US government had leveled a set of allegations against Mamdouh that, if true, would have made him one of the highest-ranking terrorists at the base. He was supposedly a senior member of al Qaeda. He had supposedly trained the 9/11 hijackers in martial arts, taken part in surveillance operations to identify other terrorist targets, and unloaded chemical weapons from a truck in Afghanistan for use against the Americans.

In 2001, Mamdouh Habib and his wife Maha owned a small coffee shop in Sydney, Australia. Born in 1955 in the Egyptian port city of Alexandria, Mamdouh left Egypt when he turned 18. Like many teenagers, he roamed a bit around Europe, living for a time in Italy and developing a fondness for Italian wine and food. Eventually, Mamdouh, a small, slightly built man, perhaps 5' 9", with receding hair and a wry smile, emigrated to Australia, where he made his home and became a citizen. In Sydney, he met and married Maha and the two of them began a family. As with young people in this country, when Mamdouh and Maha started to have children, they became more religious. As his convictions grew, he was tired of secular Australia and began considering a move to Pakistan, where he thought he could find a more observant Islamic community. In the summer of 2001, he said good-bye to his family and traveled to Pakistan, where he hoped to find a job for himself and a school for his three children. When he left, Maha was pregnant with their fourth child.[32]

In early October 2001, in the anxious aftermath of September 11, Pakistan was not a safe place for foreigners, especially foreigners who were also devout Muslims. As in the United States, security forces in Pakistan were arresting hundreds of people on suspicion that they may have had something to do with the attacks. Mamdouh telephoned his wife to tell her he was coming home. He boarded a bus in Quetta and headed for Karachi with a ticket in his pocket for his return flight to Sydney. But the police were looking for militants fleeing the approaching conflict in neighboring Afghanistan, and people leaving the country were particularly suspicious. Mamdouh's bus was stopped and searched near the small town of Khuzdar and he was arrested.[33]

He was taken to a facility near Islamabad, where he was tortured and interrogated by Pakistani agents. When I visited him at the base, he described one of the techniques used by his Pakistani interrogators. Mamdouh was suspended from hooks on the wall with his feet resting on the side of a large cylindrical drum. Down the middle of this drum ran a metal rod with wires attached to both ends. The wires ran to what appeared to be an electric battery. When Mamdouh did not give the answers that his Pakistani questioners wanted, a guard threw a switch and a jolt of electricity ran through the rod, electrifying the drum on which Mamdouh stood. The action of Mamdouh "dancing" on the drum forced it to rotate, which caused his feet to slip, leaving him suspended by only the hooks on the wall. Instinctively, he struggled to regain his balance by placing his feet squarely on the drum, which of course sent another excruciating jolt of electricity into his feet. Eventually, he was forced to raise his legs, leaving him to hang by his outstretched arms until he could stand it no longer and, exhausted, he dropped his legs back onto the electrified drum. This lasted until he finally fainted.[34]

After approximately a week in Islamabad, Pakistani guards handcuffed him, took him from his cell, placed a blindfold over his eyes, and drove him to a nearby airfield. At the field, someone approached him and began to cut away his clothes. Unsure of what was happening to him, Mamdouh, who was still blindfolded and restrained, tried to resist. Several people knocked him to the ground, yelling at him and to each other as they grappled. Mamdouh speaks English and could tell that his attackers were American. During the struggle, his blindfold was knocked askew, which allowed him to see his assailants. They all wore black, short-sleeve T-shirts with grey or khaki pants. A number of them had distinctive tattoos. One had a colorful tattoo of a woman on the inside of his forearm. Another—a large, muscular man—had a cross tattooed on his upper arm. And a third had a tattoo of an American flag across his wrist.

After the men subdued Mamdouh, they brought him to his feet. Someone continued to cut his clothes from his body while someone else took a video. Then they dressed him in a blue tracksuit and transferred him to a plane. From their voices, Mamdouh could tell that the Americans who had attacked him sat at the front of the plane. They took him to Cairo, but not at the request of the Egyptian government. Makhdoom Hayat, who was Pakistan's interior minister at the time, later reported that this was an entirely American operation. "The U.S. wanted him for their own investigations," he said, and he was taken by US agents acting on US orders.[35] On the plane, Mamdouh had duct tape placed over his mouth, a hood placed over his head, and heavy, opaque goggles strapped over his eyes—the same type of goggles he wore when he first arrived at Camp Delta.

Mamdouh spent six months in an Egyptian cell, most likely at the state security headquarters in Lazoughli Square, in the heart of Cairo. Throughout his imprisonment, he lived in a barren, windowless cell, roughly 6' x 8' and illuminated by a bare, yellow bulb that hung from the ceiling. He slept on a concrete floor with nothing but a single blanket. Cockroaches and other insects crawled across the floors and walls. Except for his interrogations, he remained in his cell 24 hours a day, though occasionally guards would allow him to use the bathroom down the corridor. For weeks on end, he did not see natural light. Three times a day he received a single glass of milk and a scrap of bread.[36]

Interrogators came for him at unpredictable times. Since he could not see outdoors, he could only estimate the time from the heat inside the prison. Sometimes it seemed they came for him in the middle of the night, other times in the heat of the day. Sometimes they would come for him not long after the last session had ended; sometimes they came for him less frequently. The sessions lasted for hours and beatings were routine. Mamdouh, who was almost always handcuffed, was kicked, punched, beaten with a stick, and rammed with what, based on Mamdouh's descriptions, must have been an electric cattle prod. If he lapsed into unconsciousness, they would revive him and continue the beatings. If they discontinued the "interrogations" and he fell asleep on the floor, they would douse him with water or kick him in the ribs and start again. These sessions typically ended only when he admitted whatever they were questioning him about at the time. Mamdouh "confessed" to it all.

Beatings were only part of the abuse. The Egyptian authorities were also adept at psychological torture. Mamdouh told me he was brought to three different rooms. In one, the guards would slowly fill the room with water. Helpless and handcuffed, Mamdouh could only watch as the water rose steadily up his body until, if he stood on the tips of his toes, he could keep the water just below his chin. He was left in this room for hours. In another room, guards filled the water to his knees. But the room had an extremely low ceiling and Mamdouh, still in handcuffs, could only stoop. If he tried to sit in the water or rest on his knees, a guard would force him to his feet. In a third room, the water only came up to his ankles. But in this room, he could see through a window to another room containing a large lever or switch. His interrogators told him that the switch was wired to an electric current and unless he confessed they would throw the switch and electrocute him.

The threat of violence was common throughout his Egyptian imprisonment. On several occasions, Mamdouh was threatened with assault by German Shepherd dogs. But this was not simply the assault we have seen at Guantánamo and Abu Ghraib. In Egypt, they told Mamdouh they could induce the dogs to sexually assault him. He does not know whether his captors had actually trained a dog to act in this fashion, as he never allowed the interrogations to reach that sadistic point. In fact, he believes the interrogations could have been even worse than he was made to endure, judging from the screams he heard from other prisoners throughout his detention. But in Mamdouh's case, he signed a number of papers, some of which were blank, and credits these "confessions" with saving his life by bringing particularly horrific sessions to a close.

The torture Mamdouh endured in Egypt did not end until days before he left the country. Without explanation, but apparently in order to allow time for his bruises to heal, the interrogations and beatings abruptly stopped. He began to receive a far better diet. He started getting meat, sweets, cigarettes, and coffee. He was taken from his cell and moved to a regular room with a bed. He was allowed to sleep as much as he wanted. He was examined by a doctor. His guards told him he was going home. Instead, he was retrieved by the Americans and brought to Bagram Air Base in Afghanistan. Three weeks later, he was transferred to Guantánamo Bay. There, he was seen by several prisoners, including Shafiq Rasul, who would later report that Mamdouh was in "catastrophic shape—mental and physical... [H]e used to bleed from his nose, mouth, and ears when he was asleep." Jamal al-Hirith, an English prisoner released in 2003, had similar recollections of the slight, balding, middle-aged Australian. He bled from the nose and ears, he recalled, and "seemed to be in pain. He was haggard-looking. I never saw him walk. He always had to be held up."[37]

When I learned what had happened to Mamdouh, I filed a declaration describing his torture in great detail, including the American role in his rendition. When my declaration was cleared for release to the public, I immediately sent it to Dana Priest at the *Washington Post*. The next morning, the *Post* ran a front-page story about the entire affair. No American official denied anything Mamdouh had told me. As it happened, the *Post* story appeared the same day Attorney General-designate Alberto Gonzales appeared before the Senate Judiciary Committee for his confirmation hearings. Senator Dick Durbin of Illinois waived the article and asked Gonzales what he thought about Mamdouh's treatment. Because the article came as a surprise to the administration, Gonzales was caught off guard. If what this man says is true, Gonzales answered, then what happened to him was against the law.

Less than 48 hours later, I received a call from the Australian government advising me that Mamdouh would soon be released. On January 28, 2005, under a bright Australian sun, Mamdouh stepped carefully down the metal stairs of a Gulfstream jet at Sydney International Airport. Stooped and weather-beaten, he looked old for his 49 years and, as he squinted in the stark Australian sun, he gazed around uneasily, unsure of his bearings. He was home. I had flown with him from Guantánamo in a plane chartered by the Australian government, west from Cuba and across the Pacific Ocean, careful not to cross over into US airspace. I am the only lawyer allowed by the US government to accompany a prisoner home from the base, a courtesy I cannot explain.

An Australian official ushered us toward another plane—a six-seat prop plane idling nearby. Unbeknownst to me, our local counsel in Australia, Steven Hopper, had arranged to fly us to a small airfield nearby in order to avoid the media scrum in Sydney. As soon as we descended the steps of one plane we were hurried up the steep steps of another. As Mamdouh stepped into the tiny six-seater, he noticed a woman sitting quietly in the rear of the plane, dressed in black pants and a plain white top, her hands nervously folded in her lap. It was his wife, Maha. He had not seen her for more than three years and, for a brief moment, he paused as if stunned by the sight. At Guantánamo, American interrogators had told him his wife was dead, and though he had spoken with her briefly since that lie, the simple sight of his wife shook him deeply. He collapsed in her arms, weeping, as the plane taxied unsteadily down the runway and then rose quickly into the crystalline sky.

I have been a lawyer for many years but few moments in my legal career have been as gratifying as the sight of Mamdouh Habib reunited with his wife. He spent more than three years in prison: six months in the prison outside Cairo, and more than two years at Guantánamo. He was never charged with any wrongdoing and the government has never defended his detention in open court. No one remotely defends the allegations leveled in October 2004, when he was just another "cunning beast" in a post-9/11 prison. As I write this, in the summer of 2012, 168 prisoners remain at Guantánamo, though more than half have been cleared for release by both the Bush and Obama administrations. Hundreds of others are held at facilities all over the world.

"Enhanced Interrogation Techniques"

When Mamdouh described the torture he endured, I had never heard anything like it and could only marvel at the ingenious, diabolical cruelty of the Egyptian and Pakistani governments. It was a moment when I could say with some pride that nothing like this would ever happen in the United States. And then it did. For many years now, we've heard and read a great deal about torture memos, waterboarding, and insects in a box. It has been the occasion for somber reflection on our past and serious deliberation about our future.

But perhaps we should also remember that there were people strapped to those boards and stuffed in those boxes. The first was Zayn al Abidin Mohamed Hussein, known to the world as Abu Zubaydah. He was arrested in Pakistan in March 2002. Because the Bush administration believed him to be a senior al Qaeda operative, his detention and interrogation produced a fistful of firsts. So far as we can tell, he is the only prisoner in US history whose interrogation was the subject of debate and direct authorization within the White House. He was the first prisoner to be disappeared into a secret CIA "black site." He was the first prisoner in the "war on terror" to experience the full gamut of Communist-inspired and Justice Department-approved "enhanced interrogation techniques." He was the first prisoner to have his interrogations captured on videotape—a practice the CIA apparently ended in late 2002. Two years later, the agency destroyed 90 videotapes of his interrogations.

Abu Zubaydah is my client. I am one of the few people in the world who actually knows what happened to him in CIA custody, most of which I cannot report. All I can say is what has been cleared for release or made public by other sources. But perhaps that is enough. Though much remains unknown, more is known about his interrogation than about the interrogation of any other CIA prisoner. As authorized by the Justice Department and confirmed by the Red Cross, they beat him senseless. They wrapped a collar around his neck and smashed him over and over against a wall. They forced his body into a tiny, pitch-dark box and left him for hours. They stripped him naked and suspended him from hooks in the ceiling. They kept him awake for 11 consecutive days. All of this was before the waterboarding. Eventually, they strapped him to an inverted board and poured water over his covered nose and mouth to "produce the sensation of suffocation and incipient panic." Eighty-three times in the month of August 2002 alone. I leave it to others to debate whether we should call this torture. I am content with the self-evident truth that it was wrong.

Abu Zubaydah's mistreatment was motivated by the bane of our post-9/11 world: rotten intelligence. They beat him because they believed he was evil. Not long after his arrest, President Bush described him as "one of the top three leaders" in al Qaeda, and "Al Qaeda's chief of operations." In fact, the CIA brass at Langley ordered his interrogators to keep at it long after the latter warned that he had been wrung dry. But Abu Zubaydah, we now understand, was nothing like what the president believed. The journalist Ron Suskind was the first to ask the right questions. In his 2006 book, *The One Percent Doctrine*, he described Abu Zubaydah as a minor logistics man, a travel agent.[38] Later and more detailed reporting in the *Washington Post*, quoting Justice Department officials, said he provided "above-ground support... To make him the mastermind of anything is ridiculous."[39] More recently, *The New York Times*, relying on current and former intelligence officers, said the initial assessment was "highly inflated" and reflected "a profound misunderstanding" of Abu Zubaydah. Far from a leader, he was "a personnel clerk."[40] The US government no longer alleges he was a member of al Qaeda or an associate of bin Laden. It no longer alleges he had any role in any al Qaeda attack, or that he knew in advance that such attacks were planned. It no longer alleges that Abu Zubaydah was even ideologically aligned with al Qaeda.

So the cunning beast turned out to be a personnel clerk. But there is more to this story that we should not leave out. No one can pass unscathed through an ordeal like this. Abu Zubaydah paid with his mind. Partly as a result of injuries he suffered while he was fighting the Communists in the early 1990s, partly as a result of how those injuries were exacerbated by the CIA, and partly as a result of his extended isolation, Abu Zubaydah's mental grasp is slipping away. Today, he suffers blinding headaches and permanent brain damage. He has an incomprehensible but excruciating sensitivity to sounds, hearing what others do not. The slightest noise drives him nearly insane. In the first two years after he came to Guantánamo, he experienced about two hundred seizures. But physical pain is a passing thing. The enduring torment is the taunting reminder that darkness encroaches. Already, he cannot picture his mother's face or recall his father's name. Gradually, his past, like his future, eludes him. He has never been charged with a crime, and so far as I can tell, never will be.

WHY I REPRESENT THOSE PEOPLE

I suppose when all is said and done, I do not know why I represent "those people." I suspect my problem is that I have never met one of them, but if I do, perhaps I'll write a postscript.

NOTES

1. The first part of this chapter will appear in Joseph Margulies, *Like a Single Mind: September 11 and the Making of National Identity* (New Haven: Yale University Press, forthcoming), and builds on thoughts that first appeared in Joseph Margulies, "Deviance, Risk, and Law: Reflections on the Demand for Preventive Detention," *Journal of Criminal Law and Criminology* 101 (3) (Summer 2011): 729–780. Some of the material in the second part previously appeared in Joseph Margulies, *Guantánamo and the Abuse of Presidential Power* (New York: Simon & Schuster, 2006), and Joseph Margulies, "Review of *In the Moment of Greatest Calamity: Terrorism, Grief, and a Victim's Quest for Justice*, by Susan Hirsch," *Polar: Political and Legal Anthropology Review* 33 (2010): 116–122.
2. David Garland, *The Culture of Control: Crime and Social Order in Contemporary Society* (Chicago: University of Chicago Press, 2001), 184.
3. Ronald Bayer, "Crime, Punishment, and the Decline of Liberal Optimism," *Crime & Delinquency*, 27 (April 1981): 169–190. This was believed

true even for African-American crime in the era of Jim Crow. Brenda Z. Seligman, "Race and Crime," *Man* 45 (March–April, 1945): 44.

4. Juvenile crime was thought particularly susceptible to environmental explanations. "The cause of the current acts of juvenile delinquency," the *Nation* wrote in 1950, "is not mysterious... They are painfully poor and since they in turn find it increasingly difficult to get part time jobs they swarm about the city streets with nothing to do, frustrated in all their desires." Ibid. at 174, quoting Carrey McWilliams, "Nervous Los Angeles," *Nation* (June 10, 1950): 570.
5. Lyndon B. Johnson, "Remarks on the City Hall Steps, Dayton, Ohio" (lecture, City Hall, Dayton, Ohio, October 16, 1964), *The American Presidency Project*, accessed August 15, 2012, http://www.presidency.ucsb.edu/ws/?pid=26621.
6. Bayer, "Crime, Punishment," 171, quoting "Crime Waves and Scapegoats," *Commonweal*, August 9, 1946, 396.
7. *Report of the National Advisory Commission on Civil Disorders*, (Washington, DC: Government Printing Office, 1968), 1.
8. Kim Phillips-Fein, *Invisible Hands: The Businessmen's Crusade against the New Deal* (New York: W. W. Norton & Company, 2010), 68.
9. Katherine Beckett, *Making Crime Pay* (New York: Oxford University Press, 1997), 35.
10. Ibid., 37.
11. "Republican Party Platform of 1968," *American Presidency Project*, accessed August 15, 2012, http://www.presidency.ucsb.edu/ws/index.php?pid=25841#ixzz1QOXYSgjy.
12. "Lurching Off to a Shaky Start," *TIME*, September 20, 1968, http://www.time.com/time/magazine/article/0,9171,838728,00.html.
13. Ibid.
14. Beckett, *Making Crime Pay*, 34.
15. "Democratic Party Platform of 1964," *American Presidency Project*, accessed August 15, 2012, http://www.presidency.ucsb.edu/ws/index.php?pid=29603#axzz1QOWXMdxn.
16. Ibid.
17. "Lurching Off to a Shaky Start"; Beckett, *Making Crime Pay*, 38.
18. Beckett, *Making Crime Pay*, 38.
19. Ibid., 48.
20. Ibid.
21. Ibid., 49.
22. Ibid., 47.
23. Ibid.
24. Democratic Party Platform of 1988, *American Presidency Project*, accessed August 15, 2012, http://www.presidency.ucsb.edu/ws/index.php?pid=29609#axzz1QPZ97ElB.
25. Republican Party Platform of 1988, *American Presidency Project*, accessed August 15, 2012, http://www.presidency.ucsb.edu/ws/index.php?pid=25846#axzz1QPZ97ElB.

26. Marshall Frady, "Death in Arkansas," *The New Yorker*, February 22, 1993, 132.
27. Jim Rutenberg and Kate Zernike, "Palin, Amid Criticism, Stays in Electronic Comfort Zone," *New York Times,* January 10, 2011, http://www.nytimes.com/2011/01/11/us/politics/11palin.html. Dupnik is quoted in Paul Krugman, "Climate of Hate," *New York Times,* January 9, 2011, http://www.nytimes.com/2011/01/10/opinion/10krugman.html.
28. Sarah Palin, "America's Enduring Strength," last modified January 12, 2011, http://www.facebook.com/note.php?note_id=487510653434.
29. Heather MacDonald, "How to Interrogate Terrorists," in *The Torture Debate in America,* ed. Karen Greenberg (New York: Cambridge University Press, 2006), 85.
30. Suggestions that inmates could be moved to the supermax prison at Florence, Colorado, for instance, touched off a political firestorm. Felisa Cardona, "Guantanamo and Supermax," *Denver Post*, January 25, 2009, http://www.denverpost.com/headlines/ci_11542867 ("I think it is completely irresponsible for [Governor] Ritter to be rolling out the welcome mat for terrorists and enemy combatants into Colorado."); Carrie Johnson and Walter Pincus, "Supermax Prisons in U.S. Already Hold International Terrorists," *Washington Post*, May 22, 2009, http://www.washingtonpost.com/wp-dyn/content/article/2009/05/21/AR2009052102009.html.
31. Alan Dershowitz, *Why Terrorism Works* (New Haven: Yale University Press, 2002), 13, 24–25, 182.
32. Megan Stack and Bob Drogin, "Detainee Says U.S. Handed Him over for Torture," *Los Angeles Times*, January 13, 2005, http://articles.latimes.com/2005/jan/13/world/fg-habib13; Raymond Bonner, "Detainee Says He Was Tortured in U.S. Custody," *New York Times*, February 13, 2005, http://www.nytimes.com/2005/02/13/international/middleeast/13habib.html. The information regarding Mamdouh is also based on personal conversations he and I had, both before and after he left Guantánamo.
33. Stack and Drogin, "Detainee Says U.S. Handed Him Over"; Bonner, "Detainee Says He Was Tortured."
34. Except where otherwise indicated, the account of Habib's torture can be found in a declaration I filed in District Court in Washington, DC. Declaration of Joseph Margulies in Support of Application for Temporary Restraining Order, Habib, et al. v. Bush, et al. (D.D.C. November 24, 2004), (No. 02-CV-1130).
35. "The Trials of Mamdouh Habib," *Dateline*, aired July 7, 2004 (Australia: SBS).
36. Declaration of Joseph Margulies; Stack and Drogin, "Detainee Says U.S. Handed Him Over" ("Habib is believed to have been imprisoned in state security headquarters in Lazoughli Square, in the heart of Cairo.")
37. Declaration of Joseph Margulies; "Statement of Shafiq Rasul, Asif Iqbal & Rhuhel Ahmed, Composite Statement: Detention in Afghanistan

and Guantánamo Bay," *Center for Constitutional Rights*, July 26, 2004, 108, http://ccrjustice.org/files/report_tiptonThree.pdf; Jane Mayer, "Outsourcing Torture," *The New Yorker*, February 14, 2005, 118.

38. Ron Suskind, *The One Percent Doctrine* (New York: Simon & Schuster, 2006), 100.
39. Peter Finn and Joby Warrick, "Detainee's Harsh Treatment Foiled No Plots," *The Washington Post*, March 29, 2009, http://www.washingtonpost.com/wp-dyn/content/article/2009/03/28/AR2009032802066.html.
40. Mark Mazzetti and Scott Shane, "Interrogation Memos Detail Harsh Tactics by the C.I.A.," *The New York Times*, April 16, 2009, http://www.nytimes.com/2009/04/17/us/politics/17detain.html?_r=4&hp.

9

Wrecking Life: When the State Seeks to Kill

William R. Montross, Jr. and Meghan Shapiro

The man sitting in the second row of the courtroom has deep creases across his face not there a year ago. His hair has turned almost entirely gray. Every day, for weeks, he has sat there—through the photographs of his wife's autopsy, the testimony of the joggers who found her decomposing body, the display of her bloody clothes. Even when others sit with him, he looks distinctly alone. His grief is so overwhelming it is a physical presence we can see and feel. It is so loud, we all hear it.

A little boy is 11 years old. He was picked by his foster father from a catalogue of the county's most vulnerable children—the kids traumatized from abuse as five-year-olds, or the ones who will always be behind in school no matter how hard they try, or the gangly teens whose bodies will never recover from the years of malnourishment. It is left to the little boy to explain to his newest "brother" that their foster father's uncomfortable touching is "normal here." So too, he says, are the rapes (though he does not know that word) and after those you might get a new toy. It's better than his last foster home, as the emergency room records of his broken wrist and alcohol poisoning show. The little boy will grow up consumed by self-loathing and various addictions. One day he will be arrested for the capital murder of a woman on a jogging path, and he will become our client.

The power and force of the widower's loss is obvious. It does not need to be uncovered or explained; it is raw and visible for all to see, and it can easily become the reason the jury sentences our client to death. The pain of the little boy, however, is very different. No one sees the vulnerable boy in the man at the defense table whose tattoos are only partially covered by his long-sleeved shirt, who looks bored during the DNA technician's testimony and distant during the medical examiner's. In this courtroom, the relevance of the little boy's story is not self-evident or easily understood. It does not fit neatly into the idea most people have about choice and consequence: that we all have the same capacity to make good decisions and refrain from making bad ones.

However, juries need to hear and understand stories like the boy's in order to return a verdict of life for someone who has caused death. Often, these stories started long before our clients were even born, well before they were making "choices," but they explain how a person gets from an 11-year-old boy to a man on trial for capital murder. They are stories that permit jurors to conclude that our clients are people—not monsters—and that, while we might kill monsters, we do not kill people, no matter how damaged they might be. But before we can even begin to tell these stories, we have to find them—and stories like these are often well-buried. Unlike the pain on the face of the widower, the scars of our clients' childhood beatings and sodomies are hidden deep inside.

Because these are the stories that can save our clients' lives, we must search and dig and probe for them. Where the rest of the world has looked away for years and years out of embarrassment or utter lack of interest, we seek out and embrace the horrors that our clients endured, often at an age when they could barely speak. No one wants to admit that he tried to hang himself at age 14 but broke the shower curtain rod, leading to the worst beating from mom yet. No one wants to talk about how he prostituted himself after three days of sleeping in a car without food. If our clients have come to understand one thing it is that they had better hide these stories of weakness if they are to survive. For some of our clients, it might be one of the few things at which they've succeeded. Yet somehow, some way, we have to breach those walls, whether invited in or by wrecking ball. Once inside we will resurrect memories and suffering no one ever wanted to think about again.

As lawyers who are drawn to capital defense out of a sense of compassion for the most damaged among us, the irony of this reality is difficult to swallow. Already, our consciences are heavy for so many reasons—the double-edged nature of our "successes" (most often, saving a client from the death chamber means he will vanish into prison for the rest of his natural life), the permanency of our failures, the constant gnawing guilt that we could have done more—but, for us, it is the pain we inflict almost every day that is our deepest wound: if we want our clients to live we will inevitably end up hurting them, their families, and ourselves in the process. People gravely ask how defense attorneys can represent someone who committed a horrible act; what would they say if they knew that as capital attorneys we deliberately follow a course of action that causes a whole new kind of pain? The irony does not end here. For the two of us, it is our clients' stories, despite all the pain they cause when resurrected, that keep us going. They wound us but also sustain us.

Our clients are already hurting when we first meet them, whether in jail just after arrest, or (in postconviction cases) after years on death row. If we enter their lives shortly after the crime, they are struggling with the enormity of having taken another person's life. Some are filled with guilt, shame, and hopelessness; some are in deep states of denial. Their lives are in ruins. If we are representing clients in postconviction proceedings, they are cut off from the rest of the world, and are scared and desperate. Almost all are self-destructive even though they may not want to be. They are downtrodden. They are hated. They hate themselves. Often, horrified at what they have done and without hope of redemption, our clients *want* to die when we first meet them. Many are mentally ill. Some suffer from cognitive impairments or organic brain damage. Others have severe medical conditions.

But as much as we want to help them with their other needs, we need their stories more. So we start asking questions. We dig. We probe. And we push onward, even when it's obvious that what we are unearthing hurts: a client so addicted to drugs that he traded the car he'd been living in for two hits of crack; a client who was forced to watch his stepfather rape his younger sister and then dump her body in a tub of cold water in an attempt to stanch her bleeding; a client who, as a small child, slept on the floor of a crack house surrounded by rotting garbage and strangers trading sex for drugs; a client so defaced by a childhood illness that his father would not touch him; a client who "permitted" grown men to perform sex on him for slices of pizza.

These are memories filled with shame, and we won't hear them unless we first gain our clients' trust—a task that is inevitably harder with our clients than with someone who has not been repeatedly betrayed by others they trusted.

Our clients were not normally the beneficiaries of professional counseling, either as children or adults, and no one ever intervened in their lives. They drowned their memories with drugs; they became alcoholics before other kids finished middle school. Few lawyers are trauma experts; we are ill-prepared to heal the wounds we are ripping open. We know that between visits our clients return to comfortless cells with nothing to do but think about the very things they have been trying not to think about most of their lives. But still we keep pushing. We wonder, "If it happened once, did it happen again?" So we dig some more.

Often the clients simply do not understand why we are digging all this up, airing their most shameful secrets. Worse still is the prospect of telling those secrets to a courtroom full of strangers. They object and protest. We explain, cajole, and assure. We promise we would choose any other course if we could, and we mean it—but then we proceed to publicly humiliate them by parading it all before their juries. Of course, we also try to console our clients as this information gushes out. We have taken our clients' hands as witnesses testified to events our clients had hoped were long buried. We have sat with them as they cried and howled once the courtroom was cleared for the day. We have been or will be with our clients for years. We can only hope that the hurt we have inflicted will perhaps be offset, to some degree, by the fidelity and friendship we show our clients in other moments.

But our clients are not the only ones we hurt, because they are not the only source of their stories. Trauma, mental illness, and cognitive impairment can leave them unable to recount their own experiences. For practical reasons they often cannot testify, and even if they could, the judge and jury would probably not believe them. So others must speak for them, or at least corroborate what they say. This means we must go to those who knew our clients and can bear witness to what happened to them long before they ever hurt anyone. We go to our clients' families, and, in so doing, we spread the harm we have already begun to do to our client.

Most of our clients don't want us to bring their families into it. Often they don't want to make their families relive what they may have, somehow, put behind them. Having already caused such harm, they don't want to cause even more. Other times, their families' self-protective response may be to turn their back on the "bad seed," and our clients may not protest. But a client's brother may be the best or only witness to abuse they both suffered, and so, despite fears that dredging up these memories could drag down the one sibling who seemingly escaped unscathed, we dredge.

For still other clients, in this moment of despair they may desperately need the very people who caused their pain in the first place. An abusive mother may now be the client's only contact with his family, the abuse forgiven or at least overlooked by both parties. As fragile as this relationship is, it might be all he has.

Yet in order to fight for our clients' lives, we end up hurting their families and friends. Our unwelcome, archeological expedition through a family's darkest secrets reignites old conflicts and brings more emotional trauma and new heartbreak. We hope that the damage we do can be mended, but we know that it may not be.

We hope that our client's sister, who we compelled to relive her stepfather's sexual abuse, will somehow find healing along the way, return to the job she struggles to keep, and continue to be the loving mother she herself never had. But even if we suspect that she will not be able to do all, or any, of these things, we nevertheless try to persuade her to tell her stories in court. We can't even promise this is the only time she'll be asked. If the case is ever retried, or winds through postconviction proceedings, we or other lawyers will be back on her front stoop asking for even more than what she has already given. Of course we worry that her world will unravel, but our chief concern has to be whether her testimony could help our client. Could it get him closer to a life sentence? If it could, we must push her to tell her story, regardless of the consequences.

Then her testimony is over. If she is unfortunate enough to sec the next day's story online, she can also see the comments of strangers who for some reason leap at the opportunity to judge her brother's life—that rape is too good for him, and maybe for her too. Her coworkers read about a life they never knew she had. Her shame spreads. She may collapse into depression, neglecting her job, her family, herself.

And then we receive the letters; she wants to kill herself; she had spent years burying these memories and now they are in the newspaper. We will write her back, and call her to say how much what she did for her brother means to him, that what she did may actually save his life. But we don't pretend that this really helps a woman on such a desperate edge. We only hope that somehow, in some way, she will, again, heal.

We will never forget the sister, just like we will never forget our clients. We know the hurt we cause, but do our best to come to grips with it: we tell ourselves we have a duty to do it—a professional duty, an ethical duty—a duty to save our client. But sometimes these rationalizations run cold, leaving us worrying that we have done more harm than good.

In our work we have uncovered horror stories that should live only in a writer's warped imagination: daughters choosing to live with fathers who rape them rather than move in with mothers who beat them; foster parents withholding water from kids as punishment; hate-filled whippings of tiny children; preteens selling their bodies for food; parents using their last dollar for crack cocaine instead of buying much-needed clothing for a six-year-old starting school; teenagers living under bridges. All of this in place of birthday parties with cake and ice cream, family vacations, high school proms, and first jobs.

It's impossible to forget these stories. We live with them—walk around with them, eat with them, sleep with them, dream about them, sometimes they are all we can talk and think about. Psychologists and psychiatrists now talk about the trauma inflicted on jurors sitting on just one capital murder trial—the emotional toll taken by witnessing the destruction both done by our client and to our client, and by bearing the responsibility of deciding whether another person will live or die. Yet capital defense attorneys are continuously exposed to the same horrors. It is our occupational hazard: the mining and recounting of horrors.

One does not end up representing people facing death by accident. Each time we take on a capital case we understand that we are exposing ourselves to the prospect of a state execution and everything that leads up to it. The responsibility of standing between a human being and a death sentence is terrifying. The question whether a client will live or die hangs over every step we take, and we can't help but gravely fear the answer. This is so not only because we have taken up the challenge of keeping a client alive, but also because, inevitably, as we have gotten to know him, we have come to care about him as a person. These dual emotions—our sense of terror as well as compassion—drive us to obsessive work. Unfortunately, this work can end up being at the expense of our families and friends (who did not necessarily choose to tether themselves to it), and sometimes at the expense of our own health.

The fear of failing our clients distorts our emotions, leading to perverse reactions to dreadful discoveries about our clients' pasts. A story from a client's aunt that she found him dirty and abandoned in his mother's apartment as a toddler prompts a happy—ecstatic, even—phone call to cocounsel. Even though part of us recoils at the thought of our client as an abandoned two-year-old, another part is celebrating the discovery of evidence that may help save our client's life. We share in each other's good news, but this is not necessarily the kind of story a partner or friend wants to hear when they ask us about our day.

Our emotional well-being also takes a beating during those critical moments when we find ourselves face to face with the people who have probably caused our clients the most pain. We sit at a kitchen table for hours, listening to someone explain that he and his wife really did love our client until his "behavioral problems" required the grown man to beat the child with a two by four. We want to scream that this man bears responsibility for the physical and emotional scars that destroyed not only our client's life, but also the lives of the victim and everyone who loved her. Instead, we sit there and nod, and shake his hand on the way out the door. Maybe something we learned can help save our client's life. We can't afford to burn any bridges here. But when we climb back into our car for the long drive home we feel disgusted with ourselves, no matter how "successful" the visit.

Ordinary criminal defense lawyers do not expose themselves to such magnitudes of trauma over and over again. We cannot think of any other "civilized" reason-based system of law that purposely endorses vengeance for vengeance's sake, or seeks to cause pain and hurt as a goal. The death penalty is expensive; it has resulted in the death of innocent people; it is barbaric and anachronistic; it is racist and classist; it sends the wrong message to our children; it stigmatizes us in the eyes of the world. It falsely promises healing and "closure" to grieving family members when there is nothing therapeutic about the process. It multiplies existing pain: where one daughter has lost a father, an execution makes it two. It makes otherwise good people cheat and destroy evidence to secure a sentence of death that advances their careers or insures their reelection. So powerful is its ability to pervert that it leads people to believe that their god wants death and not redemption.

But, from our perspective, the death penalty's greatest achievement is the hurt it has caused and will continue to cause. Absolutely nothing about it *doesn't* hurt, and we, as compassionate people serving as capital defenders feel at the same time like a sponge, a conduit, and a source of the death penalty's far-reaching devastation.

A fair question, then, may be: why in the world would we keep doing it? For the many moments of grief, doubt, anger, and despair, there are also moments of hope and joy: walking a client not only off of death row, but out of prison; a jury, against the odds, rejecting a death sentence; winning the right to a new trial based on evidence long suppressed by a prosecutor; telling a client braced for a frightening death that he is going to live. But these moments are fleeting and they are the exception.

There are other moments that take place where no one else can see. We hear clients move from the depths of self-hatred to a realization that they are more than their worst moment. We witness the gift of forgiveness from all imaginable angles and sources. We watch a man once completely estranged from his family hold his grandchild. We sit with young people as they mature and accept responsibility for their actions. We see love flowing from the most unexpected places. These precious moments do not outweigh the hurt, but they soothe it.

The reality is that often we are left feeling wounded and angry. If we relied on regular victories to rejuvenate us, we simply would not last. We know all about the hypocrisy, racism, and politics of the death penalty, but none of that explains why *we* must do this work, or how *we* will keep doing it. It is truly our clients' stories that keep us going. As much as they wound us, they also sustain us. They open doors to understanding not only our clients' humanities, but our own. Why do we hurt; why do we love; why do we do the things we do—to others and ourselves? How do we recover; how do we forgive; how do any of us move forward? We find the fragility and resilience in our clients, and in the process discover the same in ourselves. That is not only *why* we do what we do, but why we love it so much. We learn more and more that life is messy; we learn to see gray where others see black and white. Through our clients' stories, we ourselves become more human—and we are forever grateful for that.

10

"Those People" Are Us

Ann Roan

I like a good fight, as long as it's a fair one. I like fighting for poor people accused of crime and knowing that the harder and smarter I work, the fairer the fight becomes. I am a public defender because I love my country and the promise our Constitution extends to all those who step into a criminal courtroom accused of a crime—that they will not be alone.

I joined the Colorado Public Defender shortly after law school, following a brief foray into the world of big-firm civil law. I left private practice because it didn't mean anything to me. I was working really hard, but I couldn't see that what I was doing for my clients connected with the broader community or justice. Being a public defender changed all that and gave me an opportunity to fight for the kind of clients, and the kinds of stakes, I care about.

I started out in Pueblo, Colorado. Pueblo is just 70 miles north of the site of the Ludlow Massacre, an early twentieth-century showdown between striking miners and the Colorado National Guard at the behest of the Colorado Fuel & Iron (CF & I) mining company. The miners had set up a tent city to protest corporate control of the mines. Between 19 and 25 miners were murdered there on April 20, 1914, including 2 women and 11 children who were burned to death as they huddled in a hole dug beneath one of the tents.[1] It was "the culminating act of perhaps the most violent struggle between corporate power and laboring men in American history."[2]

This history is woven into the fabric of southern Colorado, making it an amazing place to learn how to defend the poor. I found that juries were appropriately skeptical of law enforcement, judges exercised their power with care, and prosecutors understood and responded to the community they served. CF & I was in the process of scaling back its operations and laying people off, but the mill and the rhythms of shift work were still a big part of the town's identity. So, too, was Ludlow's lesson: collusion between government and commerce against working people is deadly.

But even in a place sensitized to official abuse of power because of its history, people would ask me, "How can you represent those people?" Even my clients would ask me a version of that question, although they put it this way: "When are you going to be a *real* lawyer?" They meant a private lawyer who charged a lot of money (a free lawyer could never be as good as a pricey one) and had a luxurious office (rather than our dingy suite in an old building). But maybe my clients' question was closer to that other ubiquitous question than I thought. Maybe by "real lawyer" they meant a lawyer who got to choose her clients.

My clients meant their question as a compliment. They thought I was good enough to be a private lawyer for rich people. The implication—that only the rich should get the best lawyers—didn't seem to register. Likewise, those who ask how I can represent "those people" seem primarily motivated by a belief that lawyers with other, more comfortable options should grab them.

They have a point, I suppose. But I don't do this job—and I see myself as a career defender—out of martyrdom. I do it out of patriotism. As Steve Bright, the founder of the Southern Center for Human Rights—and a hero to me—once said, "Everyone who graduates from law school has to decide if he or she is going to use their law degree to help rich people get more or to help poor people get enough." I was lucky enough to figure out early on that I wanted to do the latter, and this has shaped my career.

Lawyers in the United States are in a unique position to obtain access to justice for the poor if they want to. We are literally the voice for clients in the courtroom. When a judge asks if an accused is prepared to start a trial in which he is facing loss of liberty or life, it is the defense lawyer who announces ready, not the person whose life is on the line. For whom do I want to speak? Who needs my voice more? Corporations and the rich or poor people?

It's common these days to dismiss any honest talk about the ever-widening economic divide in America as the bitter envy of those who advocate class warfare. This defensiveness and name-calling misses the point. I have the right to use my law degree where I see fit, the same way anyone else does. Corporations and rich people are doing fine, it seems to me. They certainly do not need my help. I am not driven by envy or bitterness, but by an awareness of my own freedom and what a luxury that is. I get to decide whom I stand up for in court, the same as anybody else with a law degree.

What does it mean to give poor people access to justice in the context of criminal defense? For me, it means helping them get more fairness, more due process, and more respect. It means getting the system to see them as individuals shaped by their experiences, instead of bodies in belly chains with numbers sewn on their shirts in place of their names, defined forever by a single act. Arguing for the individual—especially the economically and politically powerless individual—against the government is a value at the core of our democracy. Fighting in our courts on behalf of a poor person charged with a crime is seldom popular, but it is intensely patriotic.

Diedrich Boenhoeffer was a Lutheran pastor in Germany who fought against the Nazi regime and paid for it with his life. He rejected the idea that bearing witness to injustice was enough. "We are not to simply bandage the wounds of victims beneath the wheels of injustice, we are to drive a spoke into the wheel itself," he said.[3] Representing the poor means driving a spoke into an increasingly harsh and unjust criminal justice system. It means stopping the wheel's motion altogether if your client is in its path.

It is a sad reality that 50 years after *Gideon v. Wainwright*,[4] money makes a difference in a criminal trial—that sometimes guilty people go free and innocent people go to jail based not on the facts but their ability to pay for counsel. If you agree that justice is a human right, the way that money influences who gets it ought to keep you up at night. I represent poor people charged with crimes because I think money should matter less and the Constitution more. "Justice is not cheap in this country, and people who insist on it are usually either desperate or possessed by some private determination bordering on monomania."[5]

A private determination bordering on monomania is a pretty good description of my defender faith—that getting money's influence out of justice protects democracy and freedom. The commodification of fairness erodes what I love about my country. A system of public defenders practicing at the highest level makes fairness a matter of right, not privilege. As Clarence Earl Gideon explained to the US Supreme Court about why the Constitution guaranteed him a lawyer to defend him: "It makes no difference how old I am or what color I am or what church I belong too [*sic*] if any. The question is I did not get a fair trial."[6]

Public defenders make the Constitution come alive for those who need it most. We challenge the state's case at every turn, keeping the person we represent at the forefront, and political and popular pressures at bay. In public defender systems like Colorado's, where there are no caps on the time we can invest in a case, we are often the lawyers who litigate and create new case law. Lawyers-for-hire seldom take this on, because their clients balk at the billable hours involved. Hard work and perseverance benefit clients, and our system is set up to allow this to happen.

This is a good thing. The constitutional rights of the accused are not valued by society. Many people think individuals charged with crimes have too many rights. During jury selection, it is not uncommon for prospective jurors to describe their frustration about this. I have heard prospective jurors talk about how the system "coddles" defendants, giving them lawyers, the right to appeal, and a television in jail. In many cases, those holding the line between justice and fascism—standing up for the most reviled people without regard to the client's ability to pay—are public defenders.

This is not just a modern phenomenon. After the Boston Massacre, the British officer responsible for ordering his men to use their weapons on a mob armed primarily with snowballs was ordered to stand trial. Future US president John Adams stepped up to defend him because he realized that giving this hated British officer a fair trial was essential to the right of all citizens to be free from government tyranny. Adams won an acquittal after getting the case moved out of Boston. He gave the kind of closing argument any good lawyer would give today, telling the jury that "facts are stubborn things; and whatever may be our wishes, our inclinations, or the dictates of our passions, they cannot alter the state of facts and evidence; nor is the law less stable than the fact[.]"[7]

That's why I represent those people. The passions and wishes and inclinations of the mob can be terrifying and dangerous. Especially when a community is ripped apart by a horrific crime, people's idea of "criminal justice" is swift punishment. In Colorado and the rest of the West, punishment was historically meted out with a rope and a sturdy tree. Worrying about whether the state could prove that the rustler had stolen the cattle beyond a reasonable doubt would have taken away from the two purposes of public executions: the thrill-ride of vengeance and the stern object lesson of the dead body to would-be offenders.

The popular demand for swift, harsh "justice" mirrors the qualities that got the West settled by white people. Quick and decisive action was indispensable to getting people over the mountains before the snow came. Like pianos, sickly babies, and sewing machines, reasonable doubt didn't make it into the wagon.

Even now, with people living in close quarters from the mountains to the prairies in most of the state, there is still enormous pressure in Colorado (and the rest of the country) to speed judgments on guilt and punishment. "Justice delayed is justice denied!" goes the saying. But is it? We teach Colorado public defenders that they cannot be part of the "get along bunch," as David Wymore, one of our former chief deputies, put it a long time ago. Moving a case along simply to please the prosecution and the court is an affront to the Constitution we are sworn to serve. Litigation takes time. Figuring out the facts and law takes time. Delaying the outcome until these things happen isn't some devious defense lawyer trick: it's a fair trial.

The get-along-bunch lawyer believes that success depends on how much the prosecutor and judge like him, rather than skills, smarts, and staying power. The get-along-bunch lawyer sees every case as a plea. These are the lawyers who joke with the police, the judge, and the prosecutor, while the client watches his day in court collapse into a series of rigged outcomes.

The lure of being a get-along-bunch lawyer is not having to care about clients and not having to think about who clients are and what shaped them. Writer Kurt Vonnegut was talking about this desire to ignore human pain when he coined the word "samaritrophia" and defined it as "hysterical indifference to the troubles of those less fortunate than oneself."[8] Samaritrophia is highly communicable. It can whip through a public defender's office or defense community[9] like typhoid. Despite the tendency in some offices to blame new lawyers for perceived "generational" deficits—poor writing skills, a sluggish work ethic, insufficient attention to detail—samaritrophia carriers are generally the lawyers at the top. New lawyers come to public defender offices unsure about how to think about clients, except in the abstract. It only takes a little exposure to a lawyer who has joined the get-along-bunch to pass along the sickness. Being a public defender is a crash course in the suffering of others, all the time. Very often, defending people means figuring out what happened to them before the beginning of the prosecution's narrative, and fighting to make that truth matter in order to stop the system from making them one more criminal justice casualty.

Most people love a story about a child raised by a feckless single parent, moving from one awful apartment to another, left mostly to raise herself, but miraculously winning a full scholarship to Harvard, publishing a best-seller, or releasing a platinum album at 17. But the far more common story is that the single parent is an addict, mentally ill, or both. Unprotected, the child is raped or beaten or used as a drug mule or—sometimes—all those things. Uncared for, the child is unclean and smells bad and is ostracized by other kids. The child goes out the door in the morning with no food and no sleep and nods off in class. The teacher has too many other kids to deal with, so the child falls off the radar in school. The child gets pregnant, or gets someone else pregnant, or gets caught up in the criminal justice system. Lather, rinse, repeat. Out the other side comes a tatted-up, angry, suspicious, sometimes violent adult. If you can look at that adult and see a glimmer of the child, you have the makings of a defender. If you can still do that after the hundredth—or thousandth—time you meet a client, you are a career defender.

Children from economically disadvantaged families face challenges almost impossible to imagine for people who haven't experienced them. These children are at risk for exposure to complex trauma. "Complex trauma" refers to both the exposure to traumatic events and the impact this exposure has, both immediately and in the long term.[10] A child's exposure to complex trauma—seeing someone being shot or being physically or emotionally abused by a caregiver, for example—can cause grave neurobiological damage.[11]

Many decision makers in the criminal justice system tend to downplay this reality or reject it outright. The "abuse excuse" is societal shorthand for denying that child-abuse and neglect are real and cause serious damage to people. It is common for prosecutors and judges and jurors to observe that they personally had "tough" childhoods, or that they know people who grew up in "bad" neighborhoods and ended up being successful despite these conditions. This argument assumes two things: that reports of extreme childhood torture, rape and privation are exaggerated, and that people can choose to discard the effects of childhood trauma when they reach adulthood. Empirical research belies the first assumption and neuroscience the second. Nonetheless, some lawyers shy away from investigating a client's childhood and offering the biological and psychological effects of formative episodes to mitigate or defend the client's adult actions. They say that such presentations detract from the lawyer's standing in the eyes of the prosecutor, the judge, or the jury because it is "making excuses."

Our criminal law allows for more than outright denial in defending against criminal charges. Sometimes the law allows an explanation. Many legal defenses—self-defense, defense of others, duress, entrapment, coercion, choice of evils—can be seen as "excuses." In other words, the accused may have committed the act but is not legally responsible or perhaps less blameworthy. Defenders must use these defenses—and more—to explain a client's actions, with the goal of exoneration or mitigation or a moment of understanding.

So why do some people mock such a defense—at trial or sentencing—as an "abuse excuse?" Some argue that considering early childhood abuse in the face of adult crime is antithetical to individual responsibility and the rule of law.[12] However, as science advances and we better understand the neurobiological effects of childhood neglect and abuse, this argument shows itself as a straw man. Some experiences—being in combat, being taken prisoner of war, experiencing a traumatic event, complex childhood trauma—can have a huge impact on individual judgment and will. The *Diagnostic and Statistical Manual of Mental Disorders* (*DSM*) field trial for posttraumatic stress disorder (PTSD) "demonstrated that the age at which children are first traumatized, the frequency of their traumatic experiences, and the degree to which caregivers contribute to the event being traumatic all have a profound impact on the extent of their psychological damage."[13] Environmental factors, as well as genetic ones, can contribute to mental illness.

Colorado's state mental hospital is also in Pueblo, where I started as a public defender. I always imagined it would look like a vast, spooky castle surrounded by steep mountains. But Colorado is a young state in nonnative people's time. This youth is reflected in the architecture of its monuments and institutions. There is no gothic excess or medieval crenellation to the prisons and jails, courthouses, and madhouses. The state prison system began on the unwelcoming mesas outside Cañon City in the south of the state. The buildings of confinement are low-slung and anonymous. Only the loops of razor wire above give them away. After public hangings were finally outlawed in 1933, executions in Colorado were carried out for years in a gas chamber designed by Eaton Metal Products, in Denver. Colorado's gas chamber proved so popular that Eaton manufactured them for other states, eventually becoming the nation's leading producer of gas chambers.[14] Colorado used the same combination of chemicals—potassium cyanide capsules dropped into a mixture of sulfuric acid and water—that Nazi concentration camps favored. The state did not stop executing people with gas until 1967. The gas chamber is now part of the museum at the Territorial Prison, in Cañon City. Visitors sometimes pose in front of it for a picture, as though they're about to step inside.

So too, the state mental hospital is a series of drab buildings that stretch haphazardly beneath tough old cottonwoods on dried-out brown grass. Here, instead of poison gas, the state relied on electricity. For years, electroshock therapy was part of the treatment protocol, along with lobotomies and forced sterilizations. Being strapped down in one government building while someone threw a switch meant the state was healing you. Being strapped down in another government building while someone threw a switch meant the state was killing you.

Mental illness, like other sicknesses, is different for different people. Most people who come through the criminal courts in the United States already have or end up receiving a psychiatric diagnosis.[15] The *DSM* organizes psychiatric disorders around five axes or dimensions.[16] Axis I disorders are clinical disorders, including major mental disorders, learning disorders, and substance use disorders. Depression, anxiety, schizophrenia, and bipolar disorder, for example, are all on Axis I.

Clinical disorders are what most people think of when they think of someone who is not guilty by reason of insanity. They think of someone like Alan, one of my former clients. Alan's experience in the criminal justice system exemplifies all the ways in which arguments about personal responsibility and the rule of law fall apart in the face of what we do and do not know about the mind.

When I met Alan for the first time, he had just been arrested. All I knew about the case was the affidavit in support of arrest. These affidavits are cursory recitations of those facts the police need to persuade a judge to jail someone. I knew enough to be skeptical of the affidavit but it told an unsettling story. The affidavit said that Alan had killed his 11-year-old daughter, who had been visiting him for the summer.

When my cocounsel, Jon Bley and I went to see him in jail, he sat absolutely still. His skin had a peculiar incandescence to it; his face seemed to glow behind his overgrown beard. He was thin and looked exhausted. He stared at the table. First meetings with clients are seldom easy, especially in cases with very serious allegations. But even by that standard, this meeting was difficult. Alan appeared nearly catatonic. Jon and I had agreed that I would lead the conversation. I needed to tell him that we had been appointed to represent him, and he should speak to no one except us about anything to do with the charges. Beyond that, I wanted to start on the slow work of building a relationship, but under certain constraints. I didn't want to talk about his defense because I didn't know anything about the case yet. I didn't want to talk about the claims in the affidavit because it seemed ghoulish and voyeuristic without the semblance of a relationship. It would have been obscene to chat about inconsequential things because there was no room in that holding cell for small talk. Alan answered a few of my innocuous biographical questions, speaking very slowly and softly. Suddenly, with no warning at all, he lunged across the table, wrapped his hands around

Jon's neck and began to choke him. The guards rushed in immediately in a cloud of Mace and that ended that meeting.

It did not take much digging to learn that Alan suffered from schizophrenia and attendant psychosis. He heard voices and saw things that weren't there. He drew profound meaning from things that other people experienced as mundane occurrences. The evening that he killed his daughter, he saw a snake crawl beneath the cracked concrete front step of his apartment and after that, there was nothing he could do to stop what happened next. It was like the evening was a hula hoop rolling downhill. Inexorable. Unstoppable. And after a time, unspeakable.

Once the jail began medicating him, Alan became, as the mental health professionals put it, oriented to place and time. Whatever he saw or heard or understood that caused him to attack Jon at our first meeting receded. The medication also had the effect of making him excruciatingly aware of what he had done to the daughter he loved. He knew he had taken her life in a terrible way. After I got to know him better, he admitted that he still heard voices and saw things at the edges of his field and vision and suspected a larger import to things like a snake crawling under a porch or a bird landing on a fence or what color shirt a person on the street wore. Most of the time, with medication, he knew it was all "limp," as he described it. "But sometimes," he said, "Sometimes, I'm not so sure." By the time Alan said this in court, he had taken to sucking his lower lip in under his front teeth and running the flesh against the back of them over and over, like a child sucking an orange during halftime at a soccer game. He did it so often it looked like he was growing a second bottom lip, raw and weeping. Sometimes, his teeth punctured the scrim of scab, drawing up a bubble of blood. I mimicked the gesture when I was trying to describe it to others, and even doing it a few times hurt. But Alan seemed not to notice.

He talked a lot about the small things his daughter had asked him for during her stay with him that summer. He said no most of the time because he was trying to be a good parent and thought that meant saying no. A few days before her death, she saw a plastic horse at the grocery store and asked for it. He said no. Now he talked about how much he wished he had bought it for her. The medications had made everything in his brain take a step back. Now his head was like the Grand Canyon, ringing with the echoes and images of what they had told him to do to his daughter.

When her mother sent Alan's daughter to him for the summer, it was no secret to her that Alan was under the care of the community mental health center. A few years before, he had been found not guilty by reason of insanity for another violent act, and the state hospital had recently decided to grant him supervised release, back into the community. Those responsible for supervising him agreed that his daughter could stay with him for the summer. At the same time, though, the community mental health center decided that he needed to be more proactive and independent about his medication. Just before the police released his apartment as a crime scene, Jon and I got a court order to go through it with an investigator and a forensic pathologist. Among the things we found that the police had not taken into evidence was a letter from Alan's doctor at the mental health center, telling him that the center would no longer mail his medications to him each month and that it was now his responsibility to make arrangements to keep his prescriptions filled.

Years later, I still think about the doctor who wrote that letter. I wonder if the doctor regrets denying a very sick man easy access to the medications that kept him tethered to the real world, the way Alan regretted not buying his daughter that plastic horse. Doing either of those things would have been an effortless act of kindness.

Alan's case worked itself out appropriately on one level. He was found not guilty by reason of insanity and sent back to the state hospital. He takes his medications every day. Sometimes he sits completely still for hours. His hands and arms swell up from dangling at his sides and the orderlies have to rearrange his limbs like pieces of furniture to get the blood flowing again. He still hears the voices and sees the figures and suspects that there are signs attaching to certain events. Most of the time he is pretty sure these things are not real.

I wish Jon and I could have done more for Alan, but curing his mental illness was the only that thing that would have changed his life. Getting him sent to the state hospital instead of prison was no great feat. I am not being falsely modest about this. For the criminal justice system, Alan's case was a fairly easy one. No one disputed that he was seriously ill and was not taking his medications when he killed his daughter. In some cases, that last fact can be a stumbling block. Criminal courts are full of people with power who have no sympathy for defendants who don't take their medications. However, once the letter from the community mental health center made the rounds, it was clear that other agencies had some responsibility and everyone became eager to make the case go away quietly.

Axis I disorders, like Alan's schizophrenia, are the kinds of mental illness that criminal courts can—with effort—fold into the notion of reduced culpability. Axis II disorders, on the other hand, often yield a very different outcome.

Axis II disorders are personality disorders and intellectual disabilities. The *DSM* recognizes ten personality disorders: paranoid personality disorder; schizoid personality disorder; schizotypal personality disorder; borderline personality disorder; antisocial personality disorder; narcissistic personality disorder; avoidant personality disorder; dependent personality disorder; histrionic personality disorder; and obsessive-compulsive personality disorder.[17]

The justice system is at its least nimble when a person accused of a crime has a personality disorder instead of, or in conjunction with, a clinical disorder. Personality disorders are long-standing, deeply ingrained sets of behavior that are detrimental both to the person with the disorder and to others. Personality disorders are persistent: they often begin to manifest themselves in adolescence and continue through adulthood. People with personality disorders have rigid, inflexible coping styles. Change for them is difficult and rare.

The problem in court is that personality disorders carry with them a distinct sense of choice and agency. Alan's situation evoked pity and compassion and grief. Someone with a personality disorder is far more likely to evoke frustration and anger and the desire to punish because they are not hearing voices that tell them to do things. Instead, they seem to ignore or not care about how their actions lead to the same destructive results again and again.

The unspoken contradiction in this is that the criminal justice system is built on a foundation of causality. Punishment is meted out at least in part upon considerations of responsibility for the harm caused. The law recognizes that environmental influences, if sufficiently significant, must be weighed when determining someone's accountability.

Lay people don't have much of an understanding of what causes clinical disorders like Alan's. But the causes of personality disorders are intimately known by everyone involved in criminal cases: physical abuse, mental abuse, deprivation, cruelty, sexual abuse, abandonment, instability, and emotional starvation visited upon children by the adults who are supposed to love them and care for them. A personality disorder impacts the sufferer's cognition (ability to acquire knowledge); affectivity (expression of emotion); interpersonal functioning; and impulse control.[18]

Unlike clinical disorders, which often respond well to medication, the best hope for treating someone with a personality disorder seems to be long-term cognitive therapy.[19] But the justice system does not have the resources for this. A judge or a prosecutor can sometimes be persuaded to let a person keep her liberty in exchange for submitting to urinalysis or blood-level testing to monitor compliance with medication. Undergoing long-term cognitive therapy is poor competition against the short-term guarantee to public safety that jail provides.

Defending clients with personality disorders highlights the tension between the couch and courtroom. When a forensic psychiatric evaluation reveals an Axis II diagnosis, no one ever seems to read down to Axis IV to see what psychosocial and environmental factors contributed to it or if they do, it does not seem to impact the outcome. Judges and prosecutors often lament the fact that no one intervened during a client's childhood while the client still had a chance. But the lamentation is almost always followed by the observation that the accused is an adult now and adults must be responsible for the choices they make.

The State becomes like the doctor called in to treat Lady Macbeth:

MACBETH: Canst thou not minister to a mind diseas'd,
Pluck from the memory a rooted sorrow,
Raze out the written troubles of the brain,
And with some sweet oblivious antidote
Cleanse the stuff'd bosom of that perilous stuff
Which weighs upon the heart?
DOCTOR: Therein the patient
Must minister to himself.[20]

You start to feel a little insane yourself when you are the only person saying that people are shaped in ways they do not choose and that people can't get over a life of trauma simply by setting their minds to it.

As defenders, we have the power and obligation to start telling the story at its true beginning. Prosecutors start at the last act of an accused's story: the crime. Generally speaking, so do judges, probation officers, and parole boards. The defense lawyer insists that we start at the beginning: when the client was born or when the client was conceived. "What's past is prologue," as Antonio said to Sebastian in *The Tempest*.[21]

Some of the clients we represent are in the grips of a different kind of madness: that brought on by drugs, including alcohol. The *DSM* recognizes substance-related conditions, including substance dependence and substance abuse, as Axis I disorders. The criminal justice system is much more likely to see them as "lifestyle choices" that cannot be rewarded by decreasing culpability as a result. While drug and alcohol "treatment courts" have proliferated in recent years, the vast majority of them require forfeiting basic legal rights—the presumption of innocence, the prosecution bearing the burden of proof, the evidentiary standard of proof beyond a reasonable doubt—as a condition for admission. When a client pleads guilty in the hope of getting treatment and then does not progress to the treatment court's satisfaction, the client has no meaningful legal recourse. The ability to contest the initial allegation is over and winning a probation revocation hearing is almost impossible. The for-profit nature of the vast majority of addiction recovery programs makes it unlikely that an indigent client will be able to get help, even if he or she is willing to take the help. Some jurisdictions recognize that self-induced intoxication is a legal defense to certain crimes, but it is a hard sell to juries and to judges.

Defending addicts is hard and sad. It requires an immersion in the nightmare circumstances that shape every addict's life. On the same mesas where Colorado's prisons and mental hospital sit, and the Grand Mesa to the west, and on the beautiful, empty Eastern Plains, methamphetamine has laid its own straps over wrists and ankles in a private-market version of lethal injection. Jaws clench in teeth-loosening spasms, muscles contract, and eyes bulge as surely as those who took their seats in the old gas chamber, but the killing comes in smaller doses and stretches out over time, ravening flesh and dreams. Methamphetamine has swept across Colorado like wildfire. There does not seem to be political will to stop it—or help those who fall into its grip. The mental health system recognizes that long-term drug abuse can cause a condition called substance-induced psychotic disorder.[22] The criminal justice system calls the psychosis brought on by long-term drug abuse "settled insanity," but many states reject it as a defense. There is precious little sympathy for addicts in the halls of justice. Or rather, there is boundless sympathy for the abstract notion of addiction but none at all for the actual addict—especially when they are accused or convicted of crime.

"It was a choice to use." You hear that over and over again. That is why it is so important to really get to know the people for whom you speak, not just the facts set forth in the police report. If you rewind the clock back to when there was no choice and no free agency—back to when the child was born to addicted parents, to when the six-year-old got drunk for the first time, to when the teenager learned that meth would blot out trauma, and then learned she had to trade herself for more meth—you can start answering that facile assumption with the truth. Sometimes, telling the truth is the most revolutionary act of all,[23] but only if you keep telling it.

Of course, you can only keep telling the truth if you believe it. As a defender, you must believe in your clients—in their humanity, dignity, experience, struggle. You cannot hate your clients. You cannot badmouth them, even to other defense lawyers, because, if you do, you lose the right to stop other people from doing the same. To do this work well and for a long time, you must be able to tap into a deep well of motivation and develop an equally deep skill set. Some cases and clients need you to be a social worker as much as a lawyer. Others summon the intense, libertarian "fight the man" spirit that tilts at windmills only as a prelude to burning those windmills to the ground. The ability to balance diplomacy with street fighting is the hallmark of the successful career defender—that and an ability to combine disciplined legal analysis with pure persuasion.

But contempt for clients or their life circumstances is corrosive, as corrosive as a penny in a can of Coke. If you catch yourself disrespecting a client to increase your own credibility with a prosecutor or a judge, to show you are "easy to work with," you need to take a hard look at where your loyalties lie.[24] Acting in a way that suggests the people we have the privilege to defend are strange or scary undermines the right to counsel and our democratic ideals. "The more you can increase fear of drugs and crime and welfare mothers and immigrants and aliens and poverty and all sorts of things, the more you control people."[25]

Contempt for clients is becoming a more prevalent problem as the economy continues its terrifying slide because some lawyers are practicing criminal defense who would never do so if there was other available employment. More students than ever are leaving law school with no jobs and lots of debt. Bar associations across the country are encouraging them to "hang a shingle"—that is, take court appointments in criminal cases.[26] This is arrogant, ignorant, and ultimately hostile to the indigent accused. The arrogance comes from the implicit assumption that indigent defendants would be happy to get any lawyer, no matter how inexperienced or uncaring. The ignorance is that criminal law is so easy that any recent graduate can do it. And could there be anything more hostile than urging unqualified, uninterested people to represent the most despised and vulnerable among us? It bears an uncomfortable similarity to medical experiments performed on the poor and powerless under the guise of advancing medical knowledge.[27]

Poor people charged with crimes can choose whether to be represented,[28] but they cannot choose who will represent them. No wonder there are so many legitimate ineffective assistance of counsel claims. For all the system's desire for "finality" and "closure," there does not seem to be the will to do things right the first time when it comes to making sure appointed criminal lawyers are well-trained, properly supervised, and motivated to do their jobs right.[29]

Contempt for clients is also incompatible with an adversarial system. Unless each side is wholly committed to its goal—for the defense to the client, for the prosecution to justice, and not merely a conviction—the ideals expressed in the Constitution are defeated. Most of us who do this work are pretty lucky, at least in relative terms. We were born into some degree of privilege, some degree of stability, and had decent childhoods and educations. Being a public defender is a stern reminder, over and over, about how random life is: who gets born to whom seems to matter most and yet none of us can control our own beginnings. It is unsettling for many of us to think there are situations beyond the power of grit and hard work.

When someone asks about what we do for a living, the dialogue often rolls out like this:

Q: What do you do?
A: I'm a lawyer.
Q: What kind of law do you practice?
A: Criminal defense.
Q: What firm are you with?
A: I'm a public defender.
Q: [Moment of silence]. That must be a hard job. How can you represent those people?
A: [Some complicit, wry remark] [weird screed about the Constitution] [prompt trip to the bar for a refill]

How about this answer:

Help me understand who you think "those people" are. Because from what I've seen, it could have been me.[30] Or it could have been you. Or it might be your kid or my kid down the road, if things break bad.

I've been asked this question a lot over the years. It used to infuriate me because I heard it as a thoughtless dismissal of my professional identity. Looking back, I have become convinced that most of the time I was the one bringing animosity into the conversation. It is true that there are people who ask that question as a deliberate provocation—purposely crowding the plate—in which case I have no qualms about throwing the ball at their heads as hard as I can. But I have come to realize that, by and large, people are genuinely curious. When I can respond to the generalized "those people" with the story of an individual client (kept anonymous, of course, to maintain confidentiality), the question can lead to a thoughtful exchange instead of a caustic one. I will admit that I can't always find the patience to be thoughtful. I have answered this question more than once by saying, "Because I am very pro-crime." But the longer I do this work and the more I work with new lawyers who want to make a career in public defense, the more I believe that polarizing, snarky responses to this question are at cross-purposes with the goal of making the justice system just. The more thoughtful we can be in the face of a (usually unintentionally) thoughtless question, the more likely it is that we can get people to open their minds—and maybe change them—both inside and outside the courtroom.

I am lucky to do work that I love, lucky to be able to fight for people who truly need me. My experience has shown me that luck is all that separates me from my clients. Helping someone turn bad luck around by making sure the Constitution works as it's supposed to—no matter how destitute or damaged or reviled the client may be—is a way of serving my country. That's how I represent "those people." Because those people are us.

NOTES

1. Woody Guthrie's song "Ludlow Massacre" tells that story in a surviving miner's voice: "I will never forget the look on the faces/Of the men and women that awful day/When we stood around to preach their funerals/ And lay the corpses of the dead away/We told the Colorado Governor to call the President/Tell him to call off his National Guard/But the National Guard belonged to the Governor/So he didn't try so very hard." Woody Guthrie, "Ludlow Massacre," recorded 1944, on *Hard Travelin': The Asch Recordings, Vol. 3*, Folkways, 1998, compact disc.
2. Howard Zinn, *The Politics of History*, 2nd ed. (Chicago: University of Illinois Press, 1990), 79.
3. This was part of a speech Boehnhoeffer gave before a group of Berlin pastors in April, 1933, entitled "The Church and the Jewish Question." After he spoke this line, all the other pastors got up and left. He concluded his call to fight against the Nazis as a Christian imperative to a room of empty chairs. Dietrich Bonhoeffer, "The Church and the Jewish Question," in *A Testament to Freedom: The Essential Writings of Dietrich Bonhoeffer*, ed. B. Kelly and F. Burton Nelson (New York: HarperCollins, 1995), 130–133.
4. 372 U.S. 335 (1963) (holding that indigent criminal defendants have a right to counsel).
5. Hunter S. Thompson, *Hell's Angels: A Strange and Terrible Saga* (New York: Ballatine Books, 1996), 105.
6. Answer to Respondent's Response to Petition for Writ of Certiorari, Gideon v. Wainwright, 372 U.S. 335 (1963) (No. 890 Misc.).

7. John Adams, "Argument in Defense of the Soldiers in the Boston Massacre Trials," in *John Adams*, ed. David McCullough (New York: Simon and Schuster, 2001), 52.
8. Kurt Vonnegut, *God Bless You Mr. Rosewater* (New York: Dell Publishing, 1965), 51.
9. Prosecutors are exposed to suffering as well: the suffering of crime victims. Despite the fact that prosecutors are advocates for the government, not the individual, samaritrophia can happen to them, too. Burned-out prosecutors become contemptuous of complaining witnesses and disillusioned with the notion that they will be allowed to exercise sufficient independent judgment in a particular case to "do justice," as they define that notion.
10. "Complex traumatic exposure refers to children's experiences of multiple traumatic events that occur within the caregiving system—the social environment that is supposed to be the source of safety and stability in a child's life." *Complex Trauma in Children and Adolescents*, ed. Alexandra Cook et al. (Los Angeles: National Child Traumatic Stress Network, 2003), 5, http://www.nctsn.org/trauma-types/complex-trauma.
11. Bessel A. van der Kolk, "The Neurobiology of Childhood Trauma and Abuse," *Child & Adolescent Psychiatric Clinics of North America* 12 (2003).
12. See, for example, Alan Dershowitz, *The Abuse Excuse and Other Cop-Outs, Sob Stories and Evasions of Responsibility* (Boston: Little, Brown and Company, 1994).
13. van der Kolk, "Childhood Trauma and Abuse," 293.
14. Scott Chrstianson, *The Last Gasp: The Rise and Fall of American Gas Chambers* (Berkeley: University of California Press, 2010), 6.
15. According to a Bureau of Justice Statistics special report published in 2006, 56 percent of state prisoners, 45 percent of federal prisoners, and 64 percent of jail inmates had a clinical mental health diagnosis or treatment by a mental health professional in the preceding 12 months. Lauren E. Glaze and Doris J. James, *Mental Health Problems of Prison and Jail Inmates* (Washington, DC: Bureau of Justice Statistics, 2006), 1, http://www.bjs.gov/content/pub/pdf/mhppji.pdf.
16. This chapter relies on the *Diagnostic and Statistical Manual of Mental Disorders*, Volume IV, Text Revision (*DSM-IV-TR*) (American Psychiatric Association, 2000). The APA released the *DSM-V*, which modifies some categories and has a slightly different overall structure, after this book went to print.
17. Axis III disorders are acute medical conditions and physical disorders. Axis IV is reserved for the psychosocial and environmental factors contributing to the disorder. Axis V is the Global Assessment of Functioning for adults and the Children's Global Assessment Scale for those under 18.
18. *DSM-IV-TR*, 689.
19. See, for example, Aaron T. Beck, Arthur Freeman, and Denise D. Davis, *Cognitive Therapy of Personality Disorders*, 2nd ed. (New York: The Guilford Press, 2004); Marsha M. Linehan, *Cognitive-Behavioral Treatment of Borderline Personality Disorder* (New York: Guilford Press, 1993).

20. William Shakespeare, *Macbeth,* Act V, scene 3.
21. William Shakespeare, *The Tempest*, Act II, scene 1.
22. See *DSM-IV-TR*, 338 (definition and discussion of substance-induced psychotic disorder).
23. Howard Zinn, *Marx in Soho: A Play on History* (Cambridge, MA: South End Press, 1999), 4 ("I suppose the most revolutionary act one can engage in is . . . to tell the truth").
24. "Going to trial with a lawyer who considers your whole lifestyle a Crime in Progress is not a happy prospect." Hunter S. Thompson, in Louis Ferrante, *Mob Rules: What the Mafia can Teach a Legitimate Businessman* (New York: Penguin 2011), 47. "Loyalty and independent judgment are essential elements in the lawyer's relationship to a client." *Model Rules of Professional Conduct*, Rule 1.7 cmt. (2012).
25. Noam Chomsky, *Prison Nation: The Warehousing of America's Poor* (New York: Routledge, 2003), 58.
26. It doesn't seem that bar associations take a similar attitude toward people "hanging a shingle" in any other specialty of law. I suspect the reason is that poor people charged with crimes are seen as a captive audience.
27. For background on this, see Victoria Nourse, *In Reckless Hands: Skinner v. Oklahoma and the Near-Triumph of American Eugenics* (New York: W.W. Norton & Company, 2008).(recounting the legal battle against forced sterilization).
28. Faretta v. California, 422 U.S. 806 (1975) (affirming the right of a defendant to waive his right to counsel and represent himself).
29. For background, see Clive Stafford Smith, *The Injustice System* (New York: Viking, 2012) (death penalty lawyer recounting his unsuccessful efforts to free a man wrongly convicted of murder in a system that cares more about finality than innocence).
30. By saying this, I don't want to create the false impression that I triumphed over adversity as a child, or really, ever. From the beginning, I had material comfort, great parents, nice brothers, plenty of adults who cared about me, and no experience that could fairly be characterized as traumatic. The point is, none of that was based on anything I did. It was all just a roll of the dice: I was raised by people who loved me, were in the middle class, and weren't crazy.

11

Representing Sex Offenders

David A. Singleton

Introduction

It was February 2005, and I faced an important decision.[1] Four years after leaving my position as a staff attorney with the Public Defender Service for the District of Columbia (PDS), I was three years into my job as the executive director of the Ohio Justice & Policy Center (OJPC). The decision—whether or not to challenge Ohio's ban on "sex offenders"[2] living within 1,000 feet of schools—could repel funders and shutter the struggling organization I led. The timing could not have been worse. That month a convicted sex offender abducted Jessica Lunsford, a nine-year-old Florida girl, and buried her alive. The murder of young Jessica generated national headlines, igniting a backlash against sex offenders everywhere. I felt torn between my public defender instincts, which urged challenging the residency restriction, and the fear, expressed by some OJPC board members, that taking such a controversial case could be organizational suicide.

Guided by my public defender values, I decided to take the case. For two years we fought on behalf of thousands of men and women adversely affected by Ohio's sex offender residency restriction. We racked up defeat after defeat in the courts of law. We also got hammered in the court of public opinion. But we persevered. After a string of losses, we started to win—first in the media and then in the courts. Eventually we won a landmark decision from the Ohio Supreme Court, which held that the residency restriction did not apply retroactively to people who had committed their sex offenses before July 31, 2003, the effective date of the statute. And OJPC did not lose funding; instead we grew in both stature and size.

This chapter will tell the story of OJPC's advocacy on behalf of Ohio sex offenders. In the course of telling this story, I will share the tension I felt between fighting for individual clients, which is what I did every day as a public defender, and leading an organization whose mission was broader than any single client, and whose survival turned on our ability to appeal to the public for financial support. I will describe OJPC's sex offender residency litigation and how we used nonlegal strategies to turn a losing battle into a winning cause. Most importantly, I will explain why I am drawn to the clients people have in mind when they ask, "How can you represent those people?"

From Public Defender to Director of a Struggling Nonprofit Law Office

The question of whether to litigate Ohio's sex offender residency restriction forced me to confront two sets of competing interests. The first was already ingrained in me: as a public defender I had spent years zealously representing individual clients, one at a time, to pursue their interests. Although there were challenges in representing individual clients, there was also clarity. But now I was a "cause lawyer" heading an organization that advocated for interests broader than any single client. I felt ill-prepared to strike the right balance, if there was one.

To understand why I felt so uneasy, it is helpful to appreciate the single-minded focus I had as an attorney at a prestigious public defender office. PDS is widely considered to be one of the best public defender offices in the country. The goal of the office could not have been clearer: "Provide *better* representation than money could buy." PDS trained us to be fearless, client-centered lawyers who fought hard for each client in every case. We never worried that we would lose funding if we angered judges or prosecutors in the pursuit of our clients' interests. PDS trained its lawyers to go hard all of the time—no matter how appalling the crime. One of my clients, Thomas,[3] whose case I handled on appeal, was no exception.

Charged with first degree murder and child cruelty, Thomas was convicted of voluntary manslaughter for beating to death his three-year-old cousin Mary, who had been left in his care by her mother. After Mary wet herself, Thomas put her in a tub of water so hot it pulled the skin off her feet. Thomas then grabbed and squeezed Mary's neck as he pulled her out of the tub and punched her in the stomach to quiet her screaming. She died later that night. When questioned by the police, Thomas made incriminating statements and confessed on videotape.

Thomas won a tremendous victory when jurors convicted him of voluntary manslaughter, instead of first degree murder, and cruelty to children. His trial lawyers painted a picture of a vulnerable young man who struggled to babysit Mary and her three young siblings when the children's mother abandoned them. Testimony about the apartment's unsafe and unsanitary conditions helped the jury understand the pressure Thomas was under when he snapped and delivered the blow that eventually killed Mary.

Had Thomas been convicted of first degree murder he would have faced a minimum of 30 years up to a maximum of life in prison. Instead, his two convictions carried terms of 5 to 15 years each, which the judge ran consecutively. This meant that Thomas would be eligible for parole in 10 years but could serve a maximum sentence of 30 years in prison.

There was no doubt in my mind that Thomas had killed Mary; he said so at the trial. But the fact that he had killed his young cousin was irrelevant to me. When I met Thomas, I was fired up to help him. Though I felt for his victim, I sympathized with him too. I worried that Thomas, who was slightly built, would not fare well in prison; prisoners who harm children are especially vulnerable behind bars. It was my job to do what I could to get his conviction overturned.

As it turned out, there was much to work with. Thomas had two very strong claims to raise on appeal. The first was a possible *Edwards v. Arizona* violation. *Edwards*, a US Supreme Court case, held that once a person undergoing custodial interrogation requests a lawyer, the police must stop their questioning and cannot resume unless the suspect initiates conversation and waives the right to have counsel present. If we could convince the District of Columbia Court of Appeals that the police obtained Thomas's videotaped confession in violation of *Edwards*, then the court would have to reverse the conviction.

The second claim involved a more technical issue: the merger doctrine, under which lesser included offenses generally merge into the greater offense. For example, a person cannot be convicted and sentenced for both robbery and larceny, since the larceny is one of the elements of the greater offense of robbery. In Thomas's case we argued that the cruelty to children conviction may have been the basis for the manslaughter conviction based on the court's unclear jury instructions.

By a 2–1 vote, the Court of Appeals rejected our *Edwards* argument. But, because the government conceded our merger claim, the court vacated Thomas's child cruelty conviction. As a result of the appeal, Thomas's prison sentence was cut in half: he became eligible for parole after 5 years and would at most serve 15 years. Though I was disappointed about the *Edwards* loss—which held the possibility of making the entire case go away—I was proud of what I had done for Thomas. The case exemplified what it means to practice high-quality indigent defense.

Although I appreciated the importance of giving my all to my public defender clients, the truth is I had not been fully tested when it came to the most despised defendants. That would come later, after I moved to Cincinnati.

* * *

Crammed into an 824-foot office in the old *Cincinnati Enquirer* building, the OJPC I joined in 2002 was very different from the well-staffed and well-funded PDS I had departed. At the time, OJPC had four employees (three attorneys, including me, and a paralegal). The organization's total operating budget was $300,000, much of which was funded through grants. We brought in just enough to cover expenses. Having no reserve fund, we existed year to year.

Though both PDS and OJPC served people in the criminal justice system, the missions of the two organizations were very different. At the time, OJPC's mission, as stated in its Code of Regulations, was to "assist inmates to secure basic civil rights at prisons and jails in Ohio" and neighboring states.

OJPC's work was more than just representing individual prisoners. For example, just before I joined OJPC, the organization had launched the National Resource Center on Prisons and Communities (NRCPC) to help grassroots groups across the United States stop new prison construction. The board had also just approved a new death penalty project, which was supposed to recruit experts willing to assist capital defense lawyers during the penalty phase of the trial. The board made clear that I should focus on litigation and advocacy that was much broader than any one individual client. I was no longer a public defender but an "impact lawyer" who had to think strategically about how to use limited resources to achieve transformational criminal justice reform.

Although I worked hard, I failed miserably during my first three years at OJPC's helm. With the exception of cocounseling a class-action lawsuit to improve prison health care, our prisoners' rights litigation was virtually nonexistent. Uninspired by its narrow focus, I was unable to get the death penalty project off the ground. And in 2005, the Open Society Institute and the JEHT Foundation, both of which funded the NRCPC, withdrew their support.

The sudden loss of major foundation support threatened to shut down OJPC. At the end of February 2005, we had less than $10,000 in the bank. We struggled almost every month in 2005 to make payroll. For much of that year, I did not pay myself, to avoid laying off or delaying payment to other staff. Fourteen years out of law school, I made less than $25,000 that year. To say that OJPC was struggling is an understatement. We were on the brink of closing when a man named Joseph walked into our community legal clinic.

OJPC's Skokie Moment

Joseph had just been released from prison for two rapes he committed when he was 17. A condition of his parole was that he find stable housing. Joseph had found a place to live—a home located within 1,000 feet of a school. But Ohio law prohibited Joseph, a sex offender, from living that close to a school. Joseph was in trouble. If he did not find a place to live, he would be in violation of parole and risk going back to prison. He needed our help.

Joseph found his way to OJPC not long after we had opened the first of our Second Chance Community Legal Clinics, which provide free legal advice and representation to people returning home from prison. We started the clinics in November 2004 as a way to do work that would have a more direct impact on the Greater Cincinnati community. Our motives were partially financial. We had trouble getting support from the local community for our work helping prisoners, most of whom are incarcerated in prisons far from Cincinnati. Besides, to most people, prisoners were bad people who deserved to be treated harshly. But our Second Chance Clinic clients would have more appeal: They were people who had made mistakes, paid for them, and were now trying to become productive members of the community.

Our initial Second Chance Clinic work resonated with many community members. Our very first client, Ronald, enrolled in a paralegal school within a month after his release from prison. Ronald disclosed his conviction for felony assault on his admissions application. The school gladly accepted his money and enrolled him, but a month into classes the school's director summoned Ronald to the office. The school was now concerned about Ronald's criminal record and wanted him gone. Interestingly, the school was not worried that Ronald posed a risk to other students. It was purely a financial decision. The school feared that Ronald's record would make him unemployable, thereby bringing down its high placement rate. So Ronald was given a choice: he could either leave the school or waive placement services. Ronald objected to the school's ultimatum. He had signed a contract with the school, a part of which required it to use its best efforts to find employment for him when he graduated. He knew that there was no guarantee he would get a job but wanted the school to honor its contract. So Ronald refused to waive placement services and the school expelled him. At first we tried to negotiate. But the school's lawyer was arrogant and dismissive. He said that no judge in the courthouse would order the school to take back a convicted felon. And then he tried to intimidate me with a silly credential: "You know I am an Ohio Super Lawyer," he said.

Ronald's story ended happily. The court ordered the school to take him back, concluding that nothing in the contract permitted the school to dismiss a student for conduct committed before enrollment. And Ronald went on to earn straight A's, graduating near the top of the class. Ronald was exactly the kind of client we had in mind when we opened the clinic. His story was the type of success we wanted to trumpet when we hit the fund-raising circuit. Almost anyone could relate to Ronald's story of redemption and desire for a second chance.

Unlike Ronald's case, Joseph's situation would not generate sympathy. To the contrary, we knew it could bring serious trouble. People who commit sex crimes are pariahs—shunned by all, embraced by none. Joseph had committed not one rape, but two. Then there was the issue of protecting children from sexual abuse. That's precisely what Ohio's sex offender residency restriction purported to do—and what rational person would be against this? Sure, Joseph's victims were adults, but would people be able to make that distinction? Would the public, and more importantly the courts, favor letting a convicted rapist live near a school?

The public defender in me knew that Joseph needed a lawyer as much—and perhaps more—than Ronald did. Joseph was exactly the type of client I was drawn to: someone completely written off and despised by most people. But it wasn't just my PDS training that made me want to help Joseph.

One summer day, after my junior year in college, I traveled to the South Bronx, where I was born. The neighborhood I encountered was very different from Asheville, North Carolina, where I grew up. Asheville is idyllic; the South Bronx is not. As I walked the streets that afternoon, I saw boarded up buildings on almost every block. Broken glass and debris littered the sidewalks. Brown-skinned young men, who looked like me, stood on corners dealing drugs. Later, as I thought about what I saw, I realized that I could have easily ended up like these young men. The difference was I had parents who had the means to get us out. But even if I had become a drug dealer, I wouldn't have wanted that to forever define me. I would have wanted the possibility of redemption. So, in people like Joseph, I see part of myself, no matter the crime. I want for them what I would have wanted in their shoes—and what I want in my own: forgiveness for my wrongs.

I was also captivated by Joseph's legal issue. First, from a policy standpoint, the idea of a residency restriction seemed arbitrary. Under the statute's rationale, children would be at risk if a convicted sex offender lived 999 feet from a school but the risk would vanish if that same offender lived 1,001 feet from the school.

Second, applying the statute to Joseph, whose victims were adults, made little sense if the goal was to protect children. Although it is possible for people who commit sex crimes to have more than one victim preference, there was no proof that this was so for Joseph. Even if there were proof that Joseph posed a threat to children, would the community be safer if he lived two miles from a school but right next to an apartment building full of children? The residency restriction wouldn't protect those children.

Third, we had the law on our side—at least initially. Shortly after meeting Joseph, I read a story in the *Prison Legal News* about a successful challenge to Iowa's sex offender residency restriction, which banned sex offenders from living within 2,000 feet of schools and day-care facilities. With the exception of corn fields, much of Iowa was off-limits to sex offenders as a result of that statute. The plaintiffs in the case, *Doe v. Miller*, raised various constitutional challenges to the law. The federal district court issued a favorable ruling, finding that Iowa's statute violated a number of provisions, including the Ex Post Facto Clause of the US Constitution, which forbids the government from imposing retroactive punishment. *Doe v. Miller* was the only federal court decision at the time addressing the constitutionality of residency restrictions.

As we came closer to representing Joseph, the reality that I was no longer a public defender hit me. As the executive director of an organization with a broad mission, I had to consider not only Joseph's needs, but also the interests of OJPC. The question was not whether Joseph had a need, but whether we should take his case if doing so could jeopardize OJPC.

Unsure, I decided to talk with two board members. One of them, Paul DeMarco, who would become a close friend, told me what I knew but did not want to hear: "The case could put the organization at risk." For better or worse, he warned, representing Joseph "could be our Skokie moment," referring to the American Civil Liberties

Union's loss of support because of its high-profile representation of Nazis who wanted to march through the Village of Skokie, Illinois, where one in six residents was a Holocaust survivor. Paul never told me not to take the case. But he advised doing so only with awareness of what it could mean for the organization.

I then asked Al Gerhardstein, OJPC's founder and then board chair for his thoughts. "Go for it," he said. That was all I needed to hear. Perhaps I should have involved the board in deeper discussion. But I was more interested in the result—being able to justify filing the case—than I was in the process. So, on February 25, 2005, with the most influential member of OJPC's board supporting us, we filed Joseph's case in the federal district court located in Cincinnati. We sought an immediate court order blocking an amendment to the residency statute that would allow prosecutors to seek a court order evicting sex offenders from residences located within 1,000 feet of schools.

* * *

One of the things they don't teach you in law school is how to develop a media strategy for controversial litigation. Aside from a handful of press interviews I had done as a young lawyer with a public interest organization called the Urban Justice Center in New York City, I had very little media experience. When I was a public defender, both at the Neighborhood Defender of Harlem and PDS, office policy was to avoid speaking to the press; we had to refer all media inquiries to one of the deputy directors. The concept of using the media proactively to change public sentiment on an issue was not something I was familiar with. So we were unprepared when the media learned about Joseph's case in April 2005.

My first interview with the *Cincinnati Enquirer* was a disaster. When asked why we had filed suit, I said: "The law makes it all but impossible for sex offenders to find places to live." This was a foolish thing to say—framing the case as about the rights of my clients. Few people care about the rights of sex offenders, especially if those rights endanger children.

The law-and-order *Enquirer* seized upon my misstep in an editorial two days later: "We believe the farther child sex offenders are kept away from children anywhere, the better." It didn't matter that Joseph had not sexually assaulted children. The *Enquirer* jumped at the opportunity to tell its readers just how dangerous people who commit sex offenses are: "Unlike other types of criminal offenses, sexual offenses, especially those against children, often stem from pathological behavior that cannot be permanently corrected. Many offenders will re-offend." To drive home the point, the paper reminded readers that a convicted sex offender had kidnapped and murdered nine-year-old Jessica Lunsford, whose mother lives in Greater Cincinnati. To say that we were off to a slow start in public relations would be an understatement.

If things were going badly in the press, they were worse in court. An hour before the Ohio court was to hear our motion for a temporary restraining order (TRO), asking the court to halt enforcement of the statute pending trial, the Eighth Circuit Court of Appeals reversed *Doe v. Miller*, the Iowa federal district court case upon which we staked our entire case. We were left with no case law to support our argument.

When I entered court that afternoon, one of the state's lawyers smugly asked if we had heard about the Eighth Circuit's recent decision. "Yes," I replied, brushing past him on my way to counsel table. The court asked if we were still going forward in light of the Eighth Circuit's decision. I reminded the court that the Eighth Circuit's decision was not binding on Ohio's courts and said we wanted to proceed. The court indulged our argument but denied the TRO.

Pressing Ahead

After the TRO debacle, the court dismissed our entire case. We decided not to appeal and instead to find plaintiffs more sympathetic than Joseph, which might make a judge more sympathetic to our cause. In an ideal world we would have a Romeo-and-Juliet plaintiff, a young adult just a few years older than his or her underage sexual partner—like a high school senior who has sex with a willing freshman. Another ideal plaintiff would have been a female prison guard who commits sexual battery under Ohio law by having consensual sex with a male inmate. However, I was not sure that it would be easy to find the "perfect" plaintiff.

* * *

With our federal court challenge out of the way for now, prosecutors across the state, who up until that point had refrained from using their new enforcement powers, began filing eviction cases. There were just two of us at OJPC who could handle the resulting flood of representation requests: Stephen JohnsonGrove and I.

We asked our local legal aid office to help with the onslaught of potential cases. The office declined to assist, explaining that it needed to conserve its scarce resources for more meritorious cases. We got similar responses from other legal aid offices throughout the state. I reached out to a few large law firms in Cincinnati and tried to pitch the cases as opportunities for the firms' associates to get litigation experience. None of the firms was interested.

Although Stephen and I could not represent every sex offender who asked for representation, we did defend a dozen men from different parts of the state who faced eviction from their homes. None of our clients fit the profile of the model plaintiff. However, two of those clients, Michael and Robert, would turn out to be key players in our effort to halt retroactive enforcement of the residency restriction.

* * *

Michael lived in Green Township, a quiet suburb of Cincinnati. He had been convicted in 1995 for a sexual offense involving his sister, and in 1999 for an offense against his daughter. Michael lived with his wife and two sons in a two-story house. He and his wife purchased their home in 1991, 12 years before the restriction became law. Though not legally significant, Michael's home was 983 feet from the nearest school, measured from his property line to the school's property line; just 17 feet of the corner of his backyard fell within the 1000-foot buffer zone.

At the conclusion of Michael's day-long trial, we argued that the residency restriction could not constitutionally be applied to Michael because he committed his offenses before the effective date of the statute. On September 8, 2005, the court ruled against Michael, ordering him to move from his family home within ten days. We promptly moved for a stay pending appeal, which the court refused to grant. On October 8, 2005, Michael moved out of his home and into an apartment, while his case worked its way through the appellate process.

* * *

Robert was 75 years old when we began representing him in 2005. He and his wife, who was 91 at the time, lived in Miami County, Ohio, in a home they had purchased in 1978. Their home was located within 1,000 feet of a school.

In 1998, Robert pled guilty to attempted gross sexual imposition and was sentenced to 60 days confinement. The prosecution alleged that Robert had touched a teenage girl over her clothing in a sexual manner while she helped him walk down from the bleachers at a basketball game. Aside from this conviction, Robert had no other criminal record.

In January 2006, a trial judge ordered Robert to move. The court, however, stayed its order pending his appeal. The next stop for Robert's case was the court of appeals.

* * *

As we were preparing appeals for Michael and Robert, we learned of another potential client who lived in Akron, Ohio. His name was James. His case would lead us back to federal court.

The *Akron Beacon Journal* ran a story about James in December 2005. The news of his plight reached me in early January 2006. Although James was not the model plaintiff we had been looking for, his case was too good to pass up.

In 1986, James, who was 18 at the time, raped a woman named Ellen. James and two friends had committed a series of burglaries of unoccupied homes when they broke into Ellen's house, finding her alone. The three men took turns raping her. Not long after, the police arrested James and his accomplices. They confessed and pled guilty to rape. James received a sentence of 18 to 36 years in prison.

After his release from prison in 2004, James went to Akron to live in his family home. He met a woman, fell in love, and started a family with her. He tried to move forward with his life in a positive way. But in December 2005, the local sheriff's office notified James that he would have to move from his home because of the state's sex offender residency restriction.

Then something happened that caught the public's attention. Ellen came out publicly in support of James. She told the local press that she had forgiven James for what he had done and was worried about what would happen to him and his family if he was forced to move. Soon after, she took up a collection for James and his family, and contributed to it herself. The CBS Early Show did a two-part series on Ellen's forgiveness of James.

James's predicament and the genuine remorse he expressed for his crime moved me. He wasn't perfect, but I didn't think we would find a better client in a new federal court suit. Our search for a new plaintiff was over.

* * *

As we litigated the three new cases, we resolved to wage a more effective media campaign. Instead of focusing on how the residency restriction wronged our clients, we argued that residency restrictions were ineffective in preventing child sexual abuse, and worse, actually undermined community safety. As it turned out, we had a number of allies—some unexpected—who were willing to help frame our message more persuasively.

The Association for the Treatment of Sexual Abusers (ATSA) was our first ally. ATSA is an international, multidisciplinary professional association dedicated to treatment of sexual offenders, research, and prevention of sexual assault. ATSA supports evidence-based ways to reduce sexual violence and to manage sex offenders in the community.

We began working with ATSA in the fall of 2005, after we lost Joseph's case. We connected with ATSA through the lawyer representing the plaintiffs in the Iowa case. He was in the process of filing a petition asking the US Supreme Court to hear his clients' appeal from the Eighth Circuit's decision. He needed a lawyer to draft an amicus (or friend-of-court) brief urging the US Supreme Court to hear the case. I eagerly volunteered.

In its amicus brief, ATSA argued that the Iowa statute significantly increases the danger that sex offenders will reoffend because if you deprive them of housing, they will become isolated, depressed, and unstable, which are risk factors. ATSA pointed to a Minnesota study that found that proximity to schools or parks did not increase recidivism rates for sexually violent predators. Instead, the study suggested that offenders who committed new offenses preferred to do so far from their own neighborhood, where their identities were not known. ATSA also noted that cases of child abduction and murder by a stranger are extremely rare even though they get enormous media attention. In other words, the proliferation of residency restrictions across the country are driven by fear, not facts.

We soon had additional allies. Remarkably, the Iowa County Attorneys Association (ICAA), which represents prosecutor interests, was one of them. The ICAA called for replacing the restriction with more effective measures. It also noted the onerous effects of the restriction on the families of offenders.

By the fall of 2007, we would have even more law enforcement allies, including the Iowa State Sheriffs' and Deputies' Association. We also joined forces with victims' rights groups, like the Iowa Coalition Against Sexual Assault, and the Jacob Wetterling Foundation, which was established in January 1990, four months after someone abducted and presumably murdered 11-year-old Jacob. All of these allies shared the belief that residency restrictions did not keep children safe and actually undermined safety by creating a false sense of security.

Turning the Tide

Realizing the obvious—that law enforcement and victim's rights groups had more credibility opposing residency restrictions than criminal defense or civil rights lawyers—we began using materials put out by our allies to educate the *Cincinnati Enquirer* editorial board and its reporters about why residency restrictions are bad policy. We sent them the Minnesota Department of Corrections study and then the ICAA statement. Editorials favorable to our position soon followed.

On February 20, 2006, the *Enquirer* published a very different editorial on residential restrictions for sex offenders. Published in response to neighboring Covington, Kentucky's proposed 2,000 foot residency restriction, the *Enquirer* wrote: "Restricted zones of 1,000, 2,000, or even 2,500 feet may make us feel safer, but there's no research evidence they cut down on repeat offenses. They could increase the chances." Relying on materials we had forwarded, the editorial noted that "one Minnesota study found a sex offender was more likely to travel to another neighborhood where he could seek victims without being recognized." It noted that 90 percent of sexually abused children are molested by family members, friends, or acquaintances, not strangers. To our delight, our talking points found their way into this editorial.

Less than a month later, on March 16, 2006, the *Enquirer* published another editorial that went even further. It began: "Sex offender laws are fast becoming a national proving ground for the Law of Unintended Consequences. Lawmakers need to make sure bans against sex offenders living within specified distances of where children study or play are not giving families a false sense of security." The editorial warned legislators against "making living conditions so punitive for sex offenders, after serving their time, that they can't find jobs, can't find decent housing and are more likely to re-offend or 'disappear,' leaving the public with even less warning than if their whereabouts were known and registered." The editorial concluded by arguing that the test for new legislation ought to be whether it makes us safer. We were changing the conversation.

On December 12, 2006, the *Enquirer* published yet another editorial on the "fact and fiction" of "predators." Written in response to the city of Cincinnati's proposal to expand the state's residency requirement to ban sex offenders from living practically anywhere where children might congregate, it couldn't have been a stronger call to reason. "It's time for research to trump emotion on this issue," the editorial board wrote. The editorial derided 1000 foot limits as a shallow substitute for treatment and popular only because "they cost little more than the ink to sign them into law."

The *Enquirer* was not finished. Over the course of the next year, the paper published additional stories critical of residency restrictions. We were clearly making headway.

* * *

October 20, 2006, turned out to be an important day in our state court litigation. On that day we got two conflicting decisions, one in Michael's case, the other in Robert's. The court of appeals in Michael's case ruled that the statute could apply retroactively. The court of appeals in Robert's case held that it was unconstitutional to apply the statute retroactively because it would harm his property rights. The split decisions required the Ohio Supreme Court to take Michael's case to resolve the conflict.

* * *

On September 4, 2007, as we waited to argue Michael's case in the Ohio Supreme Court, we finally got a decision in James's case. The court ruled that the residency restriction imposed punishment for purposes of the Ex Post Facto Clause and could therefore not be applied retroactively to James. In its opinion, the court recognized that residency restrictions don't prevent the majority of child sex abuse cases involving assaults by family members or acquaintances. After weighing the onerous impact of the residency restriction compared to its minimal benefit, the court concluded that the law was punitive.

* * *

Sometimes a lawyer gets to do what might seem to others as the legal equivalent of convincing someone that the sky is green and the grass is blue. For me that opportunity came on the morning of October 10, 2007, when I stepped to the podium to argue Michael's appeal before the Ohio Supreme Court.

I started my argument by addressing the question of legislative intent. If the court found that the legislature intended the statute to apply retroactively, then the court would have to answer a second question: did the statute impair Michael's vested property rights? In light of the court's language in a recent case about the importance of property rights, we knew we had a strong chance of getting the court to rule that the statute could not be applied retroactively to a sex offender who both purchased his home and committed his offense before the statute's effective date. But we wanted a ruling that would protect nonproperty owners as well homeowners like Michael from being forced to move. To get the broader ruling we had to convince the court that the legislature never intended to apply the statute retroactively to any convicted sex offender.

We knew that our legislative intent argument would be hard to win in light of the fact that the statute, on its face, applies to any person who has "been convicted of" or who has "pleaded guilty to" a sexually oriented offense. During my practice arguments, mock judges who grilled me advised me to drop the legislative intent argument and focus solely on whether application of the restriction impaired Michael's property rights.

But OJPC board member Paul DeMarco, who initially warned that sex offender work could be "our Skokie moment," urged me not to abandon the legislative intent argument but to instead parse the statutory language to show its ambiguity.

Accordingly, I spent most of my time before the Ohio Supreme Court arguing that at best there was only a suggestion of retroactive intent and that the court needed more to find that the statute could apply retrospectively. I realized that we had a shot at winning when the court began to ask questions of opposing counsel. It was apparent that we at least had the late chief Justice Moyer's vote when he said to the other side's lawyer, "The amicus brief, as you know, from some law enforcement authorities and others who have been, who work with children who have been molested and . . . they don't like this law either. They don't think it's helpful." The chief justice was referring to an amicus brief submitted by our new allies. The brief emphasized the inefficacy of residency restrictions and how they could actually undermine public safety by creating a false sense of security and by driving sex offenders off the registry and "underground" where law enforcement could not monitor them.

On February 20, 2008, the Ohio Supreme Court ruled, in a 6–1 decision, that the legislature did not intend for the residency restriction to apply retroactively to sex offenders who had either committed their offenses or established their homes before the statute's effective date. Because the court concluded that the statute did not apply retroactively, it did not address the narrower question of whether retrospective application would have unconstitutionally impaired Michael's vested property rights. Instead of benefiting only homeowners like Michael, the court's ruling protected a much greater number of individuals who would otherwise be forced to move from their homes if the statute applied retroactively. We had won a landmark victory.

* * *

The *Enquirer* weighed in with its opinion the next day. The editorial urged treatment for sex offenders and a sensible classification system. It called the retroactive application of residency restrictions "inhumane."

We had come full circle.

Epilogue

When we began our sex offender work, many people predicted we would fail. Fortunately, we did not. Instead of drying up, OJPC's funding grew. In 2002 our annual budget was $300,000; today it is a little under a million dollars. We have 13 full-time employees today compared with the 4 we had when I began in 2002. We have also grown in prestige and influence. Although there were some who predicted we would forever be known as "those wackos who represent sex offenders," we have become well-respected locally and statewide across a broad array of criminal justice issues.

We have also become better problem solvers for our clients as a result of our residency restriction work. Whenever we litigate an impact case now, we develop complementary media, coalition-building and, if necessary, lobbying strategies. We put this strategy to use in getting the city of Cincinnati to change its blanket practice of refusing to hire people with felony records.

With our growth have come other changes. We now maintain a strategic plan for the organization, with goals, strategies, and action plans designed to achieve measurable outcomes. The plan is intended to ensure that OJPC remains true to its mission and stays focused on high impact work that makes a meaningful difference in the criminal justice reform arena.

There is no doubt that our residency restriction work was successful and had an impact. Not only did we keep thousands of people from being forced to move from their homes, but we also made significant strides in changing the conversation about how to keep children safe from sexual violence.

For two years we fought for the most despised people in the state. We refused to give up on them even when it looked like we would never win. We risked our very existence because we believed in our clients' humanity—despite the seriousness of their crimes. We gave them representation better than money could buy. Our challenge to the residency restriction is among the work I am most proud of doing in my entire legal career.

Whenever I give community presentations about OJPC, invariably someone asks how I could represent sex offenders, particularly those who have harmed children. Although I used to answer by explaining how our advocacy improved public safety, that explanation is not entirely true. The reason I come to work every day is not to make the community safer, but to be the voice of clients others would rather ignore.

So now I talk about how my faith has emboldened me to serve people others might reject. I think advocacy on behalf of people in the criminal justice system is the kind of work that Jesus would embrace. But, to me, faith is much broader than any set of religious teachings. It is about doing what's right even when others think you are wrong. Faith is what helps you persevere when you have doubts about whether you will succeed. As Martin Luther King, Jr. said, "Faith is taking the first step, even when you don't see the whole staircase." Although there were times during the residency restriction litigation that I thought we would never win, we kept going because it was the right thing to do.

What also kept me going after the early losses was my belief in the possibility of redemption. We all make mistakes, sometimes bad mistakes. My own desire not to be defined by my worst moments allowed me to feel empathy for the sex offenders I represented. I believe that everyone is capable of changing for the better, if only in small ways. That's what I now say when I am asked how I could represent sex offenders.

Notes

1. I am very appreciative of the time, insights, and assistance provided by Jessica Hunter and Trisha Cole. The work I describe in this chapter could not have been done without the tireless work of my colleagues, most notably Stephen JohnsonGrove and Marguerite Slagle. I also give thanks to the Neighborhood Defender Service of Harlem and the Public Defender Service of the District of Columbia for teaching me how to be a client-centered lawyer. I dedicate this chapter to the men and women who because of their status as sex offenders are written off as beyond redemption by mainstream society.
2. "Sex offenders" is a term I use with a great deal of reluctance. We use these sorts of labels to distance ourselves from people we deem unworthy

of full membership in our community. Despite my objections to the term, I will use it for convenience's sake to refer to individuals who have been convicted of sexual offenses.

3. Although each of the clients I discuss in this chapter was the subject of public court cases, I choose to give them pseudonyms to protect their privacy. I have also changed the names of their victims.

12

How Can You *Not* Defend Those People?

Abbe Smith

Introduction

Ronnie[1] was 16 when he got kicked out of school for the second time. First it was the local public school, now the private Christian school. His father would be furious. He had shelled out a lot of money for his kid to get himself expelled.

Ronnie had to get away. He grabbed his dad's hunting rifle and headed next door. The neighbor's car was in the driveway. He figured she'd give up the keys when she saw the gun.

Ronnie shot the neighbor, a mother of two, when she refused. He pulled the trigger again and again. The woman died instantly. Her little girl, only five years old, saw the whole thing and ran to her bedroom to hide. Ronnie followed her and shot twice at her door.

When the child thought it was over, she managed to call 911. She said, "Please come. My mommy is dead."

Ronnie was caught several hours later at his grandfather's house 300 miles away. Several shotguns, a camouflage outfit, a metal helmet, an iron cross, a swastika pin, and a copy of *The Rise and Fall of the Third Reich* were found in the car. When police asked why Ronnie had done it, he said, "They laughed at me."

He was convicted of murder, attempted murder, and car theft, and sentenced to life in prison.

* * *

Delores was accused of killing her 18-month-old baby by smothering her with a pillow. This was not the only baby that died in her care. She had already buried three other babies, all under the age of two.

She had become a familiar sight at the local hospital. She would run into the emergency room in tears, cradling a dead or nearly dead baby in her arms. Delores's children died suddenly and without warning. Some hospital staff saw Delores as a tragic figure—her babies died of Sudden Infant Death Syndrome or SIDS. Others had a less sympathetic view.

She was arrested shortly after the fourth baby was buried. The local prosecutor didn't believe in babies just dying. To him, Delores was a serial child murderer. He considered the idea that she had Munchausen Syndrome by Proxy, a pattern of behavior in which caregivers—especially mothers—exaggerate, fabricate, or induce health problems in others. But he didn't think Delores was mentally ill. He believed she knew what she was doing and did it for attention.

She was convicted of murder and sentenced to life.

* * *

After dropping out of high school, James tried trade school but couldn't stop wanting the street. He had become accustomed to the cash and women that came with selling drugs, and was good at it. He got respect. He had done some things he wasn't exactly proud of, and done some time in jail, but that was the life. You had to be tough.

He can't remember all the details of the stabbing—or doesn't want to. He knows what the prosecution says: that he and another man beat and stabbed a woman to death as payback for failing to warn a drug runner that the police were coming. The woman, a mother of two, was a crack cocaine user who sometimes worked for the same people he did. After she was stabbed in the neck and chest, she tried to make it home but collapsed on the stairs to her basement apartment.

He was convicted of murder and sentenced to life.

* * *

These are the kinds of cases that make people ask how criminal lawyers can defend "those people": a suburban "bad seed," an inner-city thug who killed young mothers, and a mother who killed her own children. Why spend one second on these monstrous criminals, much less advocate on their behalf?

Many practitioners and scholars have written perceptively about the motivations of criminal defenders, some eloquently.[2] I have my own body of work on this and related questions.

This chapter is about why I have devoted my professional career—my life, really—to defending people most would just as soon banish and forget. After 30 years of criminal law practice, my reasons are such a part of me they are nearly inarticulable: I am a criminal defender in my soul. But I have also been teaching and writing about criminal defense for almost as long as I've been doing it. I ought to be able to talk about it in a thoughtful and honest way. Let me try.

The People behind the Crimes

The crimes that Ronnie, Delores, and James committed are terrible. Ronnie's presentence report, which describes the shooting, is painful to read—especially the victim impact statements by the decedent's husband, parents, and children. Ronnie destroyed a family. What Delores did to a helpless baby is unthinkable. She gave life only to snuff it out. Equally unthinkable is what James did to a woman he knew. He purposely plunged a knife into her body, piercing her heart. He watched her stagger away and die.

But there is more to them than their crimes. And more to their crimes than the "record" reflects.

Before that day, Ronnie had never been in serious trouble. He had never been to juvenile court, much less criminal court. When he grabbed that gun he didn't intend to fire it. He was immature and impulsive. When he pulled that trigger—once, twice, five times in all—it felt like it was happening to someone else, not him.

He was different. No matter how hard he tried to fit in, he was hopelessly out of sync with other kids. They mocked and shunned him. So he did stupid stuff at school. He wrote graffiti and drew obscene pictures. He created his own identity, his own world. He wore a swastika pin on his jacket even though he didn't really know what a Nazi was.

His trial lasted only a few days. The jury wept when the little girl testified. She held her father's hand as she recounted what happened. No one paid attention to the defense psychiatrist who said Ronnie wasn't in his right mind. Ronnie's own parents sat outside the courtroom during the trial. They held hands and read the Bible with other family members.

I met Ronnie 28 years later at the maximum-security prison where he had been incarcerated for most of those years. He was now 44. He hadn't seen a lawyer in a quarter century. Legal fees had taken his parents' savings; they ran out of money after his appeal. Ronnie said he had written 1,200 letters to lawyers over the years. He didn't know why he kept count.

He had been badly brutalized by larger, older inmates in the first years of his incarceration. He was then held in protective custody—solitary confinement—for many months. After that, he somehow learned to cope with prison life.

I saw Ronnie because a prison buddy of his wrote to me about him. I found this compelling: a prisoner writing that another guy could really use a lawyer.

Ronnie still looked 16: a 44-year-old teenager. His face was soft, his skin unlined and unweathered. Of course he had barely been in weather. He was also untattooed, an unusual thing for a white prisoner, especially an alleged neo-Nazi. He worked in the prison factory making blue jeans, prison uniforms, and license plates. He had a sense of humor about this last thing: a prisoner making license plates.

I asked whether he had visitors. He said his two brothers visited once a year on "family day." His mother used to come, but she moved away some years ago and now kept in touch mostly through letters. His father died shortly after Ronnie went to prison.

I told him the clinic would take his case, but cautioned against being too hopeful. It was a difficult case. He said he knew he might never get out. He just didn't want to die in prison.

* * *

Delores was the best friend of another client, an innocent woman who had served 28 years in prison before she finally won her freedom.[3] The first client said she could not feel free while Delores was still in prison.

Delores was happily married, but sometimes felt lonely and isolated. Her husband Bill worked a lot. When he wasn't working, he was at the bowling alley or golf course. Delores had few friends and had lost touch with family.

They wanted kids but couldn't seem to have any. Delores got pregnant several times and gave birth without incident, but the babies died. Doctors told her she probably had a genetic predisposition for SIDS. She was arrested when she was still reeling from the loss of the last baby.

Delores's trial lasted only a few days, too. No medical or mental health experts testified on her behalf. When the jury found her guilty, she looked at her husband in dismay.

When Delores became eligible for release after 20 years, she had a hearing before the parole board. Despite the fact that she was often targeted for ridicule and abuse—baby killers are especially reviled in a women's prison—she had done her time without incident. She had participated in every available prison program. For most of the 20 years, she had worked in the prison hospital as a nurse's aide. She had also worked in the Catholic chaplain's office. She was a woman of faith and service.

She was denied parole because she showed "too little emotion" at the hearing.

Two years later she had her next hearing. She was now on the honors floor—a privilege given to inmates with exemplary disciplinary records. She was still working in the hospital and chaplain's office. She had learned from the previous hearing that she could not afford to be reserved. She had learned to bury her feelings to endure her incarceration, but now must reveal herself to a panel of criminal justice bureaucrats who would decide her fate. This time she let the grief pour out of her—for her dead babies, her lost life.

She was denied parole because she showed "too much emotion."

I undertook Delores's representation after her second parole hearing. I did so partly for my previous client, but also because Delores was exactly the kind of client I wanted for the clinic: a long-serving prisoner convicted of a serious crime who had done her time but might never get out.

Her account of her parole hearings also struck a chord: it was out of the movie *The Shawshank Redemption*. In *Shawshank*, Red, played by Morgan Freeman, appears before the parole board and is routinely denied parole no matter what he says or how many years he serves. After every hearing, the word "DENIED" is stamped on his file. Finally, in 1967, after 40 years, the board grants him parole:

> *Parole Hearings Man*: Ellis Boyd Redding, your files say you've served 40 years of a life sentence. Do you feel you've been rehabilitated?
>
> *Red*: Rehabilitated? Well, now let me see. You know, I don't have any idea what that means.
>
> *Parole Hearings Man*: Well, it means that you're ready to rejoin society.
>
> *Red*: I know what *you* think it means, sonny. To me it's just a made up word. A politician's word, so young fellas like yourself can wear a suit and a tie, and have a job.
>
> What do you really want to know? Am I sorry for what I did?
>
> *Parole Hearings Man*: Well, are you?
>
> *Red*: There's not a day goes by I don't feel regret. Not because I'm in here, or because you think I should. I look back on the way I was then: a young, stupid kid who committed that terrible crime. I want to talk to him. I want to try and talk some sense to him, tell him the way things are. But I can't. That kid's long gone and this old man is all that's left. I got to live with that. Rehabilitated? It's just a bullshit word. So you go on and stamp your form, sonny, and

> stop wasting my time. Because to tell you the truth, I don't give a shit.[4]

I thought it was cruel to stir up Delores's hopes by giving her a hearing every two years only to deny parole.

Another reason I was moved to take Delores's case is her husband Bill—who has stood by her all these years—paid a lawyer more than $50,000 to draft a letter for the last parole hearing. Not only did the lawyer bill for her time, she charged for every soda and candy bar she shared with Delores during the few times they met. One itemized bill included 50 cents for half a Snickers bar. It made me feel ashamed of my profession.

We hoped the third time would be the charm and put together a detailed parole petition. We prepared Delores for the hearing, pushing her to dig deeper on tough questions. We talked about "dissociation"—which might explain why she had no clear recollection of what she was doing at the time of the baby's death. We helped her to articulate what might have been going on.

This time Delores was denied parole because she "posed a danger to society" and her release would "diminish the seriousness of her crime"—even though these were the factors underlying the sentence she had already served.

We are in the process of appealing the parole board's decision. Delores knows not to be hopeful but she can't help it. She doesn't want to die in prison.

* * *

James pled guilty to murder. He regrets what he did. He knew the woman he killed, and not just as a drug associate. She was 25 years old. He had bought presents for her kids once. He wishes he could turn back the clock, make different choices. He says it all happened so fast, not exactly how the prosecution claims but close enough: an associate picked him up saying there was trouble, they confronted the woman and a man, a fight broke out, James pulled out his knife, and there was blood.

James briefly considered going to trial. However, not only would several eyewitnesses have easily identified him and his codefendant—the incident happened in broad daylight—but the prosecution would have offered evidence of prior drug-related crimes, including that the codefendant had previously beaten the decedent for stealing drug money. It wouldn't have gone well.

James apologized to the decedent's family and his own at the sentencing hearing. His mother and grandmother wept as he was taken away.

He has now served 18 years, most of it in a remote prison hours away from his family and community. He has tried to make use of the time, reading, writing, and thinking. There aren't many programs in his prison. He has found God, but is reticent about it—perhaps he senses my resistance. Now approaching middle age, he says he is a different man than the "knucklehead" who committed the crime. His favorite movie is *Shawshank Redemption*, his favorite passage when Red talks about wanting to talk sense to his younger self.

Soon he will be eligible for release, facing parole officials who will determine whether he will have a hearing every couple of years or be set free. If he gets out he would like to work with young people to help them to avoid the mistakes he made.

People in Trouble

These are three current clients. There have been many before them and hopefully many to come. These clients happen to be convicted prisoners serving lengthy sentences instead of defendants facing trial, but I would have gladly represented them at trial. Like most defenders, I represent "these people" precisely because they are *people*—people in trouble. They may have done a dreadful thing, but there is more to them than this thing they did—and almost always a story behind it.

The truth is I am drawn to people in trouble. Maybe this is because I had a little sister who was often in trouble. Once, in kindergarten, she was finger-painting. When it was time to clean up and move to the next activity, my sister kept painting, ignoring the teacher. The teacher told my sister to put the paints away. My sister kept painting. When the teacher approached, my sister picked up her paint-soaked hands and wiped them on the teacher's dress.

I grew up intervening on my sister's behalf. Sometimes I literally fought for her. There was a red-haired boy named Alan who, in second grade, called my sister a name. I gave him a bloody lip, which got me sent to the principal's office. This was my first and only visit to the principal. It was worth it.

I haven't punched anyone since. I tend to fight my battles in court.[5]

From that point on, it wasn't a great leap to others in trouble. I mean "trouble" broadly—not just the kind my sister got in (she went on to earn a master's degree in social service administration and works with the disabled), or the kind that lands people in the criminal justice system. I feel for people in difficulty or distress. It doesn't matter who they are. The fact that they are in trouble is what makes me want to defend them.

I confess that there is some irony here because patience is generally not my strong suit. I can be brusque. I have many more flaws: I can be a smart aleck; I don't suffer fools gladly;[6] I have a temper. If I am any guide, you don't need to be the nicest person to want to help people in trouble.

I seem to broadcast a certain receptiveness to trouble. I am regularly accosted by people with problems—on the street, in the subway, at the grocery store. I don't know exactly what I'm doing to invite this, but it is multiplied many times in the courthouse: the anxious person with a summons, subpoena, or son in jail manages to find me.

With people in criminal trouble there is built-in drama: something happened and something else will happen to resolve it one way or another. It doesn't need to be a serious or high-profile crime for there to be a good story—a gripping tale of comedy and tragedy.

A student and I recently represented a man I'll call Lester Johnson, who was accused of shoplifting a pair of electric clippers from a CVS pharmacy. Even though the crime was captured on videotape, Mr.Johnson refused a plea deal and insisted on going to trial. He was 49 years old. He had been in trouble in his youth, but not for years. He did a stupid, impetuous thing, but thought the store should have let him go when they recovered the clippers. He understood the system well enough to know that sometimes even strong cases fall apart: witnesses fail to appear, evidence is lost. He wanted a trial or dismissal.

The trial date happened to fall on Mr. Johnson's birthday.

When the government declared it was ready—the store security guard was present, videotape in hand—Mr. Johnson was unmoved. He was ready, too. It was unclear to me whether this was a matter of principle—the government should have to prove its case—or he had backed himself into a corner by maintaining he wanted a trial.

I tried to uncover exactly what his objectives were. We didn't have much time. We also didn't have much privacy; as often happens, we talked in the hall just outside the courtroom. The judge had given the case a brief recess and would recall us soon.

Although the original deal was off the table, Mr. Johnson still had the option of pleading guilty rather than go to trial. The judge who would hear the trial or plea was someone I'd appeared before many times. He was fair-minded. If Mr. Johnson pled guilty and expressed regret, I believed he would be sentenced to no more than a year of probation. But a pointless, time-consuming trial would test the judge's goodwill.

I explained this to Mr. Johnson. I told him we were prepared to go to trial, but he should understand that a trial here would be more like a "slow guilty plea." If Mr. Johnson's objective was to avoid jail, he should plead guilty. If his objective was to have his "day in court" no matter the consequences, he should go to trial. I acknowledged that he might still receive probation if convicted at trial.

He remained adamant. We went back and forth, but, in the end, I told him it was his decision and we would go to trial.

I went to check on a case in another courtroom. By the time I returned, things had changed drastically. A busload of middle-school children had suddenly descended upon the courtroom where the shoplifting trial would occur. There must have been 40 kids on some sort of field trip.

I grabbed Mr. Johnson and threw all that client-centered counseling[7] to the wind. Forget trial, I said. There's no way the judge won't make an example of you in front of all those kids. He'll use you to teach them not to shoplift. He'll talk about how we all suffer when people steal—shops have to hire security, consumers pay higher prices, there is greater surveillance. But if you plead guilty—if you "man up" and take responsibility for your actions—the judge will be generous. He will show those kids that judges have a heart.

I didn't give him much of a choice; he went with the plea. Mr. Johnson was so good during the plea and sentencing—he was honest and forthcoming, made no excuses, said he was ashamed of himself, and swore this would never happen again—the judge gave him only six months nonreporting probation.

When it was over, he threw his arms around me. He said he couldn't thank me enough for saving his fiftieth birthday.

Poor People, Black People, and Underdogs

Most people accused and convicted of crime are poor, a disproportionate number nonwhite.[8] This is a vivid fact in courtrooms, jails, and prisons across the country. It's been that way for a long time. The stunning news is there are now more black people under the control of the criminal justice system than were enslaved in 1850.[9]

I often tell students that I became a criminal lawyer because I read the book *To Kill a Mockingbird*—and saw the movie—too many times as an impressionable child. For me, there is no more compelling figure than Atticus Finch, the archetypal criminal lawyer defending a poor black man charged with a serious crime. Of course, Finch's client happened to be innocent.

Whether our clients are guilty or innocent, criminal defenders are, by and large, poverty lawyers: we represent the poor. We advocate for the least among us—those who live at the margins of society with the fewest resources. Too often, when accused or convicted of crime, these are "throw-away people."[10]

I have never known poverty in any immediate sense; to the contrary, I grew up with all kinds of advantages and opportunities. My own life could not be more different from my clients' lives. Still, I am drawn to the poor because no one should be destitute, lacking decent food, housing, schools, jobs, and medical care in the wealthiest nation on earth. I feel implicated by the inequality and unfairness of this.

For inspiration, I look to Martin Luther King: "I choose to identify with the underprivileged. I choose to identify with the poor. I choose to give my life for the hungry. I choose to give my life for those who have been left out of the sunlight of opportunity. I choose to live for and with those who find themselves seeing life as a long and desolate corridor with no exit sign."[11] And I also look to Eugene Debs: "Years ago I recognized my kinship with all living beings, and I made up my mind that I was not one bit better than the meanest on earth... [W]hile there is a lower class, I am in it, and while there is a criminal element, I am of it, and while there is a soul in prison, I am not free."[12]

Although I think of myself as a poverty lawyer, I confess that I am also drawn to any underdog—the little guy not the big one, David not Goliath, the Cubs not the Yankees. I often tell students that growing up a Chicago Cubs fan probably helped pave my life path.

Underdogs are not necessarily poor or black. Ronnie and Delores are white and were some version of middle class before their incarceration. But neither is college-educated nor a skilled worker—indeed, Ronnie has never held a job outside the prison walls. Neither will have an easy time on the outside if they ever get out.

There is something exhilarating about fighting for the underdog in criminal court: the stakes are high, the battle hard-fought, the outcome uncertain. The lines are also refreshingly clear: defenders fight for the accused or convicted against the state. It's the *good fight*.

What's more, we have to be that much better—tougher, smarter, more creative—in order to level the playing field. As one writer notes: "It's always a stacked deck for the State and often the defense lawyer's very best work is simply not enough to overcome the power and the might."[13] Losing is a fact of life for defenders; you have to learn to live with it. It is a terrible thing to have a human being under your care carted off to spend years in a cage or worse. But sometimes you can literally beat the government—by obtaining an acquittal at trial, getting a client into a diversionary program, winning a pretrial motion, obtaining a lenient sentence.

Moreover, if you actually win at trial—especially on behalf of a factually guilty client—you're a genius. You've accomplished a remarkable feat of derring-do. You are greeted back at the office with backslaps and high-fives. And if you don't win, there are ready condolences: the evidence was overwhelming; nobody could have won; you tried the hell out of the case; the jury had no choice but to convict.

GUILTY PEOPLE

I like guilty people. I do. I can't help myself. I prefer people who are flawed and complicated and do bad things to those who are irreproachable and uncomplicated and do the right thing. Flawed people are more interesting.

Take, for example, a recent client I'll call Renee Cooper. Ms. Cooper was African-American, in her mid-fifties, obese, toothless, and always fretting about something—how she would get to court, how she would get to the mental health clinic, the long lines at drug testing, various family problems. Ms. Cooper had been in and out of trouble much of her life. She had a long "sheet" consisting mostly of petty offenses like drug possession and prostitution, but she had also done time for selling drugs. She was doing well on parole when she "caught" a new prostitution charge.[14]

The facts of the case were memorable and not in dispute: Ms. Cooper had offered to perform oral sex on an undercover police officer in exchange for fried chicken. Ms. Cooper was only slightly humiliated to have been arrested under these circumstances. As far as she was concerned, she was hungry and a blow job in exchange for dinner was not a bad trade. But the arrest was a problem. It was a violation of her parole and meant she had to go to court on the new case.

We tried hard to get her to complete a mental health diversionary program—a "therapeutic," treatment-oriented alternative to criminal prosecution—so that Ms. Cooper might avoid a new conviction and parole violation. But she missed meetings, tested positive for drugs or "water loaded" before testing, and otherwise failed to comply with the requirements of diversion. So the mental health judge put her back on the regular criminal calendar.

This was not a triable case and Ms. Cooper knew it. Her plan was to plead guilty and throw herself on the mercy of the court. She didn't want to go to jail. By some miracle, her parole officer took pity on her and did not "violate her" for the new crime. So the only thing we had to worry about was whether the judge before whom Ms. Cooper was scheduled to appear would send her to jail for doing something as desperate as offering a blow job for fried chicken—assuming she was going to continue to test "dirty" or otherwise fall short on pretrial release.

I got a kick out of Ms. Cooper. She always greeted me with a big bear hug. She called me "Miss Abbe." She was funny and charming. She said she had heard of me, that I was known as a great lawyer. I doubted this.

Let me try to explain what I mean when I say "I like guilty people." I don't mean to be glib. Of course, there are crimes so cruel and depraved they turn my stomach. I think of child abduction-captivity-rape cases, certain hate crime, and cases featuring gratuitous meanness and violence. It is hard not to feel for the victims. It is hard not to feel revulsion toward the perpetrators.

When I say I like guilty people, I mean the vast majority of my clients, who have committed crimes for a variety of reasons but who are not evil.

This may be what every defender says: *My* clients aren't wicked, but damaged, deprived, or in distress. The reasons for their criminal conduct are both complex and simple: growing up in abusive or neglectful homes, falling prey to drugs or alcohol or gangs, being young and impetuous and lacking in judgment and resources, having cognitive or mental health problems, losing control in a moment of rage, making bad choices in a bad moment.

For the most part, my clients feel remorseful and ashamed—at least by the time they get to sentencing. If they don't or can't feel remorse it is generally not a matter of "character," but conditions and context. As famed criminal lawyer Clarence Darrow said: "We are all poor, blind creatures bound hand and foot by the invisible chains of heredity and environment, doing pretty much what we have to do in a barbarous and cruel world. That's about all there is to any court case."[15]

Moreover, as Professor Barbara Babcock has noted, the "image of the defense lawyer who uses daring courtroom skills and legal technicalities to free a homicidal maniac . . . is a fantasy almost never realized."[16] These cases are hard to win. Most plead out.

Still, I don't want to duck the question. I am often asked about what sorts of clients or cases I could not defend. It's a fair question—a subset of the familiar cocktail party question: How can you represent those people? Although I have never turned down a court appointment based on the nature of the case, some cases are harder than others, and some I wouldn't be eager to undertake. But I think I could find a way to zealously defend pretty much anyone.

The only category of criminal defendants I won't represent is police officers accused of brutality or corruption. This is purely out of loyalty to my client base. I prefer to leave these clients to others.

Ms. Cooper, the woman accused of prostitution, was ultimately placed on probation notwithstanding her less than perfect performance on pretrial release. The judge said the important thing was she had no new arrests. I think I wasn't the only one charmed by Ms. Cooper.

Ronnie says he did a terrible thing when he was 16 that he cannot undo. He wishes he could. He doesn't know why he did it; it still feels unreal. He understands why he is being punished: he destroyed two families—his neighbor's and his own. He has found some solace in his Christian faith because it holds out the promise of forgiveness.

Delores has no memory of hurting any of her babies. She has come to accept that she must have ended the life of the one child for which she was convicted. She feels sorrow, regret, and bewilderment. The bewilderment is not helpful, she realizes. It does not help to call the crime "inexplicable," a tragedy she cannot explain.

James says he will have to live with his crime for the rest of his life; it will always be part of him. He longs for forgiveness but is not sure he deserves it.

The idea of forgiveness as a key defender sensibility is intriguing. I think defenders have to have a capacity for compassion—no matter what a client is accused of—and be able to take in and respect the client, all of which might include some measure of forgiveness. However, there might be a paradox here. Some of us are more forgiving of clients for serious wrongdoing than friends and family for petty slights.

Defenders are also genuinely interested in the people we represent. We need to understand them—in a forgiving sort of way. As one of his biographers notes, Clarence Darrow "sought to make even the most hideous of crimes comprehensible . . . [t]here were no moral absolutes, no truth, no justice . . . only mercy."[17] As Darrow himself said:

> Strange as it may seem, I grew to like to defend men and women charged with crime. It soon came to be something more than the winning or losing of a case. I sought to learn why one goes one way and another takes an entirely different road. I became vitally interested in the causes of human conduct. This meant more than the quibbling with lawyers and juries . . . I was dealing with life, with its hopes and fears, its aspirations and despairs. With me it was going to the foundation of motive and conduct and adjustments for human beings, instead of blindly talking of hatred and vengeance, and that subtle, indefinable quality that men call "justice" and of which nothing really is known.[18]

Again, there are crimes that sicken me. Over the years there have been a handful of cases that have tested me: vulnerable victims, especially cruel crimes. But I strongly believe that everyone has a right to be defended. And, whatever the peculiar makeup is of a defense lawyer, I seem well suited for the task.

Also, like most defenders, I tend to believe in my clients, no matter what they may have done—in their humanity, their essential worth as a person—and want to get them off. Their guilt becomes a nonissue. Moreover, by the time of trial, I have usually convinced myself that they are not guilty at all.

Frankly, most defenders would take a guilty client over an innocent one any day. Defending the guilty is tough enough. There is nothing more "grueling," "frightening," or "desperate" than defending an innocent.[19]

Challenging Authority

The opportunity to challenge authority on behalf of another—and the duty to do so—is oddly freeing. It doesn't feel that way on my own behalf. Then I fold like a cheap tent. But for a client, I am easily indignant. I tone it down because those feelings are not necessarily effective advocacy. But I am happy to take on virtually anyone for a client.

People with authority seldom wield it well. This may be especially true in the criminal justice system. Even the judges and prosecutors I like—and there is a small handful—can't help becoming arrogant. This is probably an occupational hazard: they hold the keys and the rest of us are supplicants. It goes to their heads.

Among the most irritating authority figures are those with a tiny pocket of power who feel compelled to wield it: rude and unhelpful court clerks, imperious court bailiffs, disagreeable corrections staff. Are officious and self-important people drawn to these jobs or do the jobs make them officious and self-important?

When I visited Ronnie for the first time, I did the usual due diligence. I had never been to this prison before and wanted no problem getting in. Every prison has its own rules and regulations: some have limited hours; some don't let you wear certain clothing or colors; some don't allow you to give anything to or receive anything from prisoners, even legal documents. I was from out of state and wanted to make sure my bar card would be honored.

I telephoned the prison warden's office. The clinic office manager made a similar call to double-check. A postgraduate fellow working with me did his own checking. We reviewed the visiting rules on line. We were all assured there would be no problem.

The fellow and I got to the prison—about an hour and a half drive—on the Friday morning of a holiday weekend. We got there early because my son was playing in a baseball tournament later that day that I wanted to attend. When we walked into the outer room of the visiting area everything looked as it should, except for one thing. Taped to the metal detector was a flyer that read:

> YOU WILL RECEIVE TWO ATTEMPTS TO PASS THROUGH THE METAL DETECTOR MACHINE. IF YOU DO NOT CLEAR THE MACHINE YOU WILL BE PROHIBITED FROM VISITING.

Now, here was the problem: I was wearing an underwire bra. This sometimes sets off metal detectors. I was perfectly prepared to be "wanded"—to have one of the corrections officers use a handheld detecting wand—or hand-searched, if the detector signaled the presence of metal. This is what happens in court and other jails and prisons. But I had never encountered a jail or prison that relied entirely on a machine. Frankly, my dental work might set the thing off.

I shared my concern with the corrections officer in charge of the visiting room. I told the officer that I had contacted the warden and asked whether there was anything unusual about getting into this prison and had not been told about this metal detector rule. The corrections officer said that, in fact, the flyer taped to the machine was wrong and visitors were entitled to only *one* pass through the metal detector and if it went off the visitor would be prohibited from entering the prison.

I asked to see a supervisor.

While I was waiting, a large, heavily tattooed woman in her thirties and her six-year-old daughter arrived in the visiting area. They were coming to see the woman's fiancé. (In jails, prisons, and courthouses, everyone is suddenly a "fiancé.") An older woman was with them—maybe the fiancé's mother. The little girl and older woman sailed through the metal detector with no problem. But it went off when the tattooed woman walked through. She protested that she had no metal on her of any kind and had driven four hours to get there. The officer in charge was unmoved and said she would not be allowed in.

The woman sat down and wept. After a few minutes she whimpered, "Please. Please let me in." The officer ignored her. She wept some more and repeated her plea for admittance. This crying and begging went on for some time. It was distressing to me but seemed to have no effect on the officer.

Eventually a supervisor came. She said I might be getting worked up for no reason and suggested I remove the jewelry I had on—a couple of silver rings, small silver earrings—and see what happens. She said the other officer was wrong about getting only one try, that I was entitled to two times through, just like the flyer said. "Okay," I said, and did as she suggested. But the machine buzzed when I walked through.

I turned to the supervisor. "What now?" I asked.

"You're not getting in with that bra," she said.

So I walked out to the parking lot, took my bra off—to the enjoyment of the man sitting in a car next to mine—and threw it in my trunk. Then I walked back to the visiting area. I was met by the fellow who had accompanied me. "You won't believe this," he said. "What?" I said. He looked like he didn't want to tell me. "Now they're not going to let you in because you're not wearing proper undergarments."

You can't make this stuff up.

I walked back into the visiting area. I wanted to say any number of things but the only sign as prominent as the one on the metal detector was one that read:

> ANY PROFANITY OR ABUSIVE LANGUAGE DIRECTED AT CORRECTIONS STAFF WILL RESULT IN LOSS OF VISITING PRIVILEGES.

So I held my tongue. I asked whether they were trying to humiliate me. I asked to see another supervisor. And then another.

I would have left except that Ronnie was expecting us. He hadn't seen a lawyer in 25 years. I couldn't bear to disappoint him.

Eventually we got in to see him. I was hopelessly late to my son's tournament.

Worse still were the conditions of the visit. Legal visits at this prison were conducted by telephone in a booth with a Plexiglas screen between the prisoner and attorney. There was no physical contact whatsoever. I don't know why my bra was so important under these circumstances.

But it's a good story and it makes the point about how defenders have to constantly take on authority.

It is also a sobering lesson about prisons. If this is how corrections officers treat 50-year-old lawyers—and they also knew I was a law professor—imagine how they treat people on the inside. My clients don't stand a chance.

What's Hard about It

For all of these reasons—I can find the person behind the crime, I am drawn to people in trouble, underdogs, and the guilty, and I enjoy challenging authority—I am what might be called a "natural defender." But that doesn't mean there's nothing hard about it.

The hardest part is the randomness of justice and pervasiveness of injustice. Too much depends on the luck of the draw: which lawyer, prosecutor, judge, or jury you happen to get. And too much depends on the resources of the accused. Fifty years after *Gideon v. Wainwright* established the right to counsel in criminal cases,[20] there is still a different quality of justice for the rich and poor in much of the country—largely because we do not sufficiently fund indigent defense.[21]

Prosecutors have too much power and can be smug. Judges have too much power and can be peevish. Defenders have to play with both of them.

Then there is the harshness of punishment, often after terribly harsh lives. The United States currently locks up more people than any other nation on earth,[22] and locks them up for longer than most. In a time of mass incarceration, we also have more people under the control of the criminal justice system than any other nation—in jail or prison or on probation or parole. The total figure is staggering—larger than the size of many countries.[23]

I have already acknowledged that some especially ugly cases can also make the work difficult.

At the risk of sounding shallow, I am going to offer one more thing that has become increasingly hard: the endless waiting in court, at the jail, at prisons—usually after a desperate rush to be on time. My irritation at this obviously can't compare to the routine indignities and injustice my clients endure—after all, they are usually waiting too, in a cell block. But the older I get the harder it is.

Conclusion

In the course of writing this chapter, I accompanied a family member who was interviewing divorce lawyers. Her husband had walked out after nearly 30 years of marriage. She was devastated, in need of a good lawyer, and thought I might be helpful. When we met the first lawyer, I introduced myself as a criminal defense lawyer. My relation sobbed through the meeting, collecting herself only to apologize for not being able to collect herself. At the end, the lawyer turned to me and said, "I don't know how you do the work you do."

"Likewise!" I said.

In her classic article on criminal defense, Barbara Babcock concludes that the real question is not "How can you defend the guilty?" but "Why *don't* you defend the guilty?" She means two things by this: first, that lawyers who are supposed to be defending the accused often fail to do so because of crushing caseloads and lack of resources, and second, there should be more lawyers doing criminal defense. Babcock believes that the criminal justice system and the legal profession would be better off if more lawyers did criminal work.[24]

All of this is true. We need more lawyers proudly committed to what I like to call "The Guilty Project." But I would add one more thing: There is nothing more stimulating, fun,[25] challenging, heartbreaking, and rewarding than representing people accused or convicted of crime.

Notes

1. Names of clients and case details have been changed to protect client privacy. The essential details of the stories in this chapter are true.
2. Clarence Darrow, *The Story of My Life* (New York: Da Capo Press, 1996); Alan Dershowitz, *The Best Defense* (New York: Vintage Books, 1983); David Feige, *Indefensible: One Lawyer's Journey into the Inferno of American Justice* (New York: Little, Brown, and Company, 2006); James S. Kunen, *How Can You Defend Those People? The Making of a Criminal Lawyer* (New York: Random House, 1983); Kenneth Mann, *Defending White Collar Crime: A Portrait of Attorneys at Work* (New Haven: Yale University Press, 1985); George Sharswood, *An Essay on Professional Ethics*, 2nd ed. (Philadelphia: T. & J. W. Johnson, 1860); Seymour Wishman, *Confessions of a Criminal Lawyer* (New York: Times Books, 1981); Barbara A. Babcock, "Defending the Guilty," *Cleveland State Law Review* 32 (1983–1984); Randy Bellows, "Notes of a Public Defender," in *The Social Responsibilities of Lawyers*, ed. Philip B. Heymann and Lance Liebman (Foundation Press, 1988), 69; Charles Curtis, "The Ethics of Advocacy," *Stanford Law Review* 4 (1951); John Kaplan, "Defending Guilty People," *Bridgeport Law Review* 7 (1986); James Mills, "I Have Nothing to do with Justice," *Life*, March 12, 1971, 65; John B. Mitchell, "The Ethics of the Criminal Defense Attorney—New Answers to Old Questions," *Stanford Law Review* 32 (1980); Charles J. Ogletree, Jr., "Beyond Justifications: Seeking Motivations to Sustain Public Defenders," *Harvard Law Review* 106 (1993).
3. Abbe Smith, *Case of a Lifetime* (New York: Palgrave Macmillan, 2008) (telling the story of Patsy Kelly Jarrett, who was wrongly convicted of robbery and murder in upstate New York in 1976).
4. *The Shawshank Redemption*, directed by Frank Darabont, (Castle Rock Entertainment, 1994). The movie is based on a Stephen King novella.

Stephen King, "Rita Hayworth and Shawshank Redemption" in *Different Seasons* (New York: Viking, 1982).

5. Monroe H. Freedman and Abbe Smith, *Understanding Lawyers' Ethics*, 4th ed. (New Providence, NJ: LexisNexis, 2010), 22 ("The legal system... provides a socially controlled, non-violent process of dispute resolution. Lawyers play an indispensable part in that constructive social process.").
6. I have excellent company in this particular flaw. John A. Farrell, *Clarence Darrow: Attorney for the Damned* (New York: Doubleday, 2011), 9 (Clarence Darrow's most famous client Nathan Leopold saying, "the only things Darrow hated were... cruelty, narrow-mindedness, or obstinate stupidity").
7. Katherine R. Kruse, "Fortress in the Sand: The Plural Values of Client-Centered Representation," *Clinical Law Review* 12 (2006) (discussing the history, development, and theory of client-centered lawyering).
8. According to the Justice Department, more than 40 percent of the US prison and jail population is African-American. Heather C. West, *Prison Inmates at Midyear 2009—Statistical Tables* (Bureau of Justice Statistics, June 2010), 19, http://bjs.ojp.usdoj.gov/content/pub/pdf/pim09st.pdf (reporting that as of June, 2009, of the 2,297,500 people incarcerated in state and federal prisons or jails, 841,000 are black men, and 64,800 are black women). According to the latest census, African-Americans make up 12.6 percent of the US population. "USA State & County QuickFacts," *U.S. Census Bureau*, last modified June 7, 2012, http://quickfacts.census.gov/qfd/states/00000.html.
9. Michelle Alexander, *The New Jim Crow: Mass Incarceration in the Age of Color-Blindness* (New York: The New Press, 2010), 175.
10. See Liliana Segura, "Throw-away People: Will Teens Sent to Die in Prison Get a Second Chance?," *The Nation*, May 28, 2012, 11 (noting that Justice Ruth Bader Ginsburg suggested in oral argument in *Miller v. Alabama,* 132 S.Ct. 548 (2011) that sentencing children to die in prison renders them "throw-away people").
11. Martin Luther King, "Sermon to Ebenezer Church," (lecture, Ebenezer Church, Atlanta, GA, August 28, 1966) in *Martin Luther King, Jr.: A Life,* ed. Marshall Frady (New York: Viking, 2002), 191.
12. Eugene Debs, "Statement to the Court after Being Convicted of Violating the Sedition Act," (lecture, US District Court for the Northern District of Ohio, Cleveland, Ohio, September 18, 1918) in Max Eastman, "The Trial of Eugene Debs," *The Liberator* 1 (1918): 8–9, http://www.marxists.org/history/usa/parties/spusa/1918/1100-eastman-debstrial.pdf.
13. Michael Connelly, *The Fifth Witness* (New York: Little, Brown, and Company, 2011), 406.
14. See Paul Butler, *Let's Get Free: A Hip-Hop Theory of Justice* (New York: The New Press, 2009), 132 (noting that the expression "I caught a case"—popularized through hip-hop culture—reflects the arbitrary nature of criminal justice: a person catches a case in the same way as he or she might catch a cold).

15. Farrell, *Clarence Darrow*, 9.
16. Babcock, "Defending the Guilty," 182.
17. Farrell, *Clarence Darrow*, 9.
18. Darrow, *The Story of My Life*, 75–76.
19. Babcock, "Defending the Guilty," 180.
20. Gideon v. Wainwright, 372 U.S. 335 (1963). For a definitive account of the case, see Anthony Lewis, *Gideon's Trumpet* (New York: Random House, 1964).
21. For background, see *Justice Denied: America's Continuing Neglect of Our Constitutional Right to Counsel* (Washington, DC: The Constitution Project, 2009), http://www.constitutionproject.org/pdf/139.pdf (last visited Aug. 27, 2011) (blue ribbon commission reporting on the current state of indigent criminal defense in the US).
22. The United States leads the world in incarceration with 2.3 million people currently in the nation's prisons or jails, a 500 percent increase over the past 30 years. "Incarceration," *The Sentencing Project*, accessed August 14, 2012, http://www.sentencingproject.org/template/page.cfm?id=107. As of December, 2009, 1,524,513 people were in prison in the United States, and 760,400 people in jail. "Correctional Populations in the United States 2009," *Bureau of Justice Statistics*, modified August 14, 2012, http://bjs.ojp.usdoj.gov/content/glance/corr2tab.cfm. Our incarceration rate is six times greater than Canada, eight times greater than France, and twelve times greater than Japan. David Cole, "Can Our Shameful Prisons be Reformed?" *New York Review of Books*, November 19, 2009, http://www.nybooks.com/articles/archives/2009/nov/19/can-our-shameful-prisons-be-reformed/.
23. "Correctional Populations," *Bureau of Justice Statistics* (reporting that a total of 7.2 million people are in jail or prison or on probation or parole). For more information, see also, "One in 31: The Long Reach of American Corrections," (Washington, DC: Pew Center on the States, 2009), 1, http://www.pewstates.org/uploadedFiles/PCS_Assets/2009/PSPP_1in31_report_FINAL_WEB_3-26-09.pdf:With far less notice, the number of people on probation or parole has skyrocketed to more than 5 million, up from 1.6 million just 25 years ago. This means that one in 45 adults in the United States is now under criminal justice supervision in the community, and that combined with those in prison and jail, a stunning one in every 31 adults, or 3.2 percent, is under some form of correctional control. The rates are drastically elevated for men (1 in 18) and blacks (1 in 11) and are even higher in some high-crime inner-city neighborhoods.
24. Babcock, "Defending the Guilty," 182–184.
25. By far the most fun I ever had as a lawyer was when I was a public defender. I have never had better colleagues, or felt a greater sense of purpose, than when I was at the Defender Association of Philadelphia. There were also a lot of laughs.

13

Fair Play

Robin Steinberg

The Eternal Question

How can you defend "those people?" Like every public defender, I have been asked that question at parties, holiday meals, and family gatherings. My responses range from the frivolous to the philosophical, and from the purely political to the deeply personal. I confess that after 30 years of being a public defender—from trial attorney at The Legal Aid Society to the founder and director of The Bronx Defenders—the question infuriates me. It is frustrating that people single out criminal defense as a subject of moral inquiry and indignation. It is offensive that they think of my clients as "those people." And it baffles me that many questioners have never given the subject a moment's thought but seem so self-satisfied in their opinions about crime and punishment. I try to get past these feelings, and reply in a measured, thoughtful way because I believe in the importance of public education about public defense—primarily for my clients, their families, and communities, but also for those of us who defend the accused.

No matter how much practice I get, it is not an easy question to answer. There is no single sound bite. The simple explanations are intellectual, based in law and political theory. I have no trouble waxing on about the importance of a good lawyer when someone is facing incarceration or death. I can talk at length about protecting the individual against government overreaching and abuse. And I am skilled at explaining how the presumption of innocence is essential to our system of justice and how public defenders breathe life into that concept. All of the structural and political reasons for doing this work are also easy to recite: racial and economic disparity in the criminal justice system, this country's overreliance on jail and prison, our misguided "war on drugs," the growth of prosecutorial power and diminishment of individualized justice, the death of "rehabilitation," and the systemic underfunding of public defense. Increased media attention on wrongful convictions has made these things easier to explain, as have books like Michelle Alexander's "The New Jim Crow"[1] and documentaries like Ken Burns's "The Central Park Five."[2]

I offer these reasons sometimes. Frankly, they are the autopilot reply for a career defender. And there is truth in them. But they do not fully explain why I have chosen to devote my career to public defense. I have to dig deeper to come up with those reasons.

Love? Character? Family?

It is possible that I became a public defender because I fell in love with my criminal defense clinical professor in law school. I wanted to be as passionate, smart, and courageous as he was. I wanted to make a difference in peoples' lives as he did. He was a quirky, brilliant, and deeply committed defender. He was kind of a "pretrial motions" genius: no issue was too small to be scrutinized, developed, and creatively litigated. He was completely immersed in the work—he breathed it, ate it, and literally slept on it—since his platform bed was built above a filing system of case law, transcripts, and motions. He taught me that every case matters and, more importantly, that there is a *client* in every case.

Or maybe I was already a defender in my heart and was simply drawn to a kindred spirit. After all, I was always wary of power and authority. As early as elementary school, my report cards warned that I "needed improvement" in showing respect to teachers. Not only have I always been skeptical of authority, I have a visceral hatred of inequality. I can't really explain where this comes from but it's always been with me. This is so much a part of who I am, that if my favorite New York football team is winning by too much, I'll reflexively switch sides and start rooting for the losing team.

Growing up on New York's Lower East Side in the 1960s, I was a rebellious child, brimming with energy and strong convictions. My heroes were Gloria Steinem, Golda Meir, and other feminist giants I watched them bellowing into megaphones in front of the New York Public Library or leading braless women through Tompkins Square Park. I admired how outspoken, tough, and fearless these women were in their pursuit of justice and equality. Unlike the adult women I knew in my middle-class apartment complex of Peter Cooper Village, or my teachers at the local public schools, these women seemed free. They were unencumbered by the economic, political, and social barriers that existed for women at the time, and dedicated to envisioning a different world. Far from the kitchens and stoops where my mother and her friends chain-smoked cigarettes, drank bottomless cups of coffee, and whispered about their husbands' infidelities and abuses, these feminist activists inspired me to believe that my life could be different, and I could make a difference.

As a teenager, I dabbled in a wide variety of progressive causes in addition to women's rights. My childhood scrapbook—a gigantic, blue denim, three-ring binder—is filled with snapshots of me in bell-bottoms and tie-dye, at an anti-Vietnam War rally in DC, a pro-choice rally in Bryant Park, and an Earth Day celebration. Tucked into the plastic-covered sheets are frayed newspaper clippings of the Kent State massacre and the assassinations of Malcolm X, Martin Luther King, and Robert F. Kennedy. The bedroom I shared with my younger brother was covered with day glow peace signs and a poster warning that "War is Not Healthy for Children and Other Living Things."

Absorbed by the antiwar, feminist, and civil rights movements, I didn't give much thought to criminal justice. (The only exception was my obsessive love of "The Mod Squad," a television series about three counterculture juvenile delinquents, "One White, One Black and One Blond," who become an undercover police team determined to help troubled youth turn their lives around.) Although I was mugged several times—the inevitable rite of passage for a New York City kid back then—I never thought about who had committed the crime and why, or how the criminal justice system might respond. But, significantly, I never considered calling the police.

So maybe I was born to be a public defender. Then again, maybe it was all about my father.

A complicated and charismatic man, my father was the product of upwardly mobile Jewish parents. The success of the family's garment business catapulted them from the Lower East Side to the Bronx, and eventually, to buying a house on Long Island—the ultimate symbol of Jewish assimilation in mid-twentieth century New York. My father did not follow his parents' path. Instead, he used his charm and good looks to seduce a pretty, smart Catholic schoolgirl from Allentown, Pennsylvania—persuading her to convert to Judaism, marry him, move to New York City, and have two kids.

At first, love blinded my mother to the fact that my father was addicted to everything—coffee, cigarettes, gambling, risk, alcohol, and drugs. His addictions defined our family life. He became hopelessly dependent on cocaine, quaaludes, and, later, heroin. He was in and out of jail. He left us, disappearing for long periods of time, drifting in and out of our lives. Today, he would probably be diagnosed as bipolar and given medication to manage his intense, harrowing mood swings. Back then he was just my mother's heartbreak, a disappointment, and a "bad guy."

Children love what they get. And so it was for me. I couldn't deny that my father was damaged, but I refused to write him off. To my mind, his struggles meant that we needed to do more for him, we needed to try harder. If we did, then somehow, someday, he might change. I didn't believe in "bad people" then and I still don't. So when my mother moved us to California during my senior year of high school, hoping that I would simply forget about my father, I didn't. I kept in touch as best I could.

When I was accepted to the University of California, Berkeley, fulfilling my dream of being a full-fledged radical at that famed campus, he celebrated by appearing out of nowhere, somehow flush with cash. He insisted on buying me my first car. It was repossessed the next month.

After college, I moved back to New York to start law school. One November morning, as I was rushing to class, there was a knock on my tiny East Village studio apartment door. It was my father. He was in bad shape—exhausted and uncharacteristically unkempt—and carrying a few items of clothing. He needed a place to stay. I nervously told him he could stay with me as long as he wanted, on one condition: he was not allowed to bring drugs into my home. He agreed.

I left for class the following morning, and when I returned, he was gone. He never came back.

In some ways, it was the greatest act of love he had ever shown me. He knew how much my career meant to me and didn't want to jeopardize it. And he knew that he couldn't last without the drugs.

A few years later, he died of an overdose. He was 49.

In some ways, I have never stopped fighting for my father. I see glimmers of him in every client.

Am I a public defender because I had a drug-addicted father? Was I drawn to the work because I grew up idolizing radical feminists, questioning authority, and rooting for the underdog? Or was it that sexy law school professor? Any of these could explain my path, and probably all of them do. There are a thousand reasons to be drawn to the work defenders do, but, at the end of the day, the question may be beside the point. Whether it was love or politics or a potent combination, when I fell in love with public defense, I fell hard.

WHY STAY WITH IT?

It took a series of visits to the Bedford Hills Correctional Facility in Westchester County, New York, during law school to jump-start the process that would change me forever. I walked into the prison a women's rights lawyer and walked out a public defender.

It was 1980 and I had signed up for a law clinic called the "Women's Prison Project." The fact that the clinic served women in a maximum-security prison appealed to my radical side, but was largely incidental. I wanted to advocate for women wherever they were. Over the course of the year, I traveled to and from the prison, oddly located in one of the most affluent, bucolic towns in New York. Each visit drew me closer to the women I represented and the deeply personal stories they told me about their lives, families, and hopes and dreams for the future. All of the women were black, poor, and talked about being "railroaded," not just by the system, but by the lawyers sworn to defend them. Most complained that their public defenders didn't spend enough time with them, listen carefully, or care about them. Few could even name their defender or the crime they were convicted of, but each could tell me exactly how many days, months, and years they had left to serve away from their children and families. I went to that prison to empower incarcerated women, but came to realize that, as important as my work at the prison was, it was more important to keep these women from getting there. Listening to the women at Bedford Hills made me wonder who were these public defenders and why did they fail their clients so miserably? I joined New York University's criminal defense clinic to find out.

I will never forget the horror that I felt the first time I stepped into the Manhattan Criminal Court and saw the courtroom littered with people: the shackled men with bowed heads, hunched over the defense table, and the pained faces of their mothers, girlfriends, and children on the benches in the audience. The desperation and despair were palpable. I could not walk away. I knew that I wanted to be the person who stands up and fights not just for women but also for all those caught up in the criminal system.

Ever since that first day, I have never—not once—wavered in my decision to become a public defender. Every client I have met since has reinforced my path. It is the clients—their lives, their stories—that have compelled and inspired me to remain a public defender all these years.

For me, only clients can do that.

Of course every client is different. But what they all share is poverty and the enormous life challenges that accompany it: the deprivation and marginalization borne of insufficient housing, failing schools, inadequate healthcare, and unhealthy food. Our clients experience abuse and trauma from repeated exposure to violence, encounters with hostile police, racism, and family disintegration. Their communities are underresourced, overpoliced, and isolated. Life expectancies are short, tragedy ever-present, and hope elusive.

Despite this, I am constantly amazed that clients are able to get up every morning and face another day. I don't know how they don't sink into complete despair. I marvel at how they find reasons to hope. In this way, clients inspire me. They keep striving for better lives, some semblance of family, some feeling of connection. I am honored when they allow me to be part of that connection.

We meet our clients in their worst moments. They have been arrested, shackled, forced into a police car, taken to a police precinct, and locked in a cell where they wait for hours, sometimes days. Separated from family, friends, and community, they are harshly interrogated and subjected to degrading conditions of confinement. They are not only facing loss of liberty, but also the prospect of losing their kids, apartment, job, public benefits, and immigration status. Some are withdrawing from drugs or haven't received the medication they need. Others are battling mental illness. Everyone locked in a cage experiences some combination of depression, anger, anxiety, and fear.

There is an intimacy between lawyer and client when public defenders do their job well. We delve deeply into our clients' lives, learning about their childhoods and families, often becoming close to family members and partners. In my role as their public defender, I can often provide a client with a meaningful human bond even though the clients don't choose us to represent them. Instead, they are forced to place a tremendous amount of hope and trust in us out of need. Their blind faith in me and my abilities compels me to fight as hard as I can for every client. It takes courage for my clients to share some of the most personal details of their lives with me, and, in those moments of trust, I can't help but become devoted to them. When you open yourself up to the pain and suffering of another person—when you step into his or her shoes even for a moment—you can't help but want to do something. It's not out of guilt, a damaged father, or even (in retrospect) misguided love, it is simply a deep and unavoidable sense of shared humanity.

But There's More . . .

If personal reasons guided me to the work, and clients drew me in, what keeps me waking up and raring to go some 30 years later, is stunningly simple: unfairness. I hate unfairness and always have. It makes my blood boil. It is ironic that someone who hates unfairness as much as I do would work in the profession most steeped in it. Or perhaps it is inevitable.

Unfairness pervades our criminal justice system. We take the poorest, saddest, and most vulnerable people in our society and put them in cages. Once they are there, we offer few services, little education, and next to no assistance for a successful reentry into the outside world. The American criminal justice system applies unfair rules, in unfair ways, to those every other system in our society have already failed. The hardest thing about being a public defender is the relentless, pervasive, and institutionalized unfairness.

There is unfairness in the power disparity between those charged with crime and a prosecutorial system armed with cops, judges, and jails. Maybe this is where my years at Berkeley—reading the likes of Karl Marx, Simone de Beauvoir, Toni Morrison, Paulo Freire, and Maya Angelou—have paid off. There is no other way to understand what is happening in our criminal justice system other than as a gross abuse of power. There is no fair fight; it's a slaughter. And it makes picking sides easy for me. I will stand for the powerless against the powerful, the poor against the privileged, and the marginalized against the dominant. At the very least I will make it difficult for the other side.

Whatever the unique confluence of circumstance and Constitution that got me here, I am lucky to have found a job in which, every day, I get to stand next to a client facing down the terrifying power of the criminal justice machine. That machine is going to have to go through me to get to them. That I can spend my breath and fury and anger in defense of a person facing those odds and who—maybe, just maybe—will get the kind of second chance that all of us deserve, is a miraculous gift.

And that is why, even after 30 years as a public defender, I know I am truly one of the lucky ones. I have found a job where I can fight against unfairness every day, and where I arrive at work each morning with a mission. Being a public defender is not so much a job, but the place where I am truly and finally at home.

How can I defend "those people?"

How can I *not* defend those people?

NOTES

1. Michelle Alexander, *The New Jim Crow: Mass Incarceration in the Age of Color-Blindness* (New York: The New Press, 2010).
2. *The Central Park Five* (Florentine Films/PBS, 2012).

14

Defending . . . Still

Michael E. Tigar

I wrote the following chapter, *Defending*, in 1995, when I had been appointed to represent Terry Lynn Nichols in the Oklahoma bombing case. I have also recounted my experience in the Nichols trial in *Fighting Injustice* and *Trial Stories.*[1] Some of us thought, naively as it turned out, that the hysteria over that trial and the prosecutors' efforts to get a death verdict against Terry Nichols, represented a kind of high—or low—watermark in attitudes towards the right to a defense.

We had had more than the usual trouble getting a fair forum—a judge not affected by the bombing and a jury that could plausibly promise to heed the evidence. Those victories took months to achieve. In the hours and day after the bombing, a Jordanian was detained on the theory that Arabs must have done it.

When the federal jury acquitted Nichols of most of the charges against him and declined to impose a death sentence there was a public outcry tinged with a few pointed threats against the lawyers. All of this was before September 11, 2001. In the wake of those events, the executive branch and a complicit Congress moved quickly to establish "no-law zones" for suspected terrorists. And so we had rounds of litigation over the most elementary rights to judicial review of onerous confinement. A public official called for ostracism of lawyers who took up the cause of those accused and detained. A federal judge publicly derided the lawyers who were representing those imprisoned at Guantanamo.

Yet through it all, there were beacons of light and a reaffirmation of the most basic principles that guide what we do as defenders. These principles are more important today than at any past time. Robert McChesney and John Nichols recently commented on the dominant themes of political advertising, "wallowing in a sea of money, idiocy and corruption."

This is an apt description of what passes for public discourse about the most fundamental issues of our time.

But there are places where one has a chance to make rational arguments, based upon evidence and principle, and hope that they will be heeded. Those places are courtrooms where well-prepared advocates, seeking and obtaining access to the resources they need to prepare their cases, defend people whose liberty is in danger. They do so by invoking and insisting upon fundamental rights. In this sense, every case—no matter how seemingly trivial—is a public trial of social legitimacy. Learned Hand wrote:

> All governments, democracies as well as autocracies, believe that those they seek to punish are guilty; the impediment of constitutional barriers are galling to all governments when they prevent the consummation of that just purpose. But those barriers were devised and are precious because they prevent that purpose and its pursuit from passing unchallenged by the accused, and unpurged by the alembic of public scrutiny and public criticism. A society which has come to wince at such exposure of the methods by which it seeks to impose its will upon its members, has already lost the feel of freedom and is on the path towards absolutism.[2]

In the Nichols case, our first task was to recuse the Oklahoma judge who said he could preside over the trial even though his chambers were damaged in the bombing and some of his friends had been killed. Judge Richard Matsch, from Colorado, then heard our change of venue motion.

I argued:

> Governor Keating has been quoted over and over again, repeating his mantra, "We will give these people a fair trial. Oklahomans are independent. We want to make sure we've got the right people, but, if we do, they should be executed," as though the *Furman v. Georgia* gene had dropped out of his legal chromosome makeup.
>
> C. S. Lewis writes, in one of his letters in a wonderful collection that, "There are times, as for example on a dark mountain road at night, when we would give far more for a glimpse of the few feet ahead than for a vision of some far horizon."[3] The few feet ahead that we can see tell us that in this time and place, that a jury, in this city, charged with that decision, would be one as to which one can confidently say there is this reasonable likelihood of prejudice.
>
> Two roads, two roads, diverge before us, gathered as we are, with the decades of constitutional liberty piled so high, the anguish of the victims close at hand. To one of those roads we are beckoned, from sadness, to

> anger, to vengeance. Governor Keating beckons us along that road by what I suggest is deliberate design. The media have beckoned us along that road, simply by their desire to serve their market. The other road, I suggest to the Court, is the one the framers laid out for us while the memory of unfair trials in distant forums was fresh in their minds.
>
> We neither dishonor nor deny the grief and anger of the victims, nor even their cry for vengeance. Your Honor, this is my 30th year in the law, and I believe, more than ever, that when we summon someone, anyone, Terry Nichols, into court, to find out whether he's going to live or die, that it is our job to construct, where we best can, a kind of sanctuary in the jungle.[4]

Furman v. Georgia[5] was the 1972 case that first held that the death penalty, as then administered in most states, was unconstitutional. One of its basic precepts, later amplified by the Supreme Court, is that no offender, no matter how serious the crime, is "automatically" eligible for the death penalty. Rather, as the court has said, jurors are to make a "reasoned moral response" to the circumstances of the crime and of the human being who is on trial.[6] Thus, Governor Keating, a lawyer who should have known better, had called for death penalties in a way that debased a constitutional command and sought to usurp the jury's power and duty.

This chapter, therefore, was a tribute to those we are honored to defend and to our own role as defenders of an endangered system for controlling and regulating the state's power to punish. The nature and extent of danger can be measured by examining the title of this book, "How" can we represent "them?" Like the other contributors, I speak of the reasons I may decide to represent a client or to acquiesce in a court appointment. The background assumption in 1996, when I made that argument to Judge Matsch, was that if the executive branch believed Terry Nichols was a terrorist, there was broad agreement that his capital trial would be in a fair forum, before an impartial judge and jury, and with competent counsel. These legal ideas were expressed by Chief Justice Marshall in the trial of Aaron Burr for treason—that is, raising an army to topple the government.

Today, however, the executive branch executes people said to be terrorists without a judicial trial, using drone missiles. Never mind that in all the terrorism prosecutions arising from the Kenya and Tanzania embassy bombings and the World Trade Center bombing itself, no American jury has imposed a death sentence, even after a trial in civilian court. With drone missile executions, the question of "how can you represent" is pretermitted. Having killed these human beings found "guilty" by White House discussion, the government awaits the funeral and sends another drone to kill the mourners. We are then told that those executed have indeed received "due process," though not "judicial process." We are told that no civilians are killed in these strikes because any male of military age is defined as a combatant. And if innocent people are killed, there is a procedure for posthumous declarations of innocence.[7] These justifications are so ludicrous that satire is the best way of understanding them.[8] These events and policies sharpen the issues about which I wrote and give them a sense of urgency even greater than they had at that time.

* * *

DEFENDING[9]

The editors have asked for a chapter, a sort of travelogue of the distance between Austin and Oklahoma City, home and away, sanity and madness, hope and despair. They hinted vaguely that I might want to answer criticisms of my representing Terry Lynn Nichols. I am not responding to those hints, because I do not need to, at least not in a publication by and for lawyers. I was appointed by the court. Almost everyone I meet has been warm, supportive, and understanding. The man who ably keeps my boots repaired told me last week that he well understood what I was doing. "If people who get arrested did not have lawyers, then anybody the police suspect would be railroaded off to jail. It would be a police state."

By similar token, you will not find much in this chapter about the "facts" of the Oklahoma City tragedy. Trials are the place for evidence. The media, even a law review, is not the place for me to try this lawsuit.

The reader will, however, detect some passion and even anger in the words below. To accept a great challenge requires, at least for me, a passionate commitment to fulfill it. In litigation as in love, technical proficiency without passion is not wholly satisfying.

The call came on Thursday, May 11, 1995. I had spent the day talking about appellate practice at the Thurgood Marshall Building in Washington, DC. The audience members were federal public defenders, who do a difficult job with too little recognition, working every day to see that the line between the state and human liberty is drawn fairly.

Chief Judge David L. Russell of the Western District of Oklahoma had called my home. My 11-year-old daughter took the message. When I checked in from Washington National Airport, my daughter said I should call the judge.

Chief Judge Russell and former Chief Judge Lee West (before whom I had appeared some years ago) said they wanted to appoint me to represent Terry Lynn Nichols, the 41-year-old father of two who was being held as an accomplice in the April 19, 1995, Oklahoma City bombing.

I confess I had not followed the details in the media. I knew the government did not claim that Mr. Nichols was present in Oklahoma City on that day. I also knew that the case had been characterized as capital by the Attorney General and the President.

Judge Russell said he first had the idea of appointing me when he remembered a videotape of a mock closing argument in a capital case that I had done as part of the Smithsonian's annual Folklife Festival in Washington, DC, nearly a decade ago. He said he had checked me out with lawyers and judges, mentioning Judge Patrick Higginbotham of the Fifth Circuit by name.

When a judge tenders an appointment in a criminal case, only the most compelling reasons should make a lawyer try to avoid the assignment. We daily proclaim our commitment to the adversary system. While we have the right to pick and choose among clients who come to our doors, the indigent defendant facing death at the state's hands has a powerful claim on us. Were it not so, our protestations about the adversary system would crumble into hypocrisy and cynicism.

Judge Russell's story of how my name came to mind is probably incomplete. The Administrative Office of the US Courts has statutory responsibility for advising judges on appointments in federal capital cases, and that office has said that there was a "short list" of advocates being considered for appointment. Some lawyers had gone on national television to say they would not take such an appointment.

The charges against Mr. Nichols might make this a capital case. Hence, he is entitled to at least two experienced lead counsel. I was lucky that Ronald G. Woods, a University of Texas graduate with 30 years experience as prosecutor and defense counsel, agreed to accept appointment along with me. Ron Woods has seen law practice as few lawyers have. He was an FBI agent, an assistant district attorney, an assistant US attorney, the US attorney for the Southern District of Texas, and a lawyer in private practice. I have opposed him when he was in government service, and worked with him during his time in private practice.

During my 11 years at the University of Texas, I have been counsel in many challenging pro bono and appointed cases. Law students have worked alongside me, with the consent of the dean, and have received course credit for their work. Using pro bono cases as a learning ground for students may be reason enough to accept such responsibility. In addition, the law professor's obligation of public service demands some form of contribution to the community.

There is more. I remain a defender because I am dismayed and angered by what I see around me, and I think that as a lawyer the only way through the present terrible time is to fashion and refashion a certain image of justice.

I am not speaking now of the tragedy of April 19, 1995. I am visited every day with the sense of loss felt by all the people of Oklahoma, which is one reason I think it unfair and unreasonable to ask them to pass dispassionate judgment on those events. Nor am I conjuring up the image of the president and the attorney general rushing before the television cameras to call for the death penalty, as though no fact that could ever be found would stand in the way of deliberately taking another life as a means of doing justice for the ones already lost.

I am not talking of the storm of publicity, nor of a sense that this is a "historic" case. Every lawyer in the Oklahoma City case knows that our work will be judged, now and in time to be. It is important not to be self-conscious about that knowledge. None of us can make a bargain with history, saying, "Well, if I act in this way, can I guarantee that I will be regarded in a certain way twenty years hence?" We can only do the next right thing as best we see it. History, the past and the present, informs us, teaches us. History yet to be written cannot turn us from our honestly determined duty.

In deciding to act, one steps into a space between past and future. The past—the suffering and tragedy—are established events, to be understood as well as one can. Stepping into the moment now is a search for something called "justice." Justice or injustice, in the now and in the future, is part of a process. The past events cannot be unraveled or undone, but one can perhaps prevent people's attitudes toward those events from becoming an excuse for injustice.

I am talking of a prosaic, down-to-earth notion of justice. Something like Camus was describing when he said that our chance of salvation is to strive for justice, which is something that only the human species has devised. Justice, as Camus also reminded us, must be more than an abstract idea; it must be a reflection of compassion for one's fellow beings. In the name of *justice,* the abstract idea writ large, great wrongs have been done. Jordan and Carol Steiker have given us a compelling essay about a death row inmate weighted down by abstract and yet inhuman justice. The inmate, Karla Faye Tucker, had a T-shirt that said, "Kill them all. God will sort them out." This is one version of a cry attributed to the papal legate who presided over the massacre of some 15,000 men, women, and children at Beziers, near Marseille, in 1209. It seemed that some of these people had been adjudged (and there is the word again—derived from the same root as justice itself yet separate from it in its essence) heretics.

Today, and close by, legislators are busy terminating and trimming programs of legal assistance for the poor. The most visible casualties are the resource centers that have valiantly struggled to represent—and to help volunteer lawyers represent—defendants charged with and convicted of capital crimes. The most despised, the most endangered defendants may be without counsel. Yet their cases, as history teaches us without any reason for doubt, are the ones most likely to have excited governmental passion in ways that make judgment fallible.

Do you doubt this statement about fallible judgment? Consider the Haymarket trial, in which innocent men were railroaded, and only those who escaped the noose could be pardoned years later. Sacco and Vanzetti were swept up in the xenophobic hysteria fomented by the federal government, most visibly in the person of Attorney General A. Mitchell Palmer. More recently, a Cleveland auto worker spent years in a death cell convicted of being Ivan the Terrible of Treblinka; not only was he innocent of that charge, but our own government had defrauded the federal courts to get him extradited to Israel for trial.

In each of these cases, there were victims of crime. It was no honor to them, nor proper solace to those who mourned them, that their deaths became an excuse for crimes committed in the name of the state—in the name of justice.

Yet, in cases like these that may arise in the future, and that are now pending, there are not to be lawyers, unless something is done very quickly.

This is not to speak of the civil claims of people who simply want access to the justice system to present or protect their theoretically valid rights. These folks are to lose many of the lawyers provided by legal services offices.

In Alabama, the newspaper reports, the chain gang is back. There is no social need for it. The state gets all the gravel for its roads from commercial quarries. But rocks are being shipped at state expense to prisons, so that men in prison can be chained together and break the rocks into smaller rocks. Nobody has any proof that this degradation of humans deters anyone from crime, and there is no hint that the rock-breakers acquire a skill or do some useful labor.

Alabama's atavistic adventure is simply one example in a growing list of savageries committed in the name of justice. In 1993, 2.9 times as many people were behind bars in America as in 1980. The prison population continues to increase; sentences are longer. Yet the proportion of violent offenders among the prison population declines, telling us that prison is becoming the remedy of choice for nonviolent crime. The statistics become grimmer in the inner cities, where incarceration rates for African-American males are multiples of the already high national average. In the United States, we incarcerate a far higher percentage of the population than any country in the world, and that includes the former Soviet Union and pre-democracy South Africa.

I doubt many people feel safer knowing that prison sentences are longer and more readily handed out. To say this is not to endorse a vague commitment to finding the "social causes of crime" and doing nothing until we make the discovery. The drive for ever-sterner sentences handed out in proceedings where defendants have ever-fewer rights is simply an abandonment of rational discourse. The political success of such proposals is partly due to a gap in criminological theory. Criminologists try to tell us why people commit crimes and to describe the patterns of criminal behavior. They have had little to say about how to make people safe from criminal behavior.

It is possible to accommodate the perceived need for public safety with the dignity of all persons, but doing so will require a rational search based upon familiar values. That is, indeed, one of the most important tasks now facing us.

To look beyond our shores, we must all share a sense of horror at the waves of ethnic violence—and the incipient pogroms—that wash over nations on several continents. These tortures and murders are being inflicted by groups possessing state power, and therefore claiming a legitimate monopoly on the instruments of violence. The perpetrators are pleased to call what they are doing *justice.*

For me, the question is, "What personal responsibility do I, as one trained in the law, living the law, have right now?" Responsibility from where, from whom? Responsibility how determined? Responsibility to whom? When one says responsibility, one inevitably summons up some "other" or "others," present and not present, from the past, and in some time to come. One summons up a dialectical image of process. This sense of the other, the not present, is eloquently evoked by Jacques Derrida in his series of lectures published as Spectres de Marx.

Derrida moves from considering continuity to confront the idea of justice. Just now, I used the term "justice system." That is a mistake. It is the system-called-justice. It is called-justice in the same sense that the papal legate was sent to Beziers to dispense *justice*. The "system" is an abstraction, a machine for putting a name, the name *justice* or *judgment,* on results. The *system* is not *justice* because the system makes *justice* into an abstraction. When I say *justice,* I do not mean a name-giver. I mean what Camus meant—an idea that unites uniquely human values based upon compassion.

When I speak of a prosaic and down-to-earth idea of justice, I mean simply that one can deduce principles of right from human needs in the present time. That is, I reject the cynical, or Stoic, or no-ought-from-an-is idea that one set of rules is just as good as another. I reject the notion, as Professor Martha Nussbaum has characterized it, "that to every argument some argument to a contradictory conclusion can be opposed; that arguments are in any case merely tools of influence, without any better sort of claim to our allegiance." Rather, again borrowing from Professor Nussbaum, my notions of justice "include a commitment, open-ended and revisable because grounded upon dialectical arguments that have their roots in experience, to a definite view of human flourishing and good human functioning." One element of such views is that "human beings have needs for things in the world: for political rights, for money and food and shelter, for respect and self-respect," and so on.

By hewing to a basic definition of justice, I mean to confess a certain hesitation, perhaps humility. In times as turbulent as these, with opinions swinging widely and violently from side to side, I want to return to the most basic skills and values I know and possess. I want to live my lawyer-life in the search for, and fidelity to, this *justice* as I understand it.

I will try to derive truths from the past and present, and from a sense of responsibility to those who will come after, but I am making decisions for myself and not as an apostle of others or with a claim to lead. If the ideas appeal to you, there is plenty of work to do and all are welcome.

The sense of hesitation, and of personal quest, is also evoked by Derrida in his lectures. He begins with a translated passage from the first act of Hamlet. Hamlet sees the spirit of his father, and learns how and why his father was murdered. "The time is out of joint," Hamlet says, "O cursèd spite, That ever I was born to set it right!"

Derrida conjures with the spirit, and with various translations, of this passage to show us that thinking of justice drops us into the stream of history, the flow from past to future. In the past are the events that put time "off its hinges," or that "turn the world upside down." But to say that things are "wrong" implies that from that same past there is some idea of how things are "right-side up," or "on their hinges." This past-given sense, which is encompassed in an ideology that we can study and know, is not simply about carpentry or gravity. It is about subjective but verifiable principles of human flourishing.

And then in the present is our action, which tends into the future, toward the "set it right." To make a personal commitment to that path is not to pretend to be Prince of Denmark. It is simply to have understood the text in a certain way, and to have drawn from it certain lessons—as well as certain warnings about excessive or obsessive commitment.

This last observation is important. If the time is out of joint, the remedy is surely not to swing off one's own hinges, to become "unhinged." "And what if excessive love bewildered them till they died," Yeats wrote of the Easter martyrs, and again warned us that "too long a sacrifice can make a stone of the heart." But the dangers are not, for me, a reason not to step into the stream.

So to return to the theme, the system-called-justice dispenses "judgments" that bear the name "law" or "right"—in French "*loi*" and "*droit.*" But the term *droit* or right rarely goes out alone. Sometimes it is modified with an eye to justice, as in "human rights" (*droits de l'homme*). More often, it is qualified (and particularly in French) by words that give it an arid and abstract quality, like "civil right" as something the *law* recognizes, or "*droit criminel*" as the French would say "criminal law" and refer by those words to the system of penal rules enforced by the state. So we do best by sticking to a certain, more basic and yet more ample, sense of the term *justice.*

As law students, we studied the branches of the common-law system: contracts, torts, property, criminal law, civil procedure, constitutional law, and whatever else our law schools required. What branches of learning did you find at Harvard, Emerson said to Thoreau, who replied, All of the branches and none of the roots.

We had our chance to study the roots. Most of us did so, and from that study can come an informed judgment that the time is out of joint. Our study, and our passports to the places where the system-called-justice does its judging, adjudges, gives judgments, give us unique access. I will not say our study and our passports give us a responsibility. We must each figure that one out for ourselves.

For me, I will take my knowledge and my passport and try to advocate, in the places I am admitted, for just principles and just results. I will remember that I am lucky enough to be "admitted" to classrooms and lecture halls and street corners and byways and law journals and newspapers, as well as to places where more formal advocacy is done in the system-called-justice.

In making this decision, I am borne up by the example of my friends. Dullah Omar, a lawyer in South Africa, struggled for so many years against apartheid generally and for Nelson Mandela's release specifically. He came to be Minister of Justice in the new South Africa.

His struggle, and his decisions in it, were the product of experience, the result of stepping into the stream and not of standing beside it lost in thought.

If I see the time is out of joint, and want to help *set it right*, how shall I decide to use my energy in this, the sixth decade of my life? I am not alone on the path, so I must protect the well-being of my family in whatever I do.

Beyond that, I take my knowledge and passport to places I think I am best suited to be, not as compared to anybody else but only to how well or not-well I would do in other places where I might be.

Today, the system-called-justice poses its greatest threat to justice properly-so-called in the criminal law system. Criminal trials, particularly famous ones, are intended to be didactic. That is, the state uses the criminal system-called-justice not only to take away liberty and life, but to announce and enforce social priorities.

Taking lawyers away from people sentenced to death announces a priority—to kill inmates without ceremony, in a way that says that poor people's claims of innocence, claims for justice, are not important.

In the Oklahoma City cases, we have already witnessed some announcements of priorities. Custodial interrogations of the defendant and his family were done without semblance of process or legality. Government agents felt free to leak theories of the defendant's complicity, only to leak contradictory stories a few days later. It seemed that many people in government had decided that the stakes were high enough that the rules didn't matter.

I have seen this arrogance of power before. A federal judge asked me in oral argument why the government would commit the frauds I had alleged in an effort to condemn John Demjanjuk for a crime he did not commit. I recalled simply the rhetorical excess in which the entire government case had come to be enfolded, and summoned up Ruskin's words that there is no snare set by the fiend for the mind of man more dangerous than the illusion that our enemies are also the enemies of god.

To spare a life that might be wrongly taken, or shelter a freedom that might be wrongly abridged, is already a significant participatory act. One must bring to bear the sense of justice, and the skills learned because one is an advocate.

There is more to it. The state sees its system-called-justice as didactic, and arranges matters in the service of that goal. When the system delivers someone from the state's power, the lesson taught is not the one intended, but is a lesson nonetheless. Because the initial decision to make the system-called-justice didactic in a particular way is the state's to begin with, these deliverances have a significance all out of proportion to their number. The opportunity to weigh in that balance is an additional benefit of participating.

When the colonial newspaper editor John Peter Zenger was charged with seditious libel, no doubt colonial Governor Cosby thought to teach Zenger, his cohorts, and his supporters all a lesson. When the tables were turned, and Zenger acquitted, a far greater and longer lasting lesson was taught. When George IV sought to rid himself of his wife, Queen Caroline, by charging her with adultery in the House of Lords, her vindication had more force than the opposite result could ever have had.

When a South Carolina jury refused to condemn Susan Smith to death for killing her children, its members were expressing a community sentiment about justice, and their verdict sounded out louder than a plea-bargained life sentence would have.

These lessons—unintended from the state's perspective—redeem, refine, and announce justice and reaffirm the human commitment to it. These reaffirmations in turn help to validate norms and principles of justice, in commands and procedures. The time is out of joint, swinging on its hinges, turned upside down, dishonored; the dominant theme in every reading of Hamlet's cry is flux, change, uncertainty. "The time," the good old boy would say, "is like a hog on ice." In such a time, an image of justice—of which the human species is the only one to conceive—and of participation in a process fixed between the no-longer-there and the yet-to-be, is a guide to behavior. The option of doing nothing, a "kind of silence about injustice," as Brecht said it, is itself a participation.

So I participate because I have an inkling, and am given a means to validate it step by step.

In telling about stepping into the stream between past and future, I make clear why I part company with those who criticize my representation of this or that person. I owe those detractors no duty of explanation. My private reasonings are mine to share or not as I should wish. By focusing on some purported obligation of personal justification, these misguided souls are missing the entire point of the journey. I am not trying to set an example. I am trying to understand how to live my life. *Je voudrais apprendre à vivre enfin.*

I can say I am not trying to set an example. I realize that by making some public expression—for the lawyer as for the artist—one is condemned to signify. Neither the artist nor the advocate can plausibly claim to be tracing figures on the inside walls of his mind, for his own delectation.

But in a time out of joint, the surest signifying is done in a context provided by events. For the advocate, the event is a cry for justice, not usually spectral but from a flesh and blood human being.

I know, of course, that the rigged didactic of the criminal trial has false elements. In the courtroom arena, there is a symbolic equality of defense and prosecution. We understand that, in fact, the balance of resources almost always tips in favor of the government, and this is particularly so in high-profile cases where high officials have announced an intention to take the defendants' lives. The defendant is not given a choice whether to participate in the unequal contest. The inequality is just another device of the system-called-justice. The lawyer's job is to expose the device, deploying the signs of justice against the signs of system-called-justice. The signs of justice include empowering the jury, calling on the tribunal to respect its oath, exposing contradiction—bringing out solid reasons why the judge and jurors should go beneath the surface of things.

About 90 percent of criminal cases are disposed of on pleas of guilty, so the 10 percent of cases that are tried bear all the semiotic weight. The trial-court struggle over what will be taught covers the entire range of symbols. On one side, we see the government's reassuring sense of power and knowledge, of things as they should be, that we will be safer if another creature is jailed or put to death. On the defense side, the symbols are of individual responsibility for results; the image is one of courageous individuals standing up to superior force and using their intellect, power, and insight.

Maybe when time is rejointed, back on its hinges, right-side up, we will see more equal struggles over liberty. I can hope so.

My purpose in Oklahoma, and in whatever venue to which the case is moved, is not to justify myself. That would be an arrogant, a foolish, and a pointless act. I am and will be there to try to see that the system-called-justice respects and renders justice properly-so-called. I am there to see that done for a fellow creature whose life I am to shelter.

Where am I then? To borrow again from Derrida, *Où suis-je enfin?* Where am I finally? Not "finally" in the sense of an end, but of a moment between past and future, and about to push ahead again like feeling one's way forward in the dark. On a mountain road in the coal black night, C. S. Lewis wrote, we would give far more for a glimpse of the few feet ahead than for a vision of some distant horizon.

I am in that moment that has fascinated writers for centuries. The place between. "Your sons and daughters shall prophesy, your old . . . shall dream dreams, your young . . . shall see visions." I am old enough to be the dreamer evoked by this passage from Joel 2:28.

My dreams are of things recollected, which I flatter myself to call old truths and insights. The visions and prophesies are of the future, where those who will live there longer than I will reap the harvest of this moment in time.

NOTES

1. Michael E. Tigar, *Fighting Injustice* (Chicago: American Bar Association, 2002), 273–289; Michael E. Tigar and James E. Coleman, Jr., "A Sanctuary in the Jungle: Terry Lynn Nichols and His Oklahoma City Bombing Trial," in *Trial Stories*, ed. Michael E. Tigar and Angela Davis (New York: Foundation Press, 2008), 149.
2. United States v. Coplon, 185 F.2d 629, 638 (2d Cir. 1950).
3. This quotation was actually slightly misstated. It was originally written, "To a man on a mountain road by night, a glimpse of the next three feet of road may matter more than a vision of the horizon." C. S. Lewis to Sheldon Vanauaken, April 17, 1951, in *A Severe Mercy*, ed. Sheldon Vanauaken (New York: HarperCollins, 1980), 102.
4. Judge Matsch asked why voir dire would not serve to weed out biased jurors. I acknowledged the need for voir dire, but also noted its inherent limitations: "Nothing I have said, Your Honor, diminishes the power of advocacy nor the abilities of judges to ferret out bias and get at the truth, but my mother always told me not to eat my soup with a fork. Forks are good implements, but there are some things they're just not designed to do."
5. 408 U.S. 238 (1972).
6. California v. Brown, 479 U.S. 538, 545 (1987) (O'Connor, J., concurring).
7. "What do sterile regrets, illusory reparations matter to a vain shadow, to insensible ash?" Maximilien Robespierre, "On the Death Penalty," trans. Mitch Abdidor (Lecture, Constituent Assembly, June 22, 1791), 2004, http://www.marxists.org/history/france/revolution/robespierre/1791/death-penalty.htm. Robespierre later changed his mind, and probably changed it again before being executed.
8. Stephen Colbert has done the best job: "The Word—Due or Die," *The Colbert Report*, aired March 6, 2012, http://www.colbertnation.com/the-colbert-report-videos/410085/march-06–2012/the-word – -due-or-die; "The Word—Two Birds with One Drone," *The Colbert Report*, aired May 31, 2012, http://www.colbertnation.com/the-colbert-report-videos/414704/may-31–2012/the-word – -two-birds-with-one-drone.
9. Michael E. Tigar, "Defending," *Texas Law Review* 74 (1995). Reprinted with permission.

15

Not Only in America

The Necessity of Representing "Those People" in a Free and Democratic Society

Alice Woolley

Introduction

"How can you represent those people?" actually poses two distinct questions: "how can *anyone* represent those people?" and "how can you, *personally*, represent those people?" The first question demands an objective response, a reasoned explanation for why representing someone accused of a crime is morally justified. The second question is more personal and subjective. It asks an individual lawyer to explain and justify her decision to spend her life doing the work of the criminal defender. The questions (and responses) are of course related, since a persuasive answer to the second question will almost certainly draw on the answers given to the first. Making the case for why the life I have lived is a good one, whether to myself or to others, normally involves explaining my choices in terms of values, principles, emotions, and experiences that have some universal resonance.

The questions are nonetheless distinct. That something is worth doing for someone does not mean that it is worth doing for me, or that the life I would live doing it would be a good life for me, as judged by my own moral commitments and beliefs. The objective claims and reasons that justify being a criminal defense lawyer may not make being a criminal defense lawyer a good thing for me, personally, to do. But the point I want to make in this chapter is this: there are strong objective reasons why any free and democratic society, in which the dignity of individual citizens is respected, will have criminal defense lawyers. Further, a person who does that job, when asked to account for the value of the life she leads, will have personal reasons and motivations that connect to the objective value of the defense lawyer's role. Those reasons will not only be good reasons, but they will also be *her* reasons, what animates her life and gives it worth and value. To paraphrase the clichéd question of legal ethics: that lawyer will be a good person *because* she is a good lawyer.[1]

A Job for Someone

For decades, legal ethics scholars have debated whether the role of the lawyer can be morally justified, objectively speaking, or whether the role needs to be changed to comply better with the obligations of ordinary morality or the internal morality of the law.[2] One of the problems with that debate is that it runs the risk of being abstracted from fact, legal context, or history,[3] in part because it considers the question at the highest level—whether and in what way the role of the "lawyer" can be morally justified. Yet there is no particular reason to expect every sort of client representation to be the same, legally or morally; providing advice to a corporate client on tax efficient restructuring is as different from prosecuting a criminal case as it is alike, and any attempt to find a singular justification for the morality of both must necessarily abstract from context to the point where it runs the risk of obscuring the moral function of each lawyer's role as much as it elucidates it. An acontextual justification will, for example, not be able to consider the role a corporate lawyer plays in wealth creation, nor the role a prosecutor plays in ensuring the public interest in the fair administration of justice. Yet surely any meaningful explanation of the moral worth of what that lawyer does should take into account those sorts of reasons. Explaining why someone needs to represent "those people" requires focusing specifically on being a criminal defense lawyer, not on lawyering in general.

And when considered in the context of the criminal justice system and society as a whole, the rationale for the criminal defense lawyer becomes clear. Zealously representing the criminally accused reflects central norms of the common law and constitutional democracies like the United States, is fundamental to the achievement of a free and democratic society, and is necessary to protect human dignity.

The Rule of Law in the Common-Law Tradition

Constitutional democracies rest on the premise that the citizenry shall be governed by laws, that "governments are instituted among men, deriving their just powers from the consent of the governed,"[4] such that no state can exercise power over its citizenry without legal authority. Hence there is the US Constitution's Fifth and Fourteenth Amendments' requirement that a person be granted "due process of law" before being deprived of "life, liberty or property,"[5] or the Canadian Charter of Rights and Freedoms' requirement that no person be deprived of "life, liberty or security of the person without fundamental justice"[6] or, in antiquity, the requirement of paragraph 39 of the Magna Carta, that

> no free man shall be seized or imprisoned, or stripped of his rights or possessions, or outlawed or exiled, or deprived of his standing in any other way, nor will we proceed with force against him, or send others to do so, except by the lawful judgement of his equals or by the law of the land.[7]

While the precise details of the requirements of the rule of law can be contested, its two basic premises are clear: a person cannot be subject to state sanction unless her conduct is in fact legally prohibited, and state sanctions can only be imposed following a fair and just process. Thus in the famous Canadian case, *Roncarelli v. Duplessis*,[8] the government of Québec had revoked Roncarelli's liquor license because of his support for Jehovah's witnesses who were being subject to state persecution. Roncarelli's license was revoked "'forever'... to warn others that they similarly would be stripped of provincial 'privileges' if they persisted in any activity directly or indirectly related to the Witnesses."[9] The Supreme Court of Canada held that in so doing, the Québec government had acted unlawfully, and that "there is no such thing as absolute and untrammelled 'discretion'... no legislative Act can, without express language, be taken to contemplate an unlimited arbitrary power exercisable for any purpose, however capricious or irrelevant."[10]

For the protection granted by constitutional recognition of the rule of law to be meaningful, individuals against whom the state is acting must have some way to navigate the fair procedures to which they are entitled and to put the state to proof of its claim of legal authority. Constitutional democracies recognize this. They also recognize that the unassisted individual will not be able to meaningfully access process or be certain that only legally justified sanctions are imposed upon her. Hence there is the right to counsel in the Sixth Amendment of the US Constitution, and in Section 10(b) of the Canadian Charter. With the assistance of her lawyer the individual can ensure that only unlawful conduct, as determined through a fair and just procedure, will lead to sanctions being imposed upon her.

These legal principles mean that defense lawyers play a crucial role in the functioning of the legal system. Without lawyers, the rule of law is at best an abstraction and at worst an empty promise. Lawyers ensure that when the state says that it will only take away your life, liberty, or property after due process, that that means something, and that it is only for those unlawful acts that the state has proven through a fair and just process that you will suffer those consequences.

The Function of Legality

The strength of justifying the lawyer's role within the norms of the legal system is that it grounds its claims in the deeply rooted culture, practices, and norms of our legal system and society. Its weakness, however, is that it rests in a descriptive claim about how the law works—"since the law assumes that lawyers are important for its operation, lawyers must be important for the operation of the law"—rather than in a normative claim for how the law should work or why we might view the law as morally significant or important. If we want to claim that there is an objective, morally grounded reason for the things that criminal defense lawyers do, especially if those things might otherwise be morally objectionable—like making an honest witness look like a liar, making an argument the lawyer knows is factually untrue, or defending someone who has done a despicable thing—then we require something more than a particularistic description of the culture, practices, and norms of Western society. We need to know more than what the law says. We need to know why the law should say that rather than something else—why the rule of law, and the role of lawyers, are something that any good society, any free and democratic society, would want to have.

The reasons underlying democratic societies' commitment to legality can be stated straightforwardly. To achieve a free and democratic society there must be some mechanism to peacefully accomplish social settlement and resolve disputes while also respecting the liberty and dignity of the individual. Specifically, individuals in a society will have significantly divergent conceptions of the right way to live and of the right sort of society to have. Even on matters of apparent moral consensus like the prohibition of rape or murder, individuals may disagree radically on questions like how to define self-defense (traditionally[11] or consistent with a "stand your ground" law?[12]), consent (is marriage a form of consent? what age is too young to consent? [13]), or sanity (at what point, if any, does mental disorder excuse criminal acts?). To ensure that people can nonetheless live together without violence and that a society can pursue shared social goals and facilitate access to public goods, it is necessary to have some mechanism to resolve and settle these contentious questions and to allow disagreements to be resolved without violence.

Further, this settlement should not merely be practically effective in settling social disagreement (although of course practical effectiveness is important) but should also establish social respect and a form of "moral association,"[14] in which each individual's capacity for self-determination is acknowledged. By creating a system where the rules governing social interaction and state coercion are coherent and accessible,[15] both social community and individual freedom can be achieved. No other system permits that outcome. Tyrannies subject individual decisions to the will of the tyrant. Societies based on compromise rather than strict rule enforcement subject the individual's choices to the contingencies of a particular negotiation. "In the absence of the rule of law, there can be no area of my conduct where I can act as I choose, without regard to the fact that others may intensely object to what I am doing, relying solely upon the fact that my actions are legally permissible and will receive the protection of the law." [16]

Understood in this way, legality is of foundational importance for any free and democratic society. It allows peace. It allows the accomplishment of social goods. It allows individual freedom. But for law to achieve this purpose, it must be accessible to the citizenry. It must be possible for a person to know whether or not their actions are "legally permissible" and to resist the application of any state coercion not authorized by law.

In an ideal world, that knowledge and resistance could occur through the individual acting independently; she could read the law, understand it, and navigate the dispute mechanisms established by the state. That ideal world does not, and probably cannot, exist. The complexity necessary to establish fair and comprehensive rules and mechanisms for resolving disputes; the inherent difficulty (or impossibility) of effective self-advocacy; and the variation in individual levels of education, intelligence, and sophistication make reliance on individual self-representation impossible. To allow the legal system to serve as an effective system of social compromise and moral association requires lawyers—people who can help individuals pursue their individual conceptions of the good within the bounds of legality. And, most significantly, it requires lawyers to ensure that state action is only taken against the individual when it is legally authorized, to ensure that each person's "domain of entitlement" is in fact "secure from the power of others."[17]

Human Dignity

The role of the lawyer in ensuring the accomplishment of legality does not, however, constitute the whole of the moral justification for the criminal defense lawyer's role. The other part of the story, the part that is independent of legality, is the role of the lawyer in ensuring the protection of the human dignity of the criminal accused.

When a person is accused of a crime—whether formally through charges or informally through being the subject of an investigation—the state tells a story about that person. The story is one of guilt, illegality, immorality, suspicion, in which the accused has intentionally acted in violation of the law. But that story is not necessarily the story that the accused would tell. An innocent accused might tell the story about how he did not do the things he is said to have done, or that he did not do them intentionally, or that he did them in self-defense or as a result of provocation. A guilty accused person—guilty in the sense of being someone who did the act he is said to have done with the requisite mental state and without justification or excuse—might tell the story of the ways in which the state's story was inconsistent with the facts, of the people relied upon by the state who are lying or have reasons to lie, of the wrongfulness and unconstitutionality of the laws under which he is charged, or of the wrongful and immoral conduct of the state actors who are now seeking to punish him. He might also, if he chooses to plead guilty, tell a story of mitigation, of the facts of his life that make the imposition of harsh sanctions inappropriate.

The role of the criminal defense lawyer is to allow the accused to tell his story, to ensure that we protect the dignity of the individual[18] by allowing him to be heard whatever his own capacities for storytelling, whether he "be inarticulate, unlettered, mentally disorganized, or just plain stupid."[19] The need for an advocate to protect the defendant's dignity does not arise from the power of the state to punish a defendant if the state's story is found to be true. The need arises rather from the *fact of the state's story*, a story that is not the defendant's but that is told about the defendant. If that story is taken at face value, without hearing what the defendant has to say in response—or what the defendant might say in response—then the defendant has been treated without dignity, as if he has no story to tell and no values or beliefs worth pursuing.[20]

Further, the need for the defendant to tell his story does not arise from the fact of legality. It is not a by-product of the rule of law. A defendant's dignity was not brought into being by the Bill of Rights, even if the Bill of Rights may serve to protect it. Rather, as noted by Alan Donagan, a person's human dignity is a constant human and moral value that a society should protect if it wishes to describe itself as just.[21]

Nor is human dignity purely an abstract or theoretical aspect of the role that the criminal defendant plays. Indeed, the dignity of the criminally accused is no more of an abstraction than his physical person, his past, his weaknesses, his vulnerabilities, or any of the other complex circumstances that have brought him into interaction with the criminal justice system. In his book, *Let's Get Free: A Hip-Hop Theory of Criminal Justice*, Paul Butler describes the typical person accused or convicted of a nonviolent offense:

> Picture the guy who works in the mailroom at your office, and the men who dry off your vehicle at the car wash, and the sweaty kids who come to your house to deliver the mattress. Think of your high school classmate, the dude who didn't quite make it to graduation but who you got to know a little bit because he sold you weed. Maybe he wouldn't be your ideal companion for lunch at the Four Seasons or your first choice to marry your daughter. But he's not exactly a menace to society. He's made some bad choices, done some stupid things, but he's still young and his life is still salvageable. Spiritual folks might say, "God is not through with him yet."[22]

In her review essay about Butler's book, Abbe Smith argues further that even violent offenders can be similarly described, noting that despite the terrible things they may have done, they are often more pathetic than evil.[23] Ferdinand von Shirach, a German criminal defense lawyer, puts it this way:

> We chase after things, but they're faster than we are, and in the end we can never catch up. I tell the stories of people I've defended. They were murders, drug dealers, bank robbers, and prostitutes. They all had their stories, and they weren't so different from us. All our lives, we dance on a thin layer of ice; it's very cold underneath, and death is quick. The ice

> won't bear the weight of some people and they fall through. That's the moment that interests me. If we're lucky, it never happens to us and we keep dancing. If we're lucky.[24]

That person, the "guy who works in the mailroom" now described by the state as a wrongdoer, needs a person in his corner, someone who can ensure that the story told by the state is not presumptively accepted. That mail room guy has a voice too, even when no one seems inclined to listen to it. Through a defense lawyer, his voice may be heard.

A Job for Me

These explanations provide the criminal defense lawyer with an answer to the question, "how can anyone represent those people?" There are objective, reasonable, and morally significant justifications for the role of the criminal defense lawyer in a free and democratic society. But as Professor Allan Hutchinson once said about the issue of client selection, even if there is a good reason for a client to be represented by someone, there is no particular reason why that person has to be you.[25] The question of why I should be a criminal defense lawyer, why being a criminal defense lawyer will be consistent with my accomplishment of a life well-lived, is distinct from the objective justifications for the defense lawyer's role.

As noted by Bernard Williams, the assessment of whether one has achieved an ethical life does not terminate at the conclusion that one lived one's life in accordance with the requirements of impartial morality. Williams developed this point through his response to the hypothetical question of whether a man forced to choose between saving his wife or a stranger can rely on impartial grounds to choose his wife. Williams argued that a man who even considers the question in these terms has had "one thought too many." While impartial morality may make a claim on our actions, it is not the only claim, and other projects of importance to us—in this instance love for our family—can properly motivate our actions, and may be essential for us to achieve a well-lived life. As Williams puts it:

> This construction provides the agent with one thought too many: it might have been hoped by some (for instance, by his wife) that his motivating thought, fully spelled out, would be the thought that it was his wife, not that it was his wife and that in situations of this kind it is permissible to save one's wife.[26]

In saying this, Williams is not suggesting that the dictates of impartial morality have no relevance to our assessment of the ethical quality of our lives, but simply that such dictates cannot fully answer the case for a person trying to determine what constitutes a well-lived, ethical life.

So, why do I admire criminal defense lawyers? Why would I choose to specialize in criminal defense if I were to go back into practice, even though I have only occasionally practiced criminal law? Because criminal defense is a good thing to do. It is socially important and it involves helping people who have a legitimate need for help, and who can't entirely help themselves. It helps the kind of people I want to help: people down on their luck, underdogs, people whom everyone else has thrown on the dust heap. Many of those people have done terrible things, have injured and hurt others in ways that are revolting in addition to being legally and morally unjustifiable. But even people who have done terrible things have a story, have a reason why they got to the place they did—desires or emotions they could not control, addictions they could not defeat, mental illnesses they could not overcome. As von Shirach says, the difference between that person and me is luck, not inherent worth. Paul Bernardo, a notorious Canadian serial rapist and murderer, never seems to have had any family at his trial. No parents, no siblings, no one in his corner. His only apparent friend at his trial was his lawyer. To be that person for Bernardo, even if Bernardo did sickeningly violate (on videotape) and then murder teenage girls, would have been a person worth being.

I have a nine-year-old son who has a significant intellectual disability and autism. He looks "normal," but his behavior is not, and going to any public place with expectations for children to be quiet, or to observe social conventions—even somewhere like a grocery store—requires a carapace to protect you from the judgment of others. While my son drums on the floor with rolled up gloves and sings to himself, the man in the video store says, "When I was younger children were taught to behave." The woman in the coffee shop says "shhhhhh" repeatedly because my son is speaking too loudly. Many others look sideways at this incompetent mother and her badly behaved child. Those judgments make me rage inside (and sometimes outside) at the unfairness of it—that the difficulty the world poses for him, and the effort his dad and I and others put into teaching him are invisible. Yes, he does not always behave well, but the story of these ignorant onlookers is not the story we would tell. In those moments, no one tells our story; we silently suffer judgment. A criminal accused should not have to do the same.

The values criminal defense work supports are the values that are most important to me: living in a world that is compassionate and fair and holds people in authority to account. It takes skills I have—being pugnacious, articulate, astute at doctrinal law, and capable of processing a lot of information at once—and puts them to good use. It would earn money that helps support my family; and the structure of criminal defense work in Canada would allow me to have my own practice and give me autonomy over how I live my life.[27]

In this book, other criminal defenders give their own answer to this question, but the point I am making here is that answering the question of why one would be a criminal defense lawyer requires giving an account of one's life, of why the choices one has made were worth making, and the life one has lived was worth living. And the answer to that question will invoke objective justifications for the criminal defense lawyer's role, and it will do so through a first-person, *subjective* assertion of the importance of those justifications. That is, protecting human dignity isn't just important, it is important *to me*, and a life spent doing that will be one that I experience as worthwhile. Further, those objective justifications will be linked to other reasons and motivations held by the lawyer, things that make the lawyer's life, professionally and personally, worth living. Being a criminal defense lawyer isn't like saving your spouse from drowning; there may be reasons that motivate that choice that are obviously linked to impartial and objective reasons for action. But for them to make that lawyer's life an ethical one, their importance is not that they are impartial and objective, but that they are the individual lawyer's.

CONCLUSION

The arguments made here should not be taken as an assertion that being a criminal defense lawyer is morally uncomplicated. That there are good reasons for a society to have criminal defense lawyers, and good reasons for me to be a defense lawyer, does not mean that defense lawyers can avoid making choices with moral costs. Moral values conflict, and a person can be faced with circumstances that preclude costless solutions. Criminal defense lawyers may be faced with those circumstances more than most. My point is only this: there are deeply important moral values served by the role of the criminal defense lawyers, and each criminal defense lawyer will have her own account to give of why she does what she does. Those moral values will inform her account, but they will not wholly constitute it. Just like the criminal accused, each criminal defense lawyer will have her own story to tell, her own values and goals to pursue, and her own account of why her life as a good lawyer was the life of a good person.

Notes

1. Charles Fried, "The Lawyer as Friend: The Moral Foundations of the Lawyer-Client Relations," *Yale Law Journal* 85 (1976).
2. See ibid.; Monroe Freedman, *Lawyers' Ethics in an Adversary System* (Indianapolis: Bobbs-Merill, 1975); David Luban, *Lawyers and Justice: An Ethical Study* (Princeton: Princeton University Press, 1988); David Luban, *Legal Ethics and Human Dignity* (New York: Cambridge University Press, 2007); William H. Simon, *The Practice of Justice: A Theory of Lawyers' Ethics* (Cambridge, MA: Harvard University Press, 1998); Monroe Freedman, "Personal Responsibility in a Professional System," *Catholic University Law Review* 27 (1977–1978); Monroe Freedman, "Professional Responsibility of the Criminal Defense Lawyer: The Three Hardest Questions," *Michigan Law Review* 66 (1966); William H. Simon, "Ethical Discretion in Lawyering," *Harvard Law Review* 101 (1988): 1090; Richard Wasserstrom, "Lawyers as Professionals: Some Moral Issues" *Human Rights* 5 (1975).
3. Monroe Freedman, "A Critique of Philosophizing about Legal Ethics," *Georgetown Journal of Legal Ethics* 25 (2012): 101–102.
4. The Declaration of Independence para. 3 (U.S. 1776).
5. U.S. Const. amend. V, XIV.
6. Canadian Charter of Rights and Freedoms, Part I of the Constitution Act, 1982, *being* Schedule B to the Canada Act, 1982, c. 11 (U.K.).
7. Godfrey Rupert Careless Davis, *Magna Carta*, rev. ed. (British Library, 1989), 7.
8. Roncarelli v. Duplessis, [1959] S.C.R. 121 (Can).
9. Ibid. at 133 (Rand, J., concurring).
10. Ibid. at 140.
11. For example, the Canadian Criminal Code provides: "Every one who is unlawfully assaulted and who causes death or grievous bodily harm in repelling the assault is justified if (a) he causes it under reasonable apprehension of death or grievous bodily harm from the violence with which the assault was originally made or with which the assailant pursues his purposes; and (b) he believes, on reasonable grounds, that he cannot otherwise preserve himself from death or grievous bodily harm." Canadian Criminal Code, R.S., 1985, c. C-46 § 34(2).
12. Associated Press, "Florida: Zimmerman to Invoke 'Stand Your Ground,'" *New York Times*, August 9, 2012, http://www.nytimes.com/2012/08/10/us/florida-lawyers-for-george-zimmerman-to-invoke-stand-your-ground.html.
13. See Jeremy Waldron, *Law and Disagreement* (Oxford: Oxford University Press, 1999), 105.

14. Nigel Simmons, *Law as a Moral Idea* (Oxford: Oxford University Press, 2007), 66
15. That is, that comply with Fuller's eight precepts of legality: that (1) the law must be a set of rules that must be (2) published, (3) prospective, (4) intelligible, (5) neither conflicting nor contradictory, (6) possible to comply with, (7) stable, and (8) congruent with the action of the state. Lon Fuller, *The Morality of Law* (New Haven: Yale University Press, 1969).
16. Simmons, *Law as a Moral Idea.*
17. Ibid.
18. Freedman, *Lawyers' Ethics in an Adversary System*, 12.
19. Luban, *Legal Ethics and Human Dignity*, 69
20. Alan Donagan identifies these as the central aspects of human dignity protected by the adversary system: accepting at least provisionally that a person's beliefs are "defensibly reached and honestly held, even if mistaken" and that "no matter how untrustworthy somebody may have proved to be in the past" a story she tells now is given in good faith. Alan Donagan, "Justifying Legal Practice in the Adversary System," in *The Good Lawyer: Lawyers' Roles and Lawyers' Ethics*, ed. David Luban (New Jersey: Rowman and Allenheld, 1984), 130.
21. Ibid., 133.
22. Paul Butler, *Let's Get Free: A Hip-Hop Theory of Criminal Justice* (New York: The New Press, 2009), 30.
23. Abbe Smith, "A Hip Hop Prosecutor Sings the Blues," review of *Let's Get Free: A Hip-Hop Theory of Criminal Justice*, by Paul Butler, *Legal Ethics* 14 (2011): 261–274.
24. Ferdinand von Schirach, *Crime*, trans. Carol Brown Janeway (New York: Alfred A Knopf, 2011), ix.
25. Allan Hutchinson, "Taking it Personally: Legal Ethics and Client Selection," *Legal Ethics* 1 (1998): 178.
26. Bernard Williams, *Moral Luck* (Cambridge: Cambridge University Press, 1981), 18.
27. In Canada, the system of legal aid certificates means that the vast majority of criminal defense lawyers, even those representing indigent defendants, practice alone or in small firms.

Contributors

Barbara Babcock graduated from Yale Law School in 1963. She clerked for Judge Henry Edgerton of the DC Circuit and then joined the small firm of noted criminal defense attorney Edward Bennett Williams. After a few years of working for the interests of those who could afford the best legal advice, Babcock turned to representation of the indigent accused. As a staff attorney and then director of the Public Defender Service of the District of Columbia (PDS), she tried many jury cases and conducted the administrative work and training associated with such an office. Under her leadership, the agency grew to be one of the best defender offices in the country, noted for the dedication and skill of its lawyers. In the early 1970s, she became interested in the women's movement and taught the first courses in "Women and the Law" at Georgetown and Yale Law schools. This teaching experience led her in 1972 to join the Stanford Law School faculty as the first woman to hold a tenure track position. On leave from Stanford in 1977, Professor Babcock served as Assistant Attorney General for the Civil Division in the US Department of Justice. There she headed a staff of more than a thousand lawyers and played the complex role of political appointee and legal representative of dozens of diverse government agencies. Among Professor Babcock's early publications was the coauthorship of a now-classic text on sex discrimination law. She has also written about juries and criminal defense. Her major work is a biography of the California lawyer who invented the public defender and founded a movement for free justice for all: *Woman Lawyer: The Trials of Clara Foltz*, (2011). She is currently working on her own *Recollections*, which are reflected in the piece published here. Professor Babcock has four times won the John Bingham Hurlbut Award for Excellence in Teaching, presented to a Stanford law professor each year by the graduating class. She holds several honorary degrees, and was the recipient of the Margaret Brent Award for distinguished contributions to the advancement of women in the legal profession.

Paul Butler, professor of law at Georgetown University, is one of the nation's most frequently consulted legal scholars on issues of race and criminal justice. He is the author of the award-winning *Let's Get Free: A Hip-Hop Theory of Justice* (2009), articles in leading scholarly journals including the *Yale Law Journal*, *Harvard Law Review*, and *Stanford Law Review*, and book reviews and op-eds in newspapers like the *New York Times*, *Washington Post*, and *Los Angeles Times*. He provides legal commentary for National Public Radio, MSNBC television, and the Fox News Network. Professor Butler grew up on the South Side of Chicago and attended the prestigious St. Ignatius College Prep, followed by Yale College and Harvard Law School. After law school, he clerked for Judge Mary Johnson Lowe of the US District Court for the Southern District of New York. He then joined the law firm of Williams and Connolly in Washington, DC, where he specialized in white collar criminal defense and civil litigation. After his time in private practice, he served as a federal prosecutor in the US Department of Justice, where he specialized in public corruption. His prosecutions included a US senator and three FBI agents. Butler also served as a special assistant US attorney, prosecuting drug and gun cases, and other street crime, in the District of Columbia. Before coming to Georgetown, Professor Butler was the Carville Dickinson Benson Research Professor of Law at George Washington University Law School, where he was voted "professor of the year" three times by the graduating class. At Georgetown, he researches and teaches in the areas of criminal law, race relations law, and critical theory. He lectures regularly for the American Bar Association and the NAACP, and at universities and community organizations. He was elected to the American Law Institute in 2003. Professor Butler understands that it is high praise for a former prosecutor to be invited to contribute to a book about criminal defense.

Tucker Carrington is the founding director of the Mississippi Innocence Project (MIP) and Legal Clinic at the University of Mississippi College of Law. The project's mission is to identify, investigate, and litigate viable claims of innocence on behalf of Mississippi prisoners. MIP has also worked to advance criminal justice policy in the state, including the drafting and assisting of passage of the state's first postconviction DNA testing and preservation laws, as well as laws providing compensation for the wrongly convicted. Prior to coming to the University of Mississippi, Carrington was a visiting professor of Law at Georgetown University, a supervising and staff attorney at PDS, and a fellow in the E. Barrett Prettyman Fellowship Program at Georgetown Law. He received his BA from the University of Virginia,

MA (in creative writing) from Hollins College, and JD from the University of Tennessee. Professor Carrington has published articles in *The Federal Lawyer*, *The University of Pennsylvania Journal of Law and Social Change*, and the *Ohio State Journal of Criminal Law*, and is the editor of a forthcoming manual for criminal trials for federal trial judges. He writes and speaks frequently about criminal justice issues, particularly those surrounding indigent criminal defense and wrongful convictions. He lives in Oxford, Mississippi, with his wife, Desiree Hensley, and children, William and Glenn.

Angela J. Davis is professor of law at the American University Washington College of Law where she teaches criminal law, criminal procedure, and criminal defense: theory and practice. Professor Davis has been a visiting professor of Law at George Washington University and Georgetown University. She has served on the adjunct faculty at George Washington, Georgetown, and Harvard Law Schools. Professor Davis is the author of *Arbitrary Justice: The Power of the American Prosecutor* (2007), coeditor with Michael E. Tigar of *Trial Stories* (2007), and coauthor with Stephen Saltzburg and Daniel Capra of the fifth edition of *Basic Criminal Procedure* (2009). Professor Davis's other publications include articles and book chapters on racism in the criminal justice system and prosecutorial discretion. She received the American University Faculty Award for Outstanding Teaching in 2002, the American University Faculty Award for Outstanding Scholarship in 2009, and the Washington College of Law's Pauline Ruyle Moore award for scholarly contribution in the area of public law in 2000 and 2009. Professor Davis's book *Arbitrary Justice* won the Association of American Publishers 2007 Professional and Scholarly Publishing Division Award for Excellence in the Law and Legal Studies Division. She was awarded a Soros Senior Justice Fellowship in 2004. Professor Davis is a graduate of Howard University and Harvard Law School. She serves on the board of trustees of the Southern Center for Human Rights and the Peter M. Cicchino Social Justice Foundation. Professor Davis served as the executive director of the National Rainbow Coalition from 1994 to 1995. From 1991 to 1994, she was the director of the PDS. She also served as the deputy director of PDS from 1988 to 1991, and as a staff attorney from 1982 to 1988, representing indigent juveniles and adults. Professor Davis is a former law clerk of the Honorable Theodore R. Newman of the District of Columbia Court of Appeals.

Alan M. Dershowitz is a Brooklyn native who has been called "the nation's most peripatetic civil liberties lawyer" and one of its "most distinguished defenders of individual rights," "the best-known criminal lawyer in the world," "the top lawyer of last resort," "America's most public Jewish defender," and "Israel's single most visible defender... in the court of public opinion." He is the Felix Frankfurter Professor of Law at Harvard Law School. Dershowitz, a graduate of Brooklyn College and Yale Law School, joined the Harvard Law School faculty at age 25 after clerking for Judge David Bazelon and Justice Arthur Goldberg. He has published more than 100 articles in magazines and journals like *The New York Times Magazine*, *The Washington Post*, *The Wall Street Journal*, *The New Republic*, *The Nation*, *Commentary*, *Saturday Review*, *The Harvard Law Review*, and the *Yale Law Journal*, and more than 300 of his articles have appeared in syndication in 50 national daily newspapers. Professor Dershowitz is the author of 27 fiction and nonfiction books, including the criminal defense classic, *The Best Defense* (1983). His most recent titles include the following: *The Trials of Zion* (2010); *Finding, Framing, and Hanging Jefferson: A Lost Letter, A Remarkable Discovery, and Freedom of Speech in an Age of Terrorism* (2007); *Blasphemy: How the Religious Right is Hijacking the Declaration of Independence* (2007); *Preemption: A Knife that Cuts Both Ways* (2006); *The Case for Peace* (2005); and *The Case for Israel* (2003). In addition to his numerous law review articles and books about criminal and constitutional law, he has written, taught, and lectured about history, philosophy, psychology, literature, mathematics, theology, music, sports—and even delicatessens. In 1983, the Anti-Defamation League presented him with the William O. Douglas First Amendment Award for his "compassionate eloquent leadership and persistent advocacy in the struggle for civil and human rights." Professor Dershowitz has been awarded the honorary doctor of laws degree by Yeshiva University, the Hebrew Union College, Brooklyn College, Syracuse University, Tel Aviv University, New York City College, and Haifa University.

Monroe H. Freedman has been recognized by *The Washingtonian*, the District of Columbia's monthly magazine, as "one of [the District's] most highly regarded constitutional lawyers." His clients have included members of Congress, prominent criminal defense lawyers, and hundreds of indigent criminal defendants. During the civil rights movement in the 1960s, he represented several civil rights organizations, and became the first general counsel of a gay rights organization. He has helped to change the law on behalf of minority group members, poor people, people accused of crime, gays and lesbians, and victims of police abuse. He currently works with lawyers defending death penalty cases and Guantanamo detainees. Described in the Harvard Law Bulletin as "a lawyers' lawyer," he is frequently consulted by lawyers across the country. Professor Freedman began his academic career at the George Washington University Law School. He is the former dean of Hofstra Law School, for 30 years he lectured annually on lawyers' ethics at Harvard Law School's Trial Advocacy Workshop, and from 2007 to 2012 he was a visiting professor at Georgetown Law School. He has written many books and articles, including *Understanding Lawyers' Ethics* (with Abbe Smith) (2010), *Lawyers' Ethics in an Adversary System* (1975), and his classic 1966 *Michigan Law Review* article on criminal defense ethics, "Professional Responsibility of the Criminal Defense Lawyer: The Three Hardest Questions." Among his many awards, he has received the American Bar Association's highest award for professionalism in recognition of "a lifetime of original and influential scholarship in the field of lawyers' ethics," and received an award from the American Board of Criminal Lawyers, an exclusive national society for criminal trial lawyers, for "a lifetime of extraordinary service to the criminal defense bar." He received his AB, LLB, and LLM at Harvard University.

Vida B. Johnson has been a visiting professor at Georgetown Law School since 2010, where she teaches and supervises fellows in the E. Barrett Prettyman Fellowship Program and students in the Criminal Defense & Prisoner Advocacy Clinic and the Criminal Justice Clinic. She also visited Georgetown and taught in the Juvenile Justice Clinic in the spring of 2009, and was an adjunct professor teaching trial skills and case theory to Prettyman fellows from 2008 to 2010. Prior to coming to Georgetown, she was a supervising attorney in the trial division at PDS, where she worked for eight years. At PDS, Johnson tried numerous cases, including homicides, sexual assaults, and armed offenses. Johnson's responsibilities at PDS also included supervising other trial attorneys and serving as one of the agency's two representatives to the DC Superior Court Sentencing Guidelines Commission. Before joining PDS, Johnson was a fellow in the E. Barrett Prettyman Fellowship Program at Georgetown University Law Center. Johnson is the author of "A Plea for Funds: Using Padilla, Lafler, and Frye to Increase Public Defender Resources," in the *American Criminal Law Review*, "A Word of Caution: Consequences of Confession," in the *Ohio State Journal of Criminal Law* (2012), and "Effective Assistance of Counsel and Guilty Pleas" (2013) and "A Primer on Crossing an Informant" (2011) in *The Champion* (the magazine of the National Association of Criminal Defense Lawyers). Johnson earned her law degree from New

York University Law School in 2000, where she was a Hays Fellow and Public Service Scholar, and she earned her BA in American History from the University of California, Berkeley, in 1995.

Joseph Margulies is an attorney with the Roderick MacArthur Justice Center and a clinical professor at Northwestern University Law School in Chicago. He began his legal career in 1989 in Texas, where he defended men and women on death row. In 1994, Margulies entered private practice in Minneapolis, specializing in civil rights and capital defense. In 2002, he was the distinguished practitioner in residence at Cornell University Law School, and in 2004, he joined the MacArthur Center. Margulies was counsel of record in *Rasul v. Bush* (2004), involving detentions at the Guantanamo Bay Naval Station, and in *Geren v. Omar & Munaf v. Geren* (2008), involving detentions at Camp Cropper in Iraq. Currently he is counsel for Abu Zubaydah, whose interrogation in 2002 prompted the Bush administration to draft the "torture memos." In June 2005, at the invitation of Pennsylvania senator Arlen Specter, Margulies testified at the first Senate Judiciary Committee hearing on detainee issues. Margulies writes and lectures widely on civil liberties in the wake of September 11, and his commentaries have appeared in numerous publications, including the *Washington Post*, *Los Angeles Times*, *Chicago Tribune*, *National Law Journal*, *Miami Herald*, *Christian Science Monitor*, *Virginia Quarterly Review*, *Legal Times*, and *The New Republic*. He is also the author of two books, *What Changed When Everything Changed: 9/11 and the Making of National Identity* (2013) and *Guantanamo and The Abuse of Presidential Power* (2006). *Guantanamo* was named one of the best books of 2006 by The Economist magazine. It received the prestigious Silver Gavel Award of 2007, given annually by the American Bar Association to the book that best promotes "the American public's understanding of the law and the legal system." It also won the Scribes Book Award of 2007, given annually by the American Society of Legal Writers to honor "the best work of legal scholarship published during the previous year." Margulies has also won numerous awards for his legal work since September 11.

William R. Montross, Jr. joined the Southern Center for Human Rights (SCHR) in Atlanta, Georgia, in 2003. In his present capacity as a senior capital attorney, he represents individuals in Alabama and Georgia charged and/or convicted of capital offenses at trial, on direct appeal, and in the postconviction process; consults with lawyers throughout the country on capital cases; and works with other organizations and individuals in efforts to end the use of the death penalty. Mr. Montross is also a faculty member at the Southern Public Defender Training Center, teaching client-centered representation and mentoring young public defenders practicing in the Deep South. Prior to joining SCHR, he was a public defender at the Defender Association of Philadelphia, the Bronx Defenders, and the Office of the Appellate Defender in New York City. Mr. Montross lectures and writes extensively on matters of criminal justice and capital punishment, including "Virtue and Vice: Who Will Report on the Failings of the American Criminal Justice System?" published in the *Stanford Law Review*, "Go, Witness, and Speak," which appeared in the *Journal of the Society of Christian Ethics*, and "The Calling of Criminal Defense" (cowritten with Abbe Smith) in the *Mercer Law Review*. Mr. Montross received his BA from Fordham University, JD from Harvard Law School, and LLM from Georgetown, where he was a fellow in the E. Barrett Prettyman Fellowship Program from 1995 to 1997.

Ann Roan was born in Denver and grew up in a northern suburb. When she was 16, she began cooking Sunday dinner for the guests at Denver's Catholic Worker homeless shelter. The guests and workers at the shelter taught her the truth of Dorothy Day's observation that "our problems stem from our acceptance of this filthy, rotten system." Ann graduated with honors from the University of Iowa in 1986 with a BA in political science and earned her JD from the University of Colorado School of Law in 1989. After a brief stint with a big law firm, she joined the Colorado State Public Defender in 1990, and tried cases all over Colorado, ranging from theft of cattle in the south to aggravated assault near the Wyoming border and first degree murder in the Denver metro area, before joining the system's appellate division in 1998. Since 2004, she has been the state training director. The Colorado PD's training program is a model for excellent indigent defense, and Ann is regularly called upon to consult with other defender trainers across the country. She teaches the "Colorado method" of both capital and noncapital voir dire to defense lawyers nationwide and is a frequent guest lecturer on jury issues at the University of Denver and the University of Colorado law schools. She is a faculty member of the National Criminal Defense College and the National Association of Criminal Defense Lawyers (NACDL) Death Penalty Voir Dire College, and has written for *The Champion,* NACDL's monthly magazine. She is also an adjunct professor at the University of Colorado Law School. She was elected to the American Board of Criminal Lawyers in 2011. She lives in Boulder with her daughter Molly, her son Patrick, and her husband Jim Jenkins.

David A. Singleton is the executive director of the Ohio Justice & Policy Center (OJPC) in Cincinnati, Ohio, a nonprofit law office that works for productive, statewide reform of the criminal justice system by promoting rehabilitation of incarcerated people, enabling them to successfully reintegrate into the community, and eliminating racial disparities in criminal justice. He is also an assistant professor of law at Northern Kentucky University's Salmon P. Chase College of Law, where he teaches the Constitutional Litigation Clinic and other courses. Singleton received an AB from Duke University and JD from Harvard Law School. Upon graduation from law school, he received a Skadden Fellowship to work at the Legal Action Center for the Homeless in New York City. He then worked as a public defender, first with the Neighborhood Defender Service of Harlem and then with PDS. Singleton practiced at Thompson Hine in Cincinnati before joining OJPC in 2002. In 2010, Mr. Singleton received the first annual Canary Award, which honors a person championing social and economic justice in the United States. He is the author of "Sex Offender Residency Restrictions and the Culture of Fear: The Case for More Meaningful Rational Basis Review of Fear-Driven Public Safety Laws," in the *St. Thomas Law Review*; "Interest Convergence and the Education of African-American Boys in Cincinnati: Motivating Suburban Whites to Embrace Inter-district Education Reform," in the *Northern Kentucky Law Review*; and "The Disenfranchised of the Re-enfranchised: How Confusion over Felon Voting Rights in Ohio Keeps Qualified Ex-Offender Voters from the Polls," available at http://www.ohiojpc.org/text/ publications/disenfranchisement.pdf. In addition to his OJPC and teaching duties, Mr. Singleton volunteers with Gideon's Promise (formerly the Southern Public Defender Training Center), and the National Public Defender Training Project. Mr. Singleton also serves on the boards of the New York City-based Urban Justice Center and the Management Assistance Group in Washington, DC.

Meghan Shapiro is a criminal defense attorney in Alexandria, Virginia, whose practice consists mainly of representing individuals charged with capital murder, on death row, or serving life without parole. She has published articles in the *American Journal of Criminal Law*, *The Champion*, and *Virginia Lawyer Magazine*. She has litigated and written about each of Virginia's methods of execution, lethal injection, and electrocution. Formerly with the office of the Northern Virginia Capital Defender, a trial-level public defender's office exclusively representing men and women facing capital murder charges in state court, she also served as a law clerk to the Honorable Leonie M. Brinkema of the Federal District Court for the Eastern District of Virginia from 2009 to 2010. she earned her law degree from the University of Texas School of Law in 2009, and her BA from the College of William and Mary in 2006. While in law school, she studied and worked at the Capital Punishment Center and the William Wayne Justice Center for Public Interest Law, received a number of public interest scholarships and awards, worked as a research assistant to Professor Jordan M. Steiker, and had internships at the Texas Defender Service, the Capital Habeas Unit of the Federal Community Defenders for the Eastern District of Pennsylvania, the Federal Capital Resource Counsel's Office at the Federal Public Defender for the Eastern District of Virginia, and the Equal Justice Initiative of Alabama. Ms. Shapiro is a graduate of the Southern Public Defender Training Center and is on the board of directors for Virginians for Alternatives to the Death Penalty.

Abbe Smith is director of the Criminal Defense and Prisoner Advocacy Clinic, codirector of the E. Barrett Prettyman Fellowship Program, and professor of law at Georgetown University. Before Georgetown, she was deputy director of the Criminal Justice Institute, Clinical Instructor, and lecturer at Law at Harvard Law School. She has also taught at the City University New York School of Law, Temple University School of Law, American University Washington College of Law, and the University of Melbourne (Australia) Law School, where she was a Senior Fulbright Scholar. Professor Smith teaches and writes on criminal defense, juvenile justice, legal ethics, and clinical legal education. In addition to numerous law journal articles, she is the author of *Case of a Lifetime: A Criminal Defense Lawyer's Story* (2008), coauthor with Monroe Freedman of *Understanding Lawyers' Ethics* (2010), and coauthor with Charles Ogletree, et al. of *Beyond the Rodney King Story: An Investigation of Police Conduct in Minority Communities* (1994). Smith began her legal career at the Defender Association of Philadelphia, where she was an assistant defender, member of the Special Defense Unit, and senior trial attorney from 1982 to 1990. She continues to be actively engaged in indigent defense as both a clinical supervisor and member of the Criminal Justice Act panel for the DC Superior Court, and frequently presents at public defender training programs in the United States and abroad. Smith is on the board of directors of the Bronx Defenders and the National Juvenile Defender Center and is a longtime member of the National Association of Criminal Defense Lawyers, the American Civil Liberties Union, and the National Lawyers Guild. In 2010, she was elected to the American Board of Criminal Lawyers. She is also a published cartoonist. A collection of her cartoons, *Carried Away: The Chronicles of a Feminist Cartoonist* was published in 1984.

Robin Steinberg, a leader and pioneer in indigent defense, has been honored by the National Legal Aid and Defender Association for her "exceptional vision, devotion and service in the quest for equal justice," and by the New York Bar Association for her "outstanding contribution to the delivery of defense services." She was also awarded Harvard Law School's Wasserstein Fellowship in recognition of her "outstanding contributions and dedication to public interest law." A 1979 graduate of the University of California, Berkeley, and a 1982 graduate of New York University School of Law, Robin has been a public defender her entire career. Starting as a criminal trial lawyer with the Legal Aid Society, continuing her career as a founding member and deputy director of the Neighborhood Defender Service of Harlem, and ultimately creating the Bronx Defenders in 1997, Robin has extensive experience in every aspect of public defense—from representing individual clients to creating a nonprofit organization. Today, Robin advocates nationally and internationally for holistic representation—delivering papers, conducting trainings, providing technical assistance to defender offices moving toward holistic defense, and hosting visitors from around the world. Robin has taught trial skills at various law schools and created Columbia University School of Law's first externship in "Holistic Defense," which she currently teaches. Robin is the author of "Heeding Gideon's Call in the 21st Century: Holistic Defense and the New Public Defense Paradigm" in the *Washington and Lee Law Review*, "Unprotected: HIV Prison Policy and the Deadly Politics of Denial" in the *Harvard Journal of African-American Public Policy*, and "Beyond Lawyering: How Holistic Lawyering Makes for Good Public Policy, Better Lawyers, and More Satisfied Clients" in the *NYU Journal of Law and Social Change*. Robin lives in New York City with her husband, David, and her two children, Jacob and Emma.

Michael E. Tigar is emeritus professor of law at Duke Law School and emeritus professor of law at American University Washington College of Law. He formerly held the Joseph D. Jamail Chair in Law at the University of Texas, and has taught at several other law schools in the United States, France, South Africa, Switzerland, and the Netherlands. He received his BA and JD from the University of California, Berkeley, and was editor-in-chief of the California Law Review and Order of the Coif. He was an associate and partner at Williams & Connolly, and then a partner in his own firm, Tigar & Buffone. Since 1996, he has been associated in law practice with his wife Jane B. Tigar. He is the author or editor of more than a dozen books, including *Nine Principles of Litigation—and Life*; *Thinking about Terrorism: The Threat to Civil Liberties in Times of National Emergency*; *Fighting Injustice*; *Examining Witnesses*; *Persuasion: The Litigator's Art*; and *Law and the Rise of Capitalism*. He has also written three plays and dozens of articles and essays. In law practice, Tigar has represented *The Washington Post*, John Connally, Angela Davis, Senator Kay Bailey Hutchison, Scott McClellan, Representative Ronald Dellums, Mobil Oil, Fernando Chavez, John Demjanjuk, Lynne Stewart, and Terry Lynn Nichols. He has tried cases in many courts across the country, argued dozens of federal appeals, and argued seven cases in the US Supreme Court. In 1999, the California Attorneys for Criminal Justice held a ballot for "Lawyer of the Century." Mr. Tigar came in third, behind Clarence Darrow and Thurgood Marshall. In 2003, the Texas Civil Rights Project named its new building in Austin the "Michael Tigar Human Rights Center." Of Mr. Tigar's career, US Supreme Court justice Brennan wrote that his "tireless striving for justice stretches his arms towards perfection."

Alice Woolley is professor of law at the University of Calgary. She is the author of *Understanding Lawyers' Ethics in Canada* (2011) and coauthor and coeditor of *Lawyers' Ethics and Professional Regulation* (2012). Professor Woolley's scholarly work focuses on the intersection between professional regulation, moral philosophy, and moral psychology. She has published academic articles on lawyer billing, the good character requirement for bar admission, regulation of extra-professional misconduct, legal ethics teaching, access to justice, regulation of lawyer civility, lawyer self-regulation, and the theoretical foundations of the lawyer's role. She is the book reviews editor for the journal *Legal Ethics*, the secretary of the International Association of Legal Ethics, and the executive vice president of the Canadian Association of Legal Ethics. Prior to joining the University of Calgary law faculty in 2004, Professor Woolley practiced law in Calgary, Alberta, and has been a member of the Law Society of Alberta since 1997. From 1995 to 1996 she was a law clerk to the then chief justice of Canada, the Right Honorable Antonio Lamer. She has an LLM from Yale, and a BA and LLB from the University of Toronto. At the University of Toronto, she was awarded the gold medal in law and the Dean's Key for contribution to extracurricular activities of an academic nature.

INDEX

Printed in the United States of America